Arab and African Film Making

Lizbeth Malkmus and Roy Armes

Zed Books Ltd
London and New Jersey

Arab and African Film Making was first published by
Zed Books Ltd, 57 Caledonian Road, London N1 9BU, UK, and
165 First Avenue, Atlantic Highlands, New Jersey 07716, USA,
in 1991.

Cover designed by The Third Man, London.
Cover picture adapted from a still of *Askndrie . . . Lie?*
supplied by courtesy of the British Film Institute.
Typeset by EMS Photosetters, Thorpe Bay, Essex.
Printed and bound in the United Kingdom
by Biddles Ltd, Guildford and King's Lynn.

A catalogue record for this book is
available from the British Library

US CIP data can be obtained from the Library of Congress

ISBN 0 86232 916 7 Hb
ISBN 0 86232 917 5 Pb

To
James and Reven Malkmus,
Caroline, Helen, Philip and Alison Armes

Contents

Acknowledgements

Between them, both authors have quite a few people to thank. For reading parts of the text and, frowning or laughing, at least saying that they would now like to see some of the films, Lizbeth Malkmus would like to thank Reven Malkmus, Betty Owsley, Nidal Ashgar and Linda Hulin. For introducing her to images thanks go to Douglas Lowndes and, for intellectual provocation, to Professor John Wansbrough. Particular gratitude from both authors goes to Samir Nasri, who compiled much of the documentation section. Roy Armes is further grateful to Eric Liknaitzky, Friday Thompson, Christine Whitehouse, Nigel Algar and Sylvia Marshall for help with film viewing. Finally, for help with stills, the authors express their thanks to the Association des Trois Mondes, the festivals of London, Nantes, Carthage and Ouagadougou and, above all, the film makers themselves.

Introduction

In its studies of Arab and African film, this book proposes an analysis via cinema's two main constraints: external conditions and internal forms. Thus, in the first section of the book, two chapters sketch the emergence of cinema in these regions, following it from the era of colonialism to that of independence, examining the political, economic and social pressures brought to bear on it. Not just a producer of autonomous artefacts, cinema is treated as only one of many mass media, in collusion or in competition with the publishing, broadcasting and recording industries, and, like them, more or less vulnerable to state support, private exploitation and local endorsement. These material considerations inevitably entail questions of elitism, cultural archaism and the perennial duality of popular models.

The second and third sections of the book are a series of essays on film form itself, in the cinema of the Arab world and in that of black Africa. In Part Two, in analyses which move from problems of narration to those of representation, film in the Arab world is considered by focusing on that major story component, the hero/ines. If chapter 3 follows straight on, in their wake, chapter 4 watches them slip momentarily out of place, and chapter 5 contemplates their slide downhill. The shots in which they are shown, the discourses in which they are heard, and the traces signifying their voyage are surveyed in chapters 6, 7 and 8. In Part Three some of the key issues raised by black African cinema are considered. Chapters 9, 10 and 11 describe how the African world is constituted in/as cinema. The initiation of and participation in narration provide the point of entry, and then this cinema's particular extensions and ellipses in space are explored. Finally, within the time structures of film, voice and space are seen as engaged in a dialectic leading to the familiar and yet unfamiliar patterns of the African film story.

Parts Two and Three are both formalist and speculative. As a way around the disappointments inherent in a chronological approach, the determinisms of a topographical one, or the sanctions of one centred on individual genius, the authors study formal issues. But genre and convention are proposed only in order to study their transmutations. To dilute taxonomic rigidities further, axes and conflictual organizations are emphasized, and the essays are at times contentious, at times tentative, and occasionally hazard analogies with present norms of Western cinema or with past traditions of the East or the South. The essays do not pretend to historical or regional conclusions but attempt instead to plot out patterns in Arab and African cinema, both those already realized and those of future potential.

The book concludes with a further section offering documentation on Arab and African film-making. For reasons closely argued in the text, the concept of a 'national cinema' is not useful for a consideration of Arab and African film-making. The documentation therefore supplements and updates existing (mostly French-language) sources by proposing an alphabetical listing of the directors of the 1980s, both new ones and those whose work has continued from an earlier period.

It should be noted that *Arab and African Film Making* is intended as a book of analysis, not of criticism, so that the authors rarely use epithets, whether of praise or of blame. The book sets out to suggest lines of approach and enquiry only, and does not pretend to exhaust them. The authors' principal concern has been to shift discussion of Arab and African film-making away from the customary concentration simply on questions of theme and content, so that the equally crucial issues of form can be highlighted. While the Introduction and Dictionary of Film-makers have been jointly authored, Parts One and Three were written by Roy Armes and Part Two by Lizbeth Malkmus.

A note on film titles and dates

A film's first occurrence in the text is accompanied by mention of director, country, date, English and foreign title. Where no translation or transcription occurs it is clear that the title (usually a proper name) is the same in both languages. The date given is normally that of the film's release, but often the date can be no more than approximate since a number of films have never been shown in their country of origin and some have never received a commercial distribution anywhere.

It is impossible to be totally consistent with regard to film titles, their translation or transliteration. Often films are shown at festivals and reviewed by critics under titles subsequently changed for more general foreign screenings. Many films are known by titles which are only approximate renderings of the original, often because the title has first made a detour into English through a French version. The practice adopted here is to use the title and/or translation by which the film is most likely to be known. In the case of Arab films, the first mention in the text is accompanied by a transliteration in a literary but simplified, non-scholarly form, the only unfamiliar letter retained being the 'ain of Arabic, marked here by an apostrophe. Subsequent references use the English title only, but the transliteration can be found by reference to the index. In the case of African films, subsequent references are mostly in English, but the original title is retained when it is likely to be more familiar to the reader: *Yeelen*, for example, rather than *Brightness* (the festival title) or *The Light* (UK release title).

Part One

Context

1.   Cinema Under Colonialism

The advent of the cinema

The first stage in the development of the modern media took place towards the end of the nineteenth century, with the birth of amateur photography (thanks to Thomas Edison's Kodak camera in 1888), the invention of the cinema by Louis Lumière in 1895, the patenting of Edison's new 'improved' phonograph in 1888 and of Emile Berliner's gramophone in 1887, the beginnings of the popular press with the founding of the *Daily Mail* as the first halfpenny newspaper in 1896, as well as the early work by Guglielmo Marconi and others on wireless transmission. This period was also characterized by the height of the European empires and the US government's first overseas imperial involvements in Cuba and the Philippines. Key dates in the last great outward surge of European imperialism, which extended up to the outbreak of war in 1914 and had a particularly strong impact on Africa and the Arab world, include the British occupation of Egypt in 1882 (which was to last seventy-four years); the Berlin conference of European powers on the partition of Africa in 1884–5, which was followed by the establishment of the Congo Free State in 1885, the failed Italian invasion of Ethiopia in 1894–6 and the successful British conquest of the Sudan in 1898; the creation by France of French West Africa (1904) and French Equatorial Africa (1908) and the establishment of French protectorates in Tunisia (1908) and Morocco (1912); the unification of Nigeria in 1914; and, after the destruction of the Ottoman Empire during World War One, the granting of League of Nations mandates over Lebanon and Syria to France and over Palestine and Iraq to Britain. Not surprisingly there is a clear connection between the development of the modern media, such as cinema, in Africa and the Arab world and the existence of the European colonial system. However diverse the four geographical areas covered by this book may be, black sub-Saharan Africa, the Arab West (or Maghreb), Egypt and the Arab East (or Mashreq) all share the mark made on their political, economic and cultural development by colonialism.

The companies in Europe and the United States involved in the new media developments were mostly small by modern standards – so that film production, for example, could remain a family business for a decade or more – but the owners were accustomed from the start to think in terms of a world market for their products. As a result, the cinema, as a dazzling new example of Western technology, was demonstrated worldwide within a few years of its invention. Shows of the Lumière cinematograph were arranged in Egypt – in the backrooms of cafés in Cairo and Alexandria – as early as 1896.[1] In autumn of the same year the cinematograph was also demonstrated in the two Algerian cities where the greatest number of European settlers lived, Algiers and Oran.[2] In Tunis in 1897 the pioneer film-maker Albert Samama (also known as Chikly) and his friend the photographer Soler arranged the first ten-minute showings of the early Lumière films (including *La sortie des usines Lumière* and *L' arrivée d'un train à la Ciotat*), backed up with magic lantern slides.[3] The same year – 1897 – saw the first showings at the Royal Palace at Fez in Morocco.[4] In black Africa, the first show was in Dakar, the capital of Senegal and centre of all French activities in West Africa, in 1900. It was apparently arranged by a travelling showman, who subsequently took the films on tour.[5] In Anglophone black Africa the first screenings seem to have been in August 1903 at the Clover Memorial Hall in Lagos, Nigeria. According to the *Lagos Standard*, the show included:

> scenes of a steamer moving through water; a conjugal dispute; a steeplechase; acrobats and other pictures . . . shown with the vividness of life; and scenes of the coronation of King Edward VII at Westminster Abbey (the royal procession alone, according to the newspaper, being worth the price of admission).[6]

Elsewhere in Africa early showings seem to have been limited. But in the Belgian Congo (now Zaire) a beginning was made in 1910 with screenings arranged by missionaries in Leopoldville, a Méliès programme put on by an Italian in Stanleyville, and a further showing organized in Elizabethville.[7] In Libya, a first film theatre was set up by Italians in 1912.[8] The introduction of the cinema into the Ottoman Empire was also delayed, but there was a first showing in Syria – at Aleppo in 1908 – arranged by some Turkish businessmen,[9] and in Iraq – on 26 July 1909 – when films of unknown origin were shown at the al-Shafa House in Baghdad.[10] The audiences for these showings were drawn largely from settler communities and members of an emergent Westernized elite, interested in all things European.

Often those who imported the cinematograph were local businessmen who also introduced other Western novelties. Chikly, for example, who brought the cinematograph to Tunisia, also introduced the bicycle, still photography and the radio. Elsewhere, those who promoted the new leisure medium tended to be locally based Europeans. Showings in Lagos, for example, were organized by a European merchant, Stanley Jones, who was praised in the press 'for relieving the monotony of Lagos through interesting and innocent entertainment'.[11] Similarly it was a Frenchman resident in Egypt, De Lagarne, who in 1912 commissioned a foreign cameraman to shoot the first scenes of Alexandria in order to add local interest to showings there.[12] This involvement of Europeans was common throughout the non-Western world and reflects their general predominance in such modern industrial development as occurred at this time in Africa and the Arab world.

It is in colonial Africa that we see most clearly the extent to which the impetus for developing a market for films was initially a response to the entertainment needs of settler audiences and the tiny bilingual elites which shared their tastes and values. In colonies without large settler communities, developments in film distribution were generally slow and distinctly limited. A typical example is Libya, where only twenty or so cinemas were constructed in almost forty years between 1912 and the granting of independence in 1951. A dozen of these were in the capital, Tripoli, and all concentrated on an Italian-speaking audience, offering imported films without Arabic subtitles.[13] In Algeria, too, film was at first slow to take root and the press records the names of only a few pioneers who came from France to show films: a certain Professor David, who gave a demonstration of Méliès films to the Société littéraire de la ville d'Oran in 1899, for example, and a showman named Godard who toured in 1900. It was 1908 before a specialist film theatre was established and in 1914 there were still only seven cinemas in Algiers.

But as the European population in Algeria rose, from some 781,000 in 1912 to around 1 million (compared to just under 9 million locals) at the time of the Algerian War, film theatres mushroomed. In 1933 there were 150 and that figure had doubled to 307 by 1956 (in addition to 360 16mm installations). But almost all the 35mm cinemas were in the major cities inhabited by the settler community, over 100 in Algiers and Oran alone (where almost half the Europeans lived). A few cinemas catered for local audiences, but provision was strictly limited and the Egyptian films they favoured were heavily taxed. The total film audience in 1955 is estimated to have been 22 million, but the proportions of the two types of distribution were very unequal. Of the 1,400 film titles handled at that time by the 37 distribution companies (all based in Algiers), only 70 were Egyptian.[14]

The case of Algeria is perhaps extreme, but distribution systems of this kind existed throughout the colonized world. There was no impetus for local film production and the imported films reflected almost exclusively the tastes of the colonizer. As a result, under colonialism, cinema served as a socially divisive force, a mode of leisure from which the bulk of the population was excluded. Even after independence this situation could not be instantly transformed, since the crucial exhibition infrastructure (the film theatres themselves) and all the structures of the profitable distribution system reflected cinema's role as an imported urban entertainment medium. Such an infrastructure needs hundreds of films a year – more than can possibly be produced locally – and so remains open to foreign-based international distributors. The only alternative is state intervention but, outside the socialist bloc, governments have seldom intervened successfully to shape the production and distribution structures of a commercial entertainment cinema (though they have, of course, often been concerned with documentary and newsreel production).

Thus a single pattern of European dominance is to be found in the emergent film distribution system throughout Africa and the Arab world. In the early 1920s, when Egyptian feature film production was hesitantly getting underway, the distribution market was largely dominated by French and Italian films. Since the sales of US films to French agents usually included the rights for Egypt, Palestine and Syria, US distribution companies did not become directly involved in the Egyptian market. But though the suppliers remained European, US films came to take an increasing share of screen time, reaching an estimated figure of 70 per cent by 1929.[15] The African market was generally considered too small to be of direct interest to US distributors, and it was not until the 1960s that the Motion Picture Export Association of America (MPEAA) set up specific affiliates to exploit the market in sub-Saharan Africa: AMPEC for Anglophone countries and AFRAM for Francophone West Africa.[16]

The best-documented case of the operation of tight monopoly control over film distribution in colonial Africa is the system established in French West and Equatorial Africa by two French companies, themselves subsidiaries of Monaco-based holding concerns: COMACICO, established in 1926, and the Société Archambault, later restructured as SECMA, which followed a few years later. These two companies divided the market amicably between them, refusing to compete when buying films in Paris for the African market and following a policy of acquiring only the cheapest, least demanding titles. The distribution market they controlled was only 5 per cent as large as that of France but they managed to make it highly profitable. The system they devised of circulating films through three regional centres (Dakar, Abidjan and Douala) and changing the programme virtually daily, was highly efficient but depended for its profitability on the constant flow of a large number of copies of films through the region. As a result, when French West and Equatorial Africa was eventually split into 14 separate independent states, it proved impossible for any one of these states, acting unilaterally, to challenge successfully the power of the foreign distribution duopoly. For this reason COMACICO and SECMA were able to continue their market dominance beyond independence and, indeed, up to 1974.[17]

The other new media

The film industry – as an instance of classical 'free enterprise' capitalism – has generally continued to be open to market forces, and it is instructive to compare its introduction and development with the history, in Africa and the Arab world, of the press, the gramophone and broadcasting. The press was introduced into these areas long before the promotion in the 1890s of a popular daily press in Europe with the *Daily Mail* and the *Petit Parisien*. In Africa and the Arab world the press was initially seen as a form of purely official communication and as such it was first brought into being, in a French-language form, in Egypt by Napoleon during his campaign of 1798 with the *Courier de l'Egypte* and *La Décade Egyptienne*. Thirty years later, in 1827–8, it was reintroduced in Egypt through the official Arabic-language journals *Jurnal al-Khadyu* and *Al-Waqai'*, which set out the policies of Muhammad Ali.[18]

Similarly the official press in Algeria dates from the years immediately following the French conquest of 1830. Other Arab states also have a long press history with official journals widely published in the latter part of the nineteenth century: *Al-Anba* (1858) in Lebanon, *Al-Raid* (1860) in Tunisia, *Tarabulus al-Gharb* in Libya, *Suriya* (1865) and *Al-Zawra* (1869) in Iraq, *San'a* (1879) in Yemen, and *Al-Maghreb* (1899), *Al-Gazette* (1899) and *Al-Hijaz* (1909) in Sudan.[19] Even today it is common for the press to continue to be seen as part of the state bureaucracy throughout much of Africa and the Arab world. But there is also a long tradition of independence, spearheaded in Algeria by *Al-Akhbar*, which was founded as a French-language paper in 1839 and became bilingual in 1903, and in Egypt by *Wadi al-Nil* (founded in 1867) and especially by *Al-Ahram*, which was founded in 1875 and continues today as Egypt's leading newspaper.

In some rare instances, newspapers were in existence before colonialism finalized its hold. For example, the first known newspaper in Nigeria, *Iwe Iorhin*, was published in the Yoruba language for the Christian Missionary Society in Lagos as early as 1856, even before the British obtained full control over the area. It was followed in Nigeria by a number of other privately owned papers which gave some voice to nationalist sentiment and protest against colonial rule, particularly the

Lagos Weekly Record, which for thirty-nine years from 1891 'inveighed against the government and white men in general, calling for independence'.[20] In Morocco too there was an active Arabic- and French-language press long before the protectorate was established: the first of four Arabic-language papers was founded in 1889 and the French-language *La Vigie Marocaine* started publication in 1908. When they took charge, however, the French put a stop to all non-official Arabic news publication in Morocco for twenty-five years, until 1936.[21]

In the formally colonized parts of Africa the newspapers founded in the late nineteenth and early twentieth centuries tended to be either official journals or expressions of settler concerns. Often Africans were forbidden to own newspapers. Thus three French newspapers were founded in Senegal before 1900 – *Le Réveil du Sénégalais* (1885), *Le Petit Sénégalais* (1886) and *L'Union Africaine* (1896) – but the editor of the latter could have been speaking for all three when he said that his paper's role was to 'serve on the one hand as a link between the traders of the metropolitan country and those of the colonies, and on the other hand among those of the colonies themselves'.[22] Similarly in Kenya the weekly *African Standard* was founded in Mombasa in 1902 and, as the *Standard,* survives as one of two foreign-owned Kenyan dailies, continuing to put the views of foreign commercial interests as well as those of local inhabitants.[23]

The 1930s saw an intensification of foreign involvement in African and Arab markets and a huge increase in media development. In French West Africa, for example, Charles De Breteuil, who already had interests in Tangier and Casablanca and was later to start newspapers in Guinea and Cameroon, founded *Paris-Dakar* as a weekly in Senegal in 1933 (it became a daily, *Dakar-Matin,* two years later) and *France-Afrique* (later *Abidjan-Matin*) in the Ivory Coast in 1938. These were two of only three dailies still in existence in French West Africa at the time of independence, as the lives of most newspapers lasted a few months or a year or two at best.[24] But Africans did begin to own and operate newspapers: a trio of shortlived papers was founded in Dakar and Rufisque during the 1932 political campaign in Senegal, and *L'Éclaireur* was founded in the Ivory Coast in 1935. The year 1936 saw the re-emergence of a non-official Arabic newspaper, *Al-Atlas,* in Morocco, and in the following year Nnamdi Azikiwe, later to become president of Nigeria, founded the *West African Pilot* in Lagos as the first stage in the establishment of West Africa's first African-owned newspaper chain.[25]

During these years the gramophone also spread throughout the Arab world, where it became not only a domestic luxury but also a feature of café life. In one of the early fusions of local music and the modern recording media, the gramophone allowed the wider diffusion of a new musical form initially developed as an elite style, the *dwar.* As exemplified in the work of the Egyptian singer Sayyid Darwich, the *dwar* was to become 'the musical model and melodic reference of the era'.[26] As Mustapha Chelbi points out, the new music united the linguistically divided Arab world from Morocco to Iraq and played an important social role: 'At a particularly painful moment when the whole Arab world was under colonial domination, the *dwar* appeared as a point of affirmation.'[27]

The 1930s also saw the introduction into the African market of recorded music, in the form of the wind-up gramophone and the cut acetate-coated 78 r.p.m. disc. Wole Soyinka's memoir of his years of childhood, *Aké*, gives a marvellous picture of the impact of this first example of Western technology introduced into African homes. He and his sister were fascinated by the His Master's Voice trademark with its picture of Nipper the dog:

Tinu and I had long rejected the story that the music which came from the gramophone was made by a special singing dog locked in the machine. We never saw it fed, so it would have long starved to death. I had not yet found a means of opening up the machine, so the mystery remained.[28]

The records recalled by Soyinka give some idea of the range available in an African middle-class household:

The voices of Denge, Ayinde Bakare, Ambrose Campbell; a voice which was so deep that I believed it could only have been produced by a special trick of His Master's Voice, but which father assured me belonged to a black man called Paul Robeson . . . Christmas carols, the songs of Marion Anderson; oddities such as a record in which a man did nothing but laugh throughout, and the one concession to a massed choir of European voices – the Hallelujah Chorus.[29]

Aided by the consumer boom caused by World War Two, the period up to 1950 saw an enormous growth in both the quantity of records and the quality of the recorded sound. But, as Ronnie Graham notes, Africans were largely excluded from the profits to be made in the new music industry:

Lacking access to capital, African businessmen failed to capitalize on the opportunities opening up to the major European record companies who, through their African subsidiaries, monopolised the market for 78 rpms. These companies recorded a great deal of local music, both traditional and urban, which was then sent to Europe for pressing into discs. The final products were then exported back to

Africa in a lucrative double trade which guaranteed handsome profits.[30]

The other major communication medium to make its appearance in Africa and the Arab world during the colonial period was radio. The very first broadcasting stations, in Algeria in 1925 and Egypt in 1926 (like the one established in Tunisia in 1935), were private commercial operations, set up to make a profit from the sale of radio sets and air time. But states quickly intervened to take command, and virtually all subsequent introductions of broadcasting capacity into Africa and the Arab world were state-dominated operations. States kept control, seemingly mistrusting private enterprise and advertisement-funded systems, though sometimes the responsibility for the actual running of the operation might be given to a foreign company. This was the case in Egypt (where broadcasting was run by the British Marconi Company from 1934 to 1948) and in Tunisia (where the French broadcasting authority set up the state system in 1938 and had a total monopoly from 1948 to 1957). At first the introduction of radio was slow. Only Morocco and Kenya joined Egypt and Algeria in possessing radio systems in the 1920s (in each case a start was made in 1928), and in the following decade only five further states developed a broadcast capacity. But the potential propaganda power of the medium was recognized by colonial administrations in World War Two, during which a further dozen states set up broadcasting stations. After the war the possession of such a system became the norm and an additional twenty states had acquired a broadcast system of some kind by the time they gained independence.[31]

Radio had a complex impact on colonial societies. European governments could not fail to become aware – particularly in the early 1930s – of the new medium's political importance, as exemplified by the powerful way in which radio brought Hitler's message to the German people. It is therefore not surprising that they took care to control the development of broadcast systems in the colonies. They did not prohibit or impede their introduction, however, since they could see radio's potential value for their own propaganda purposes. Colonies in Africa tended to have borders which, though they certainly seemed neat and tidy to those carving up Africa at the 1884–5 Berlin conference, made little sense on the ground. Colonial administrators were conscious of a need to unify their territories in some way. Most colonies were multilingual and composed largely of illiterates, so there could be no question of following the paths to nation-building familiar in Europe, where nationhood and printed languages had so often gone hand in hand. Benedict Anderson, whose definition of nations as 'imagined communities' provides fascinating insight into the ideological construction of nationalism, points out that, 'multilingual broadcasting can conjure up the imagined community to illiterates and populations with different mother tongues'.[32] This was, of course, precisely the aim of colonial administrators and the reason why they promoted the development of radio.

But broadcasting can also convey the sense of an alternative imagined community, for example, a politically free, non-colonized state. Frantz Fanon's chapter 'This is the Voice of Algeria' in his book *A Dying Colonialism* spells out the role of radio propaganda in the Algerian War of Independence. Writing in 1959, Fanon noted that:

> Since 1956 the purchase of a radio in Algeria has meant, not the adoption of a modern technique for getting news, but the obtaining of access to the only means of entering into communication with the Revolution, of living with it.[33]

On a different level, the existence of radio broadcasting transmitters powerful enough to go beyond the physical boundaries of a single colony or state led to a new awareness *between* African and Arab communities. This had important political implications, but in terms of culture it became particularly apparent in popular music. Here radio speeded up a process which had been under way for centuries, but only through the personal migrations of itinerant musicians. The spread of Egyptian popular song – as exemplified by such star performers as Oum Kelthoum, Mohamed Abdel Wahhab and Farid al-Attrache – owed much to Cairo's powerful radio station, though films and records also played a key role. Music plays an important part in Arab life. As Chelbi observes:

> In the twentieth century Arabs have given more applause to singers than to thinkers. . . . Oum Kelthoum has had more importance – in social impact – than Taha Husayn. Rabah Drissa has been more important in Algeria than Yacine Kateb.[34]

The fusion of the new media – cinema, record industry and broadcasting – in Egypt allowed Cairo to become the cultural centre of the whole Arab world throughout the period when colonial dominance was being confronted, thereby increasing immeasurably Egypt's political influence.

A precise delineation of the new awareness opened up by the new media in those growing up in Africa is given, again, by Soyinka's *Aké*. The book's narrator notes the radio's immutable schedule – 'the box could not be made to speak or sing at any time of the day'[35] – and its indifference to any response. This latter earned it the Yoruba name *As'oromagb'esi*, 'one who speaks without expecting a reply'.[36] Radio introduced for the narrator's elders a new object of worship – 'THE NEWS' – and brought new patterns of entertainment into the African home, most curious of which were:

> the wranglings of a family group which were relayed every
> morning, to the amusement of a crowd, whose laughter shook the
> box. We tried to imagine where this took place. Did this family go into
> the streets to carry on their interminable bickering or did the idle
> crowd simply hang around their home, peeping through the windows
> and cheering them on?[37]

Above all, in the 1940s, there was the propaganda force of the radio as
exploited by the British and only partially comprehended by young
listeners:

> Hitler monopolized the box. He had his own special programme and
> somehow, far off as this war of his whim appeared to be, we were
> drawn more and more into the expanding arena of menace. Hitler
> came nearer home every day.[38]

European filming and recording

So far we have looked at what might be described as the external impact
of the new media: their relations with the structures of colonial power
and their impact on the growing urban population increasingly drawn to
Western definitions of news and entertainment. But the new media, and
particularly the cinema, were also employed to create representations of
African and Arab life for Western informational and entertainment
purposes, as objects of European academic study and – it must be said –
as expressions of colonial 'superiority'. Only in rare instances before
independence were these media used to offer genuine expression of
African or Arab values and concerns. The European-dominated media
production of representations of African and Arab life has a history
almost as long as that of media consumption, as exemplified – in cinema
– by the development of distribution and exhibition structures.

A considerable amount of documentary and newsreel material was
shot in Africa and the Arab world during the colonial era.[39] But apart
from the Lumière material, which was customarily used by the Lumière
operators to give a local touch to their presentations (as well as being
added to the general catalogue in Paris), most of this footage was not
intended for African or Arab audiences. Rather, the supposed objectivity manifested by the still or movie camera was consciously
used, in Europe and elsewhere, to support the colonial cause. Guido
Convents notes the key part played by film images of the colonies – as
information, scientific record and novelty – in a colonial propaganda

drive which also embraced the press, education, art, international exhibitions and popular entertainment. He concludes:

> Between 1895 and 1918 the propaganda power of the cinema was gradually recognized by a number of groups which did not hesitate to introduce this medium into the range of their activities. The colonialists were among this number.[40]

This propaganda use of the new medium of film has to be seen within the context of the power and prestige of the European science and learning which underpinned the economic strength of the European powers. But science was far from being objective during the colonial era where racial issues were concerned, and recent scholarly investigation has drawn attention to numerous instances of blatant bias and what has been termed 'pseudo-scientific racism'. Stephen Jay Gould, a specialist in evolutionary theory, has pointed out that racism – in the form of notions of Aryan supremacy – was a key factor which prevented most scientists from accepting Darwin's correct surmise that the human race evolved in Africa.[41] Gould notes, moreover, that for decades any new evidence concerning evolution was systematically adjusted to support existing racial prejudices. An a priori belief in black inferiority shaped theoretical speculation and coloured all interpretation of the data.[42] In a similar fashion, Martin Bernal's investigations into Western views on Egypt's role in the origins of Greek civilization have uncovered a striking series of shifts in the successive models (or basic structures of knowledge) used to shape the efforts of European scholars. The model universally accepted until the beginning of the nineteenth century, and indeed based on the writings of the Greeks themselves, asserted that the Greeks had been colonized around 1500 BC by Egyptians and Phoenicians. Though this model had, in Bernal's view, no major internal deficiencies or weaknesses in explanatory power, it came to be replaced first by an approach which denied the truth of Egyptian settlements in Greece and then, 'during the twin peaks of anti-Semitism in the 1890s and again in the 1920s and 1930s', by one which denied even Phoenician cultural influence:

> For eighteenth- and nineteenth-century Romantics and racists it was simply intolerable for Greece, which was seen not merely as the epitome of Europe but also as its pure childhood, to have been the result of the mixture of native Europeans and colonizing Africans and Semites.[43]

A new discipline of Egyptology now grew up, dealing with Egyptian culture as something essentially alien and separate from the civilization of the Greeks. But this new discipline was merely one aspect of the systematic downgrading of the Arabs and their culture and religion, that formed one of the supporting pillars of colonial thought. As Edward Said observes:

> The Orient is not only adjacent to Europe; it is also the place of Europe's greatest and richest and oldest colonies, the source of its civilizations and languages, its cultural contestant, and one of its deepest and most recurring images of the Other.[44]

Said traces the way in which the potential challenge of Arab culture was confronted in Europe during the colonial era, through the welding together of various European doctrines and strands of thought into a single system – Orientalism – which came to occupy so authoritative a position that, 'no one writing, thinking, or acting on the Orient could do so without taking account of the limitations on thought and action imposed by Orientalism'.[45] In this sense, Orientalism is not a structure of lies or myths, or even an airy European fantasy about the Orient, but 'a created body of theory and practice in which, for many generations, there has been a considerable material investment'.[46] As such, from the early nineteenth century it shaped the thought of European poets and painters, economists and philosophers, politicians and colonial administrators. Said's lucid analysis makes cautionary reading for anyone in the West engaged in analysing Arab or African culture, since we cannot, logically, escape the problem: the Orient must remain, for us, the Other. But the problem is in many ways more intense for African and Arab writers and film-makers who have trained in the West and who, in their work, set out to recover their own past. Said intends his analysis to illustrate, 'specifically for formerly colonized peoples, the dangers and temptations of employing this structure upon themselves or upon others',[47] since European-devised models of thought invite them to see *themselves* as the Other.

Parallel to the documentary filming of various aspects of African and Arab life – newsreel footage of foreign interventions, rebellions and royal visits, wildlife compilations and records of rural crafts – were the expeditions by anthropologists and musicologists intent on recording traditional music. Graham gives a compendium of those who, equipped with a single microphone but also perhaps half a ton of fragile recording equipment, ventured to record African traditional music: there was Carl Meinhof in German East Africa from 1902, Pater F. Witte in Togo in 1905, N. W. Thomas in Sierra Leone and Nigeria in 1908, Sir Harry Johnson in Buganda and Alice Werner in Kenya and Tanzania before World War One, and Hugh Tracey in fifteen countries of East, Central and Southern Africa for forty years from the early 1930s.[48]

Worthy as the impulses behind these efforts undoubtedly were, and fascinating as the recorded results may be, this recording activity points to one of the crucial cultural effects of European colonialism: the denial of the essential fluidity of traditional African or Arab cultures. In traditional societies like those of pre-colonial Africa, individuals were not characterized by a single 'tribal' identity. Instead they

> moved in and out of multiple identities, defining themselves at one moment as subject to this chief, at another as a member of that cult, at another moment as part of this clan, and at yet another moment as an initiate of that professional guild.[49]

The custom and continuity valued in traditional societies were never rigid, but instead loosely defined and infinitely flexible, allowing 'an adaptation so spontaneous and natural that it was often unperceived'.[50] The European colonizers, however, brought to bear a very different definition of custom and tribal identity. As far as they were concerned:

> People were to be 'returned' to their tribal identities; ethnicity was to be 'restored' as the basis of association and organization. The new rigidities, immobilizations and ethnic identifications, while serving very immediate European interests, could nevertheless be seen by the whites as fully 'traditional' and hence as legitimated.[51]

It is clear that the preservation of a musical tradition at a single point in time – when it is accessible to the intrepid recordist but still uncontaminated by the modernizing forces of colonialism – represents an equivalent ossification of tradition. From our present perspective we can see that, though music was wedded to virtually every key moment of African life – from birth, through work, family and religion, to death – it was not itself immutably fixed. The various seasonal and permanent migrations of groups and individuals, combined with the constant impact of foreign influences (Chinese, Indian, Arab and European), all created a music which was both traditional and in a constant state of flux. It is this essential fluidity which the recording process denies if it is cited as incontrovertible evidence since, by freezing the traditional in one of its transitory manifestations, the record denies the validity both of current variants and of future modifications. This is precisely in accord with the (often unwitting) manipulation of African traditional values by European colonizers who, by classifying what they took to be African tradition, in fact *invented* it. As Terence Ranger has noted, 'What were called customary law, customary land-rights, customary political structure and so on, were in fact *all* invented by colonial codification.'[52] Again, the danger for African writers and film-makers who repudiate the Westernized culture of the bourgeois elite is that they may unwittingly end up embracing another set of colonial inventions instead.[53]

European fictional approaches

In addition to the material gathered by film documentarists and musicologists, during the colonial era a great deal of fictional film was shot partly on location in Africa and the Arab world by Europeans. Examples of imperialist rhetoric are to be found in the film production of most of the colonial powers. With regard to black sub-Saharan Africa, one might cite as particularly significant Alexander Korda's British production *Sanders of the River* (1933), the French *L'Homme du Niger* (1939) by Jacques de Baroncelli and, from Nazi Germany, Herbert Selpin's *Die Reiter von Deutsch-Ostafrika* (1934) and, especially, *Carl Peters* (1941). All these concentrate on their European-born heroes, who are depicted as dedicating or sacrificing themselves to the good of Africans seen from a totally paternalistic perspective. A stance untroubled by any questioning of European dominance is characteristic of all such works, and their principal role, as the Tunisian critic Ferid Boughedir has pointed out, was 'to supply a cultural and ideological justification for political domination and economic exploitation'. The roots of their mythical portrait lay in the falsification of reality, whereby the colonizer was 'a technician, a man of progress, from a superior culture and civilization, while the native was a primitive, incapable of technical progress or of mastering his passions'.[54]

Of course, most films set in the colonies were no more than adventure films, but the ideology was the same whether they were shot on location or entirely in the studio. The same myths are propagated by Julien Divivier's *Pépé le moko* (shot in 1937 partly on location in Algiers) and John Cromwell's Hollywood remake *Algiers* (made the following year using merely background transparencies). Similarly, as Jeffrey Richards notes:

> Ideologically, the American films of Empire were little different from British films of Empire. The one major difference seems to have been the unusual preponderance of Canadians who turn up in the British Imperial service, a device necessary to explain away the American accents of members of the cast.[55]

The actual setting of the story – whether it is, say, India, Burma or Africa – is of little consequence, since these are essentially tales of the colonizer and his adventures, a pattern reflected in the categories which Richards uses to organize his analysis of the 'Cinema of Empire': The Old School Tie, The Imperial Archetype, The White Man's Burden, etc.

Of the hundreds of feature films produced in the colonial era throughout the Arab and African worlds, the best-documented are the 210 features made by American and European (mostly French) companies in the Maghreb between 1911 and 1963: about 100 in Morocco, over 80 in Algeria and a couple of dozen in Tunisia. This colonial cinema – for which, as Pierre Boulanger notes, 'the talent expended was inversely proportional to the number of camels employed'[56] – is largely mediocre, and even great directors, such as Jean Renoir with *Le Bled* (1929), produced some of their weakest works here. Most of the films, as Guy Hennebelle points out in his preface to Boulanger's book:

> have become in part intolerable because of their latent racism, their paternalism or their warlike mentality. All, or thereabouts, seem at present like the archaeological relics of a bygone era during which Europe thought itself able to impose definitively on to the world a domination which it thought legitimized by its civilization's claim to universality.[57]

British imperial films set in Africa did offer parts – if only in supporting roles – to black actors like Robert Adams, Orlando Martins and Earl Cameron.[58] But for the Arabs of the Maghreb even that consolation was lacking. In addition to the falsity of the myths and the inauthenticity of the life depicted, there was a virtual absence of Arab players on the screen: all substantial roles were played by Europeans, so that the Arabs themselves were reduced to mere silhouettes, essentially a part of the landscape. Abdelghani Megherbi, who is able to find only six appearances by Arab performers in the eighty or so films shot in Algeria,[59] stresses the way in which the invisibility of the Arabs in this filmed fiction was in one sense a perfect reflection of the Algerian's insignificance in the life of the colony:

> The correspondence between the two is crude, brutal, continuous, total. In conformity with the implacable logic of colonization, the Algerian is virtually absent everywhere.[60]

Of course, in economic terms this use of location filming constituted no more than a minor facet of the interaction between the film industries of the West and the colonial world. The great bulk of films distributed dealt only with European and North American lives and fantasies. For African peoples, as Boughedir observes,

[T]o watch these films that neither spoke their language nor had any connection with their society brought a double alienation, one that was both ideological and, more especially, cultural.[61]

While Boughedir's strictures have their justification – and point to the immense cultural importance of the films made in local languages by Arab and African film-makers after independence – this is only part of the truth. The Hollywood style of film-making was a universally accessible form of narrative. The mechanics of the storytelling allowed all viewers the enjoyment of the action and the thrill of identification. Many future African and Arab film-makers learned a love of cinema, not cultural alienation, from Western movies. Thus the radical power of the Ethiopian-born documentarist Haile Gerima's work is in no way diminished by the fact that, as a child in the provincial town of Gondar, he identified with Tarzan, shouting warnings against 'them', that is the Africans.[62] Films can also be read in ways not intended by their makers, so that the Senegalese director Ousmane Sembene claims to have realized the power of the cinema from seeing the feats of the black American athlete Jesse Owens in Leni Riefenstahl's Fascist-inspired documentary on the 1936 Berlin Olympics, *Olympiad*.[63]

Given the unquestioned assumption of Western superiority expressed in virtually every European or Hollywood film set in Africa or the Orient, one might have expected colonial settlers and administrators to have welcomed the distribution of feature films in the territories of the European empires in the 1920s and 1930s. In fact we find an immense unease at the depiction of white cultural stereotypes, particularly in Hollywood films. Edward Thompson, for example, saw the cinema as 'India's overshadowing menace' and complained that 'already films have left little respect for our (supposed) ways of living in the West'.[64] Sir Hesketh Bell, who felt that the conception of white civilization that 'the backward races within the Empire' were receiving from third-rate melodramas constituted 'an international menace', wrote:

The success of our government of subject races depends almost entirely on the degree of respect which we can inspire. Incalculable is the damage that has already been done to the prestige of Europeans in India and the Far East through the wide-spread exhibition of ultrasensational and disreputable pictures.[65]

In the House of Commons, a former Chancellor of the Exchequer, Sir Robert Horne, said:

I do not suppose that there is anything which has done so much harm to the prestige and position of Western people and the white race as the exhibition of films which have tended to degrade us in the eyes of peoples who have been accustomed to look upon us with admiration and respect.[66]

But such protests had little impact on the policies of the dominant Western film distributors, who continued to seek all possible means of expanding the world market for their products.

The colonial film units

The paternalistic attitude adopted by the colonizers was particularly strong when directed towards Africans. As late as 1958, William Sellers, a pioneer in the use of instructional films in Nigeria and subsequently a key figure in the Colonial Film Unit, gave the following response to the question 'Why should not entertainment films made for Western audiences be distributed through cinemas in Africa?'

> There is overwhelming evidence that this would be a disastrous policy. Such films more often than not deliberately set out to falsify the facts of life, and would not only be misleading but even dangerous when shown to illiterate rural audiences in Africa.[67]

But the underlying sense of the power of film to shape ideas and attitudes did lead to a number of attempts to make 'positive' use of films in the colonies. One project that aimed to explore the potential of cinema for education in Africa was the Bantu Educational Cinema Experiment undertaken in 1935–7, the report on which set out:

> to elucidate for all who have the advancement of the African at heart those principles which govern the use of the motion picture as an instrument of education and an aid for tribal society in the two-fold struggle it is making to preserve the old traditions and to adapt itself to the modern world.[68]

These worthy aims were to be attained by making films in Africa *for* Africans. One of the principal conclusions reached was that:

> [T]he moving picture is understood by quite unsophisticated Natives to a degree which astonishes people who have experienced their comparative inability to recognize still pictures.[69]

But the organizers showed a paternalistic approach in their very limited view of what even an intelligent African could achieve:

[I]ntelligent young Africans can be trained to do much of the routine work of the darkroom and the sound studios, and even some of the semi-skilled work. Also . . . Africans can be trained to operate small cinema units and to deal satisfactorily with most of the simpler difficulties that arise.[70]

There was no recognition in the report that Africans could, in the foreseeable future, actually *make* films. The Bantu Educational Cinema Experiment in East Africa was funded by the Geneva-based International Missionary Council, and attempts to interest the Colonial Office in funding an immediate follow-up were unsuccessful. It was not until 1939 and the outbreak of war that the Colonial Film Unit was set up as part of the Ministry of Information. Its aim was to tell 'the story of the War with the right propaganda',[71] in parallel with similar efforts to use the propaganda power of the radio broadcast. The unit was run by William Sellers and veteran silent-film director George Pearson. Together the two devised a remarkable theory of film-making for 'primitive audiences':

Their basic assumption was that perception of moving images on film is something learned rather than inherent. The Unit's films were required to be simple in content, slow in tempo and have considerable pictorial continuity. It was recommended that film techniques should not go beyond the viewer's experience and that the use of montage, flashbacks and magnification be avoided.[72]

Despite the lack of suitable African footage and adequate funds to send a crew to shoot on location, the Colonial Film Unit was the most sustained attempt to date to exploit film's educational potential in Africa. But it retained the traditional paternalist attitude to Africans, with Sellers arguing against the appointment of Africans to the staff of the unit on the grounds that 'an African with the necessary qualifications would be too out of touch with conditions among the most illiterate sections of the community for whom the films were principally designed'.[73] Though the actual effectiveness of film as part of a (notably successful) multi-media campaign to ensure African support for the war effort is uncertain, and the impact of the special simplified film style remains controversial, the unit's perceived success led to the setting up of various film units in postwar Africa. When the Colonial Film Unit itself was disbanded in 1955, the staff set up the Overseas Film and Television Centre to offer similar services in London on a purely commercial basis.[74] A film training unit in Ghana, later to be known as the Accra Film School, was set up and in 1949 led to the establishment of what was to become the Ghana Film Industry Corporation.[75] A Central

African Film Unit – to serve Northern Rhodesia, Southern Rhodesia and Nyasaland[76] – and a Nigeria Federal Film Unit were both set up in 1948, the latter staffed by Nigerians who had trained in Ghana.[77] In Kenya, the Institute of Mass Communications began its valuable work in educational and informational film-making. The effect of such organizations has been to give a firm focus to documentary film activity in Anglophone Africa. But this has occurred at the expense of feature film-making which, receiving no official encouragement, has tended to be scattered and sporadic.

World War Two drew the attention also of the French authorities in Algeria to the propaganda potential of film. The Service de diffusion cinématographique (SDC) was set up in 1943, though it did not begin to function until 1946. It concentrated on bringing films to rural communities, using mobile *ciné-bus* units, and between June 1946 and December 1948 gave some 786 showings attended by over 1 million spectators.[78] Most of the films shown were documentaries; some were made in France, others were produced by the French through a production organization – the Service algérien du cinéma (SAC) – set up alongside the SDC. There were also showings of classic French feature films in Algerian schools and, whatever the intended propaganda purpose of these, they in fact served to introduce a number of future Algerian film-makers to the art of the cinema.[79] Later, in the 1950s, during the Algerian War, the French army made extensive use of newsreel footage specially edited to put the case for 'pacification' to the Algerian people. Shots of Algerian combatants were naturally omitted, but it was not possible to avoid all aspects of Algerian reality. The ironic result, as Megherbi points out, was that Algerians saw their own lives – the squalid living conditions of the colonized rural masses, for example – depicted realistically on the screen for the first time, thanks to the propaganda efforts of the French army.[80]

The Belgian authorities in the Congo followed the example of the British in attempting to 'protect' Africans from normal commercial films and conventional film style on the grounds that:

> The African is, in general, not mature for cinema. Cinematographic conventions disrupt him; psychological nuances escape him; rapid successions of images submerge him.[81]

In 1947 the Belgian Ministry of Information set up the Bureau ciné-photo under L. van Bever to make films specifically for the Congolese, using a simplified technique similar to that employed by the British Colonial Film Unit. As a result, by 1957 the number of screenings arranged by the government had reached 15,000 a year, with the number of spectators estimated at 8.6 million.[82]

Another organization set up at the same time with similar aims was the Centre congolais d'action catholique cinématographique (CCACC), which founded three film production centres in the Congo. The head of the missionary organization, Father Van den Heuvel, believed like Sellers and Pearson that a special style was required for films addressed to African audiences, and proposed a technique 'analogous to that used in making films for children'.[83] These Belgian efforts, especially those of the missionaries, have received considerable praise from certain European critics, but the verdict of the young African critic Manthia Diawara is severe:

> The Belgian officials and missionaries were producing a paternalist and racist cinema, and in the process they shut out the Zairean as film maker. Their fetishization and/or mystification of the technological apparatus prevented them from having a human to human rapport with Zaireans. They treated Zaireans as 'non-évolués', with lower mental capacities; it would therefore have been contradictory for them to picture these Africans in unsupervised positions of film makers and producers.[84]

Indigenous culture under colonialism

Despite the wide variations in the form and severity of foreign dominance, it is reasonable to see the whole of Africa and the Arab world as colonized, to a greater or lesser degree, until at least the 1950s. Egypt, it is true, had been granted its independence in 1922, but only unilaterally by Britain, on terms that no Egyptian politician was prepared formally to accept. The occupation of Egypt by British troops continued for a further three decades. In the Arab East, the Mashreq, it was the most socially, culturally and economically backward parts of the Arab world, such as Saudi Arabia, which achieved their independence on the break-up of the Ottoman Empire, while the more developed areas, such as Lebanon, Iraq and Syria, were placed under European mandate.[85] In the Arab West, the Maghreb, Libya achieved independence in 1951, Morocco in 1952 and Tunisia in 1956, but the influence of the former colonizing powers remained strong. In black Africa only Sudan, Ghana and Guinea gained independence in the late 1950s, while the bulk of colonized Africa had to wait until the 1960s for even formal political sovereignty. Nevertheless, the difference between settler colonies, such as Kenya or Algeria, and those areas controlled by indirect rule, such as Northern Nigeria, was significant in terms of cultural development. It is fair to see the emergent literature and cinema of Egypt, for example, as a reflection of both the country's growing economic strength, which made it virtually self-sufficient in consumer products by the end of the 1930s,[86] and the three decades of national awareness and struggle which were to find their culmination in the 1952 revolution.

In Africa and the Arab world, the modern literary forms of drama, the novel and the short story, together with the cinema and the record industry, have their origins under colonialism or imperial dominance, and this has had a considerable effect on their development even after independence. In analysing cultural forms of this kind it is conventional to distinguish between three broad categories: traditional, popular and elite. Karin Barber, in a stimulating piece of analysis, has offered useful definitions of these categories in African terms. Traditional arts are 'transmitted more or less intact, though slowly changing, from a pre-colonial past', while elite arts, by contrast, are 'produced by the educated few who have assimilated European languages, forms and conventions more or less thoroughly'.[87] After independence both may form part of the official state culture, traditional arts being used for state ceremony (in the form of, say, dance displays put on for visiting dignitaries) and elite arts being taught in state schools and colleges (as when French- or English-language novels and plays are used as part of the curriculum). Popular arts – of which music is a striking example – are more difficult to define: hybrid, syncretic, often despised and always unofficial. They are very much 'the new unofficial arts of colonialism and post-colonialism, produced by the profound and accelerating social change that has characterized these periods'.[88] They may borrow from elite forms and be grounded in the traditional, but popular arts are constantly evolving, unfettered by rules and able to use for their diffusion the most modern media forms such as radio, record and cassette. An analysis of cinema in these terms shows very clearly its particularity as a cultural form: produced by an elite well aware of European approaches, often drawing self-consciously on traditional themes and sources, but aiming almost always at the widest popular audience.

A key factor shaping cultural developments was the nature of the colonial educational system. Once the internal dynamics of traditional society had been brought to a halt and the living continuity of the community had been broken by colonization, the colonizer was able to begin to impose his image on the colonized. This was a key factor in colonial society because, as the Kenyan-born academic Abdul R. Jan Mohamed observes, the colonizer has a spiritual dependency on the colonized which, to some extent, matches the latter's economic dependence on him:

While he sees the native as the quintessence of evil and therefore avoids all contact because he fears contamination, he is at the same time absolutely dependent upon the colonized people not only for his privileged social and material status but also for his sense of moral superiority, and, therefore, ultimately for his very identity.[89]

The essential aim of the colonizer was to have the imposed image of inferiority 'accepted and lived with to a certain degree by the colonized'.[90] Education was a key means of attaining this aim. Among other things, education would teach the student a history which was not that of his own people. As Albert Memmi, who grew up under the French protectorate in Tunisia, writes, the student was given an alien (and alienating) perspective:

> Everything seems to have taken place out of his country. He and his land are nonentities or exist only with reference to the Gauls, the Franks or the Marne. In other words, with reference to what he is not: to Christianity, although he is not a Christian; to the West which ends under his nose, at a line which is even more insurmountable than it is imaginary.[91]

More seriously still, the colonized's own native tongue was undermined. To quote Memmi once more:

> [T]he colonized's mother tongue, that which is sustained by his feelings, emotions and dreams, that in which his tenderness and wonder are expressed, thus that which holds the greatest emotional impact, is precisely the one which is the least valued. It has no stature in the country or in the concert of peoples.[92]

From widely differing regions of Africa two novelists – Bernard Dadié from the Ivory Coast[93] and Ngugi wa Thiong'o from Kenya[94] – have recalled the treatment meted out at school to pupils foolish enough to use their native tongue. In each case the humiliation involved being compelled to carry or wear a symbolic object (in Ngugi's case a metal plate with an inscription such as 'I am stupid' or 'I am a donkey') until the end of the day, when a thrashing would be administered. The same practice was apparently also common in French-language schools in Lebanon and Syria.[95] To add to the impact, pupils would be actively encouraged to denounce each other for what the teachers regarded as linguistic malpractice. The colonizer's aim in these educational practices was of course to produce a bilingual administrative elite. But they also formed the context for the emergence of the literatures in the languages of the colonizer which began to emerge throughout Africa, particularly after World War Two.

African and Arab literature

African literature in French got underway with a cluster of fictional works in the 1920s,[96] but developments in the 1930s were sparse: the occasional novel, some amateur theatre production at the Ecole William Ponty in Senegal (one of the key educational institutions with French as its language of tuition) and, most important, the laying in Paris of the foundations of the black consciousness movement, *négritude*, by Caribbean and African students led by Aimé Césaire and the Senegalese Léopold Sédar Senghor. The movement, which drew its inspiration from both surrealism and Marxism, was to come to prominence after World War Two with the publication of Césaire's *Cahier d'un retour au pays*, written in 1935 but not published until 1947, and Senghor's *Anthologie de la nouvelle poésie nègre et malgache* (1948) with its preface, 'Orpheu noir', by Jean-Paul Sartre.

The idea of *négritude* as developed by Senghor, a major French-language poet who became both first president of an independent Senegal and a member of the Académie française, met with considerable resistance in the 1960s, especially from writers in Anglophone Africa. But what is striking in retrospect is the way in which this first literary movement under colonialism parallels the subsequent political movements for liberation in black Africa. Just as the latter constitute a form of revolt shaped as a kind of mirror image of the colonial state (seeking independence in Western political terms, rather than through a return to tradition), so too *négritude* asserts black values as a counter-myth to European racism but in a European, not an African, language. As Abiola Irele has pointed out: 'It is important to note that for Senghor, the answer does not consist in a systematic rejection of Western racist theories, but rather a modification of the terms in which they are set out.'[97]

Some early African prose writers using French as their means of expression sought to preserve African literary forms (see, for example, the collections of folktales published by Birago Diop from the 1940s onwards). But most writers who adopted the French language also chose to shape their fiction into the Western form of the novel. By the mid-1950s the novel had become the dominant form of literary expression in Francophone Africa, with the autobiographical works of Fernand Oyono and Bernard Dadié, the satires of Mongo Beti, Camara Laye's romantic visions of an African past and Ousmane Sembene's politically committed studies of contemporary African workers. These writers set the pattern for the steadily increasing output of novels which marks the early years of independence.

Though *négritude* was never a potent factor in Anglophone Africa, in other respects the development of an English-language African literature resembles that in French. In Ghana, which led sub-Saharan Africa into independence in 1957, there were a number of early pioneering works, such as Joseph E. Casely-Hayford's novel *Ethiopia Unbound* (1911) and Kobina Sekyi's play *The Blinkards* (1915). But this early impetus was not maintained in Ghana and no major writers emerged there until after the 1966 coup which overthrew the independence leader, Kwame Nkrumah. In Nigeria, Amos Tutuola's idiosyncratic retelling of traditional African stories, beginning with *The Palm-wine Drinkard* (1952), offers a parallel to Birago Diop's French folktale collections, and a number of major English-language writers emerged in the last years of the colonial regime, among them the novelists Chinua Achebe and Cyprian Ekwensi and the poet Gabriel Okara. What differentiates the Anglophone areas from their Francophone counterparts is the existence in the former of a large quantity of writing in modern forms but in local languages: the Swahili poetry and novels of Shabaan Robert in Tanganyika (now part of Tanzania), the early Luo verse of Okot p'Bitek in Uganda, as well as the mass of prose fiction in both Hausa and Yoruba in Nigeria and in Ndebele and Shona in Southern Rhodesia (now Zimbabwe).[98] The area of indigenous language output which eventually proved most relevant to the cinema is the Yoruba folk opera-cum-drama, beginning with the work of Hubert Ogunde in the mid-1940s.

But the bulk of major African writers continued to work in European languages and their struggles have been graphically conveyed by Gabriel Okara:

> In order to capture the vivid images of African speech, I had to eschew the habit of expressing my thoughts first in English. It was difficult at first, but I had to learn. I had to study each Ijaw expression I used and to discover the probable situation in which it was used in order to bring out the nearest meaning in English.[99]

In North Africa, where French influence on a predominantly Arab culture has been so strong, the language question is not merely a linguistic struggle, but an issue of cultural identity. The debate has been particularly strong in Algeria. There, an Arabic-language literature preceded a literature in French, which did not emerge until the 1950s, but the writers educated in French and choosing it as their medium of literary expression – such as Mohamed Dib, Mouloud Mammeri, Kateb Yacine and Mouloud Feraoun – were both fully committed to the struggle for national liberation and also forceful in their view that French formed part of the cultural heritage of contemporary Algeria. Whilst recognizing that they themselves belonged to a transitional generation, they defended their French-language work spiritedly. As

Mammeri put it:

> The French language is for me not at all the shameful language of an
> enemy, but an incomparable instrument of liberation and, secondly,
> of communication with the rest of the world. I consider that it
> translates us (*traduit*) more than it betrays (*trahit*) us.[100]

But the particular situation of such writers, and their Moroccan
counterparts, such as Driss Chraïbi and Mohamed Khair-Eddine, often
residents of France and married to French wives, remains problematic,
particularly when they feel compelled to point out that the forces of
Arabization iń North Africa are often extremely conservative and closed
to notions of modernization.

Those concerned with the creation of a modern literature in Egypt
faced linguistic problems of a rather different kind: the unsuitability of
literary Arabic to the adopted Western forms of literary expression and
the unacceptability to literary critics of writing in the vernacular. Ali B.
Jad traces the 'acceptance and cultivation of a functional non-rhymed
prose as a literary idiom' to the growth of newspapers from the 1880s
onwards.[101] But prose fiction was slow to emerge in Egypt. Mohamed
Husayn Haykal's pioneering novel *Zaynab* (1913) had few immediate
successors and, in the period up to the emergence of Naguib Mahfuz in
1939, critics point to only a handful of significant lengthy prose works:
novels such as Ibrahim al-Mazini's *Ibrahim al-katib/Ibrahim the Author*
(1931) and Tawfiq al-Hakim's *Awdat al-ruh/The Return of the Spirit*
(1935), and the first two volumes of the critic Taha Husayn's
autobiography, *Al-Ayyam/An Egyptian Childhood* (1925) and *The Stream
of Days* (1939). In contrast, the 1920s and 1930s saw a succession of
lively and inventive short stories, whose emergence Sabry Hafez has
explicitly linked to the growth of Egyptian nationalism after 1919:

> Just as Egyptian nationalism used elements of western thought
> blended with elements of classical traditional culture in its attempt to
> express itself in this phase, so the early beginnings of the Egyptian
> short story emphasised the importance of the genuine marriage
> between the inherited traditional elements . . . and the western short
> story.[102]

Both novel and short story gained momentum in the 1940s and 1950s.

The situation is somewhat different with respect to drama. European
conceptions of dramatic form were first introduced into the Arab world
in the mid-nineteenth century, with a translation of Molière, and from
this stemmed, fairly unproblematically, a tradition of popular Egyptian
vernacular comedy, exemplified successively by Ya'qub Sanu and Naguib

al-Rihani. Serious drama, by contrast, was hampered from the start by both the traditional Arab involvement of drama with music and singing (a tradition of great relevance to the Egyptian sound cinema) and the problem of language. Traditional literature was composed in a style of classical Arabic still written but no longer spoken, and many critics (and writers) refused to consider as literature anything written otherwise. The construction of a modern theatre dealing with contemporary issues in a non-spoken language is clearly a contradiction in terms, but at the same time the Egyptian vernacular both lacked status as a potential literary language and reduced the potential audience to Egyptians alone, since it would be quite incomprehensible to Arabic speakers in, say, Morocco or Kuwait. The difficulties are exemplified by the career of the man widely recognized as Egypt's greatest dramatist. Tawfiq al-Hakim's output of plays – marked by an interest in intellectual debate and the clash of ideas – is essentially designed to be read rather than performed. And even Hakim was driven to propose a 'third way', 'a kind of all-size Arabic especially for the drama and for dialogue in general that would be at once read as classical and spoken as vernacular'.[103] Little came of this, but the general difficulties in establishing both a tradition of the novel and a style of serious drama coincided with the early years of fictional film-making in Egypt. This too, after 1932, also had to confront the problem of language.

The beginnings of Arab film-making

In the years between World Wars One and Two commercial feature film production gradually established itself in Egypt, within the context of the country's general industrial development. But elsewhere the cinema's appearance was fragmentary – the result more of exceptional endeavour by isolated individuals than of any underlying social necessity. Pre-independence cinema was very much a cinema of pioneers, and was rare in the Arab world and totally lacking in sub-Saharan Africa. Silent film production had barely got under way in the Arab world by the time the sound film arrived in 1932 – in sharp contrast with the situation in India, China or Latin America. After pioneering short films by the Egyptian Mohamed Bayoumi (*The Civil Servant/Al-bash kateb*) and the Tunisian Chikly (*Zohra*) in 1922, only a handful of silent features were made in the subsequent decade. In Tunisia the enterprising Chikly made the sole North African silent feature film, *The Girl from Carthage/Ain al-Gheza*, as early as 1924. In Egypt just thirteen silent features were made between 1926 and 1932, beginning with *Kiss in the Desert/Qubla fil-sahara*, directed by a Chilean émigré of Lebanese origin, Ibrahim Lama, and *Leila*, directed by Istephane Rosti and

Wedad Orfi and starring the actress Aziza Amir. While *Leila* is generally
considered by critics to be the first 'national' film (in that it was
conceived and realized by Egyptians), the film singled out by Samir
Farid as the most important of these silent features is Mohamed Karim's
1930 adaptation of the novel *Zaynab*.[104] In Syria two features were
made: *The Innocent Victim/Al-muttaham al-bari* (1928), with a plot
'much influenced by the adventures of gangland so favoured by the
American cinema',[105] and *Under the Damascus Sky/Taht sama Dimashq*,
which had to compete with the first Egyptian talkies when it appeared in
1932 and was a financial disaster. In Lebanon, the first silent feature was
an amateur effort, *The Adventures of Elias Mabrouk/Mughamarat Elias
Mabrouk* (1929) which 'was not presented in any motion-picture
house',[106] a fate which did not deter the director, Jordano Pidutti, from
attempting a second film, *The Adventures of Abu Abed/Mughamarat Abu
Abed*, the following year.

During the thirteen or so years from the screening of the first Egyptian
sound film in March 1932 to the end of World War Two, the feature film
established solid roots in Egypt – along with the short story and the
novel – though developments elsewhere in the Arab world were sparse.
In all some 150 features were made in Egypt during this period; output
passed double figures for the first time in 1935–6 and reached a first
peak of 25 features in 1944–5. Just as the first important silent film,
Zaynab, had been based on the first significant Egyptian novel so, too,
close links were established between the sound film and the emergent
Egyptian theatre. The three dominant figures of the Egyptian stage[107]
were all involved in film-making in the early 1930s: the actor and pioneer
of prose drama Georges Abyad worked on one of the very first sound
films; Yusuf Wahby, the stage advocate of the musical melodrama and
verse drama, set up the Ramses studio (named after his theatrical
troupe) in 1932; and Naguib al-Rihani appeared in his stage persona as
Kish Kish Bey before directing the first Franco-Egyptian co-
production, *Yacout Effendi* – an adaptation of Marcel Pagnol's *Topaze* –
in 1934. Wahby's production of Mohamed Karim's *Sons of Aristocrats/
Awlad al-dhawat*, a version of one of his stage successes shot partially in
Paris, was the first Egyptian sound film. Released on 14 March 1932, it
enjoyed a great success.[108]

The theatricality of the early Egyptian sound cinema was enhanced by
the development of films offering songs and dances as their prime
attraction. The second Egyptian sound film to be released in 1932 (and
the first actually to be shot with sound) was *The Song of the
Heart/Anshudat al-fuad*, made in Paris by an Italian director, Mario
Volpi, using songs by the writer Abbas al-Akkad and starring some of
Egypt's leading singers and performers. Though the film was a
forerunner of the most successful Egyptian film genre, the musical, it

was a commercial failure.

The reason seems to lie in the fact that at this time the stage presentation of the traditional Arab song had not been modified to the needs of the new forms of diffusion. In Egypt, one of the key media for the popularization of song throughout the Arab world, the radio, was as undeveloped as the cinema at the beginning of the 1930s. Though some private commercial radio stations had been set up in Cairo and Alexandria from 1926, it was not until 1934 that the Egyptian Broadcasting Corporation was inaugurated and even then it proceeded only slowly with the development of a nationwide network.[109] In its traditional form the Arab song consisted of two parts: a musical overture of perhaps three minutes' duration leading to the song itself, slow-rhythmed and heavily marked by repetition, lasting another fifteen minutes. Clearly such a format could not be viably inserted into a basically narrative film form and some modification was required. In view of the enormous impact Latin American rhythms were to have subsequently on sub-Saharan popular music, it is interesting to note Yves Thoraval's assertion that the Arab song needed the introduction of new, Latin American rhythms before Egyptian musical films could acquire a true filmic rhythm.[110] Gradually the necessary adaptations were made and Egyptian musicals, featuring such singers as Mohamed Abdel Wahhab (beginning with Karim's *The White Rose/Al-warda al-baidaa* in 1934), Oum Kelthoum (first seen in Fritz Kramp's first Misr production *Wedad* in 1935) and later Farid al-Attrache, established their popularity throughout the world, assisted by records and the increasing power of Cairo radio.

The Egyptian cinema of the pre-1945 period was more a cinema of genres than of auteurs, though it did possess one individual film-maker of widely acknowledged exceptional status in Kamal Selim who, after making his debut as a scriptwriter, went on to make one of Egypt's most important and innovatory realist films, *The Will/Al-azima*, in 1939. Thoraval notes that far from being a contribution to some timeless stream of filmic realism, *The Will* has a precise political import, as 'a reflection of the social situation of the period demonstrating the indispensable alliance of the work of the urban petit bourgeoisie and the capital of a corrupt and declining aristocracy'.[111] Selim did not succeed in surpassing this film before he died in 1945 at the age of 32, while working on his tenth feature. Otherwise the Egyptian cinema of the period is characterized by the musicals, the series of farces produced by Togo Mizrahi, the Bedouin tales of love and adventure by the Lama brothers, and Yusuf Wahby's stage adaptations.

In 1935 came the opening of the Misr studio, after which one can talk meaningfully of a film industry in Egypt. The studio, founded by Egypt's leading financial institution, the Bank Misr, had the resources to purchase modern equipment and hire foreign technical expertise. It funded training in France and Germany for directors and technicians and offered posts to those who returned from abroad with privately acquired qualifications. In short, it set out to meet the call, made in 1925 by the Bank Misr's director, Talaat Harb, for a company 'capable of making Egyptian films with Egyptian subjects, Egyptian literature and Egyptian aesthetics, worthwhile films that can be shown in our own country and in the neighbouring oriental countries'.[112] The Misr studio's first production, the musical *Wedad*, was an outstanding success and it was well placed to play a leading role in the continuing growth of Egyptian film production.

The real boom in Egyptian cinema came in the period between the end of World War Two and the 1952 revolution. The number of cinemas rose steadily from around 100 in 1935 to some 244 in 1949; production averaged more than 50 films a year (a level maintained into the 1980s) and by 1952 the export of films was surpassed only by that of cotton.[113] Though the bulk of this output had no more than commercial aspirations, the period did see the debuts of two major directors who, in their very different ways, were to dominate Egyptian cinema for decades to come: Salah Abou Seif and Yusuf Chahine. Samir Farid, who has dubbed this period 'the cinema of war profiteers', has attributed the boom to the combination of three factors: the very low cost of film production, an increase in purchasing power and the accessibility of capital acquired, often illegally, from speculation. In Farid's view, film-making at this time was the simplest, quickest and surest way of making a fortune in Egypt.[114]

Elsewhere in the Arab world, production had still hardly got under way in the two decades since the coming of sound. Chikly's pioneering efforts in Tunisia had no real successors. Abdelaziz Hassine's 1935 feature, *Tergui*, was completed but never shown[115] and the most specifically national film produced, the Tunisian-dialect production *The Madman of Kairouan/Majnun al-Kairouan* (1939), was directed by a Frenchman, M. J. Creusi. The remaining ten or so films of the colonial era which were technically Tunisian or Moroccan productions were all foreign-directed films and sought more to imitate the European features shot on location in the Maghreb than to give any expression to local life and culture.[116] Though Lebanon steadily developed its key role in film distribution throughout the Arab world, production there was stagnant. The pioneering 1935 sound film by Julio de Bucci and Karim Bustany, *In the Ruins of Baalbek/Bayn hayakel Baalbek*, was followed by only three features in the 1940s and a mere dozen in the 1950s, none of which had any international impact. In Syria, like Lebanon free of French troops only in 1946, only four features were made in the first two decades of sound, all of them, seemingly, amateur efforts. In Iraq, a more solid start was made after World War Two, with two Egyptian co-productions in 1945 followed by a dozen or so 'national' productions in the years up to the 1958 revolution which finally broke British dominance. Most of these films were made by small companies which vanished after producing just a single feature, and the Iraqi critic Shakir Nouri singles out only two of them – Abdel Jabar Wali's *Who is Responsible?/Man al-mas'oul?* (1956) and Kameran Hassani's *Saïd Effendi* (1957) – for special mention.[117] Elsewhere in the Arab world, and throughout the whole of sub-Saharan black Africa, there was no indigenous film-making until after independence.

Developments in popular music

It is interesting to contrast the general lack (outside Egypt) of indigenous film-making under colonialism with the very positive progress made in the recording industry, especially in sub-Saharan Africa. In West Africa even before 1914, representatives of the Gramophone Company were seeking outlets for their products in Sierra Leone, Ghana and Nigeria. No sooner was a market established than the Gramophone Company began recording indigenous popular music through its subsidiary Zonophone. In East Africa, the Gramophone Company first established a market for records imported from Europe in Uganda, Kenya and Tanganyika and then began distributing Indian music recorded in its Bombay studio to the trading community throughout the area.[118] The recording of indigenous African music soon followed, with initial sessions in 1929–30 in Nairobi by four European companies – the Gramophone Company and Columbia from Britain, the French Pathé and the German Odeon. A first recording studio was established in the Belgian Congo in 1929, and was followed the next year by the setting up of Radio Congo-Belge. From the early 1930s onwards, the spread of recorded music and the development of radio stations throughout Africa went hand in hand.

One characteristic of the growth of African popular music is that it involved economic exploitation. As Graham notes:

> The years between 1930 and 1950 can be characterized as years of intense exploitation of African music and African musicians by expatriate companies. Royalties were seldom paid and the companies preferred to operate on the basis of single session fees. The protection afforded musicians by copyright and publishing laws was almost entirely lacking.[119]

The foreign-based companies recorded indiscriminately, mixing traditional songs and modern dance music, Christian mission hymns and Islamic chants, locally developed styles and imitations of Western approaches (there was even, Stapleton and May observe, a version of 'The Coon's Lament').[120] The various African instruments and languages were also used indiscriminately and there seems to have been little attempt to develop any sort of coherent policy. As a result, though some records sold well and circulated widely, many were total flops. In addition to their involvement in local recording, the foreign record companies continued to import material of all kinds from outside Africa. Of particular importance were the 200 or so titles in EMI's GV series of Latin American music, reissued for the African market after World War Two. Many early imports, such as vaudeville and classical music, waltzes and swing, had been distinctly Western, and this Latin American music made an immediate impact, particularly in French West Africa and the Belgian Congo.[121]

Far from destroying the special identity of African popular music, the imported Latin American music had an invigorating and positive effect, since its essentially African rhythms allowed the kind of synthesis so important to the development of popular forms of culture. As Stapleton and May observe: 'Since the 1930s, the forms that have had the biggest impact in Africa have all come from there in the first place: calypso, reggae and, most significantly, rumba.'[122] The rediscovery of African roots through this imported music was crucial to post-independence musicians such as Fela Anikulapo Kuti, who was to remark of his own experience, 'I had been using jazz to play African music, when really I should have been using African music to play jazz. So it was America that brought me back to myself.'[123]

The importance of this interaction of African and imported music is shown by the geographical differences in the spread of popular music: its influence was strongest in such points of interaction as the Western coastal towns and the urban industrial centres, and weakest in settler-dominated areas and where Islam hindered Western influence. But wherever meaningful creative developments occurred, these were the result of the reworking of the imported material:

> Music was never copied as an end in itself. Instead it served as a catalyst for the creation of new forms, like highlife, soukous and juju, that drew their strength from local as well as foreign music.[124]

In the mid-1950s, on the eve of independence, African popular music, which had earlier incorporated imported instruments like the acoustic guitar, began to unite African rhythms with electric guitars and amplification. As the music industry slowly shifted its emphasis from 78 r.p.m. to extended and long-playing records, the African sounds with which we are familiar today emerged.

Conclusion

It is clear that any colonial system, as an extreme form of political, social and economic domination, will inevitably have a distorting and inhibiting effect on cultural developments, both during the colonial era and in its aftermath. At one extreme, the colonial system may lead to the paradoxical creation of an elite national literature from which the bulk of the population is excluded by illiteracy and which can find publication and a readership only within the colonizing power. At the other extreme, colonial domination may prevent any self-expression whatsoever, as when racist attitudes of superiority led officials of the Colonial Film Unit and missionaries in the Belgian Congo to see Africans as basically children, to be protected from Western commercial cinema and offered only simplified, overtly educational films made specially for them. It is also clear that in general colonial governments were as hostile to the idea of African film-making as they were to African rural capitalism, seeing it – to adopt John Iliffe's telling phrase – 'not only as socially and politically dangerous but as somehow improper for Africans, like guitars or three-piece suits'.[125]

In such a context, popular arts that were outside direct colonial control and required little or no capital investment could flourish. In the case of popular music, its diffusion and the development of new syncretic forms were enhanced by the new broadcasting and recording media established under colonialism. But local film-making could occur only where colonial dominance was weakest and indigenous economic activity was most advanced. Such developments as did occur were inevitably limited. But the nature of these developments does offer clear insight into the factors which were to continue to shape film-making after independence, since the economics of cinema remain the same whether in a colony or in a state subjected – after formal independence – to neocolonial domination. Though we customarily think of the film industry as a single phenomenon, the various sectors – production, distribution and exhibition – are not necessarily linked to form a unified, coherent whole within any single nation, since the film market is a global one. For this reason, the existence in a particular country of a well-organized distribution network and a large audience for imported films – as, for example, in Algeria under colonialism – does not of itself lead to local film production. Able to acquire a popular product regularly and at advantageous rates from abroad, local distributors and exhibitors have no need to foster local production. Indeed they may even be hostile to it, since a change in audience viewing habits might threaten the profitability of the whole operation.

As the case of Egypt demonstrates, a film industry can come into existence only when a number of favourable factors are all present: a general industrial infrastructure, an urban mass audience with money to spend on entertainment, an organized system of film distribution, and access to capital for investment in facilities as well as in production itself. Even then self-sufficiency cannot be assured, since the profitable operation of the system needs several hundred films a year – far beyond the capacity of most national film production industries. Thus Egypt's output of some fifty films a year ranks it fairly high in the list of film-producing nations – in the 1950s akin to Mexico or Argentina – but leaves it vulnerable to imported films, particularly from the United States with its mass production cinema. Moreover, a breakthrough to largescale production in a single country does not mean that its neighbours will now be able to follow suit more easily. As Egypt's relationship with the other Arab states shows, it is more likely that these neighbouring states will be developed as markets, so that their audiences acquire an increased taste for imported – in this case, Egyptian – films.

The role of language is crucial here. The linguistic diversity of spoken Arabic is a key factor in inhibiting the widespread development of Arab film production. The language used in Egyptian movies by producers aiming at the whole Arab market could be neither classical Arabic – now largely confined to intellectual use – nor the authentic local Cairo dialect, which is largely incomprehensible in the wider Arab world. Instead, film-makers initially had to adopt their own language – what Victor Bachy has called 'a nonexistent language, a cinema-speak, a synthetic product invented by scriptwriters'[126] – in which a surface coating of colloquial Egyptian is given to an essentially literary structure. Only gradually could spoken Egyptian, backed up by other media such as radio and recorded song, impose itself so widely that to audiences it eventually came to seem the *natural* language of Arab cinema. As Farid Jabre notes, 'The audiences in the Arab countries, without understanding every word of the Egyptian dialect, have got used to it and feel uncomfortable when faced with another Arabic dialect'.[127] In this way imported Egyptian films may well have become even more of an inhibiting factor holding back production in other Arab states than imports from the West. Yet despite all the difficulties inherent in importing a Western-originated technology and Western forms of dramatic and narrative organization into Africa and the Arab world, the innovators could take comfort from one certainty: films found enthusiastic audiences wherever they were shown. The film-makers of the post-independence era were able to use this popularity when they gave expression to the new sense of cultural awareness that came with the ending of the colonial system.

2. Cinema After Independence

Introduction: national identity

One of the lasting heritages of imperialism proved to be the structure of the state, established under colonialism and bequeathed to their successors by the departing colonizers in the era after World War Two. The precise nature of the colonial state varied from colonizer to colonizer, differing in accordance with the various traditions and stages of development in Europe. But it was always an imposed, imported model which owed little or nothing to local traditions. It lacked any accountability to those it ruled and over whose lives it exercised a power akin to that of the most powerful absolutist monarchy. At the same time it was an interventionist state, imposing strong European influences, aiming 'to mould the populations it included in its domain according to clearcut European images'.[1] Only where existing social structures were underwritten by strong religious traditions (as in the Islamic societies of North Africa and the Middle East) could lasting resistance be offered, though individual revolts were far more prevalent than contemporary colonial history allowed.

A further key factor – regardless of the pomp and ceremony with which the governor might choose to surround himself – was that the colonial state was essentially a bureaucratic state. Ultimate power lay not with the governor but with the ministry and specialist bureaucracy in the colonizing country. Moreover, as the colony developed, there was an accompanying increase in bureaucratization (one of the major features of state development everywhere in the twentieth century). As Anderson observes, 'Alongside the old district officer appeared the medical officer, the irrigation engineer, the agricultural extension-worker, the school-teacher, the policeman and so on.'[2] Where these posts were occupied by Europeans, they had to be supported by a mass of locally recruited clerks and officials who came to constitute an educated, bilingual elite 'capable of mediating linguistically between the metropolitan nation and the colonized peoples'.[3]

The state's need to recruit such people – combined with its self-proclaimed civilizing mission – inevitably led to a spread of European-style education, through which selected pupils could hardly fail to pick up European ideas of democracy and nationalism which contrasted strongly with their everyday experience of colonialism. As Alistair Horne notes of the situation in Algeria:

> With its traditional emphasis on the grandiose liberal traditions of the 'Great French Revolution', French education could hardly help but divert perhaps otherwise passive minds to the nobility of revolt. M'hammed Yazid, one of the more intellectual FLN leaders, notes that school heroes for his generation included Mustapha Kemal, Gandhi and the Irish rebels of the First World War. At their best, the French schools provided an admirable breeding ground for revolutionary minds.[4]

An ironic reversal is at work here. There was an undoubted missionary zeal in the idea of offering a Western education to subject peoples, exemplified by Thomas Babington Macauley's memorably stated aim of creating in India 'a class of persons Indian in blood and colour, but English in taste, in opinions, in morals and in intellect', and thereby eliminating Hinduism among the 'respectable' classes within a generation.[5] But in following this project, the colonizers were in fact creating the one social group which could offer them a viable opposition. The bilingual educated elite, aware of its own status though humiliated in its daily contact with the colonial state, was able to articulate an opposition conceived not in terms of tradition, indigenous religion or so-called tribalism, but in Western political forms, that is, as a nationalism which took the colony's often arbitrary borders as a given and proclaimed the need to offer Western rights of citizenship to all the colonized.

Various reasons have been advanced for the speed with which nationalism universally took hold in the various colonies of Asia and Africa, even in those whose boundaries were arbitrarily defined and which contained populations of highly diverse religions, social formations and ethnic origins. One of the most fascinating explanations for this phenomenon has been offered by Anderson. Noting the link between the intellectual endeavours of linguists, the rise of vernacular languages to state use and the impact of the printing press, Anderson is able to map out one pattern of emerging nationhood – that particularly characteristic of Europe:

> The convergence of capitalism and print technology on the fatal diversity of human language created the possibility of a new form of imagined community, which in its basic morphology set the stage for the modern nation.[6]

Anderson contrasts this pattern with a second more relevant to Africa
and the Arab states, namely the emergence between 1776 and 1838 of
sovereign nation states in the old Spanish empire of South America. The
impulse for a national assertion of independence came largely from the
sense of humiliation experienced by the American-born Spaniards (or
creoles) who were treated as second-class citizens by European-born
Spaniards. The terms of the creole's exclusion were turned on their head
to become the basis of a new, positively affirmed national identity: 'Born
in the Americas, he could not be a true Spaniard; *ergo*, born in Spain, the
peninsular could not be a true American.'[7] But a surprising corollary of
this logic was that within the new 'imagined political community' of the
American nation state, the creoles allied themselves as fellow citizens
with the indigenous and mulatto groups who shared the fact of birth in
the Americas, rather than with the mainland Spaniards with whom they
had so much more in common culturally. The territorial definitions of
the new nations echoed precisely the boundaries of the old administrative
units of the Spanish empire because, Anderson argues, these were the
limits which circumscribed the experience – and hence the imagination –
of those who struggled, often at the expense of life or fortune, to create
the new independent nation.

The same is true of the emergence of a national identity in the often
arbitrarily defined colonies established, particularly by France and
England, in Africa and the Arab world from the late nineteenth century.
Anderson sees the roots of national identity in the two trajectories
followed by members of the bilingual elites who were to be the future
architects of African and Arab nationalism. The first of these
trajectories comprised the travels undertaken within a pyramidal
educational structure which drew the pupil further and further
(physically, linguistically and intellectually) from his home town or
village to the capital. Second, even for those who acquired the final
accolade of a university degree in the metropolis, there was a parallel
trajectory in the service of the colonial state, which, if successful, would
similarly progress from provincial administrative postings to eventual
promotion to a post in the colonial capital – but never in the metropolis
or in a neighbouring colony. As Anderson notes, 'The interlock between
particular educational and administrative pilgrimages provided the
territorial base for the new "imagined communities" in which "natives"
could come to see themselves as "nationals".'[8]

Film and literature

The African and Arab film-makers of the immediate post-independence
era were virtually all shaped by this process of development which

linked foreign-language education and a growing sense of independent national identity. In this respect they shared a personal trajectory with the writers, musicians and broadcasters of the period and it is important to see their work in relation to the broad context of post-independence cultural developments. There were, it is true, comparatively few direct links between film and literature. The new film-makers did not seek to adapt the work of their literary contemporaries, and only Sembene Ousmane managed to combine over twenty-five years the roles of practising film-maker and French-language novelist. Other potentially promising developments have been largely stillborn: the Algerian novelist Assia Djebbar made just two features at the end of the 1970s, the Kenyan novelist Ngugi wa Thiong'o's film training in Sweden has not as yet led to any feature film production and the Nigerian dramatist Wole Soyinka's first and only feature film, *Blues for a Prodigal*, failed to be released. But if we are to understand fully the forces shaping post-independence African and Arab film-making, it is important to consider the trajectory followed by the parallel generation of writers.

If the origins of the paradoxical concept of *négritude* – 'the essence of African-ness expressible only in French' – can be traced directly to French-language tuition in colonial schools,[9] so too the elite African literature of novels and plays in French and English is similarly one expression of the generation which led the African and Arab colonies to independence. The writers may disagree profoundly with the politicians and deplore the direction in which the nation is being led, but this disagreement rests on shared understanding derived from similar social and cultural experiences: writers and politicians quite literally speak the same language, and this sets them apart from the mass of the population. The intertwining of literature and politics is symbolized by the two very different African figures who shared the dual identity of poet and president: Léopold Sédar Senghor of Senegal and Antonio Agostinho Neto of Angola.

Writing in 1957, the Tunisian Albert Memmi prophesied that 'colonized literature in European languages appears condemned to die young'.[10] But just as Memmi continued to write novels in French – while living in Paris – so too all the major writers who had found their literary voices in Africa under colonialism continued to write and publish in European languages after independence, when they were joined by newcomers of equal talent. Alongside the explorations of personal identity amid a clash of cultures, there appeared a strong current of criticism of the colonial past, as writers in Algeria, Senegal or Nigeria confirmed their commitment to the cause of the people and sought to affirm a national identity for the newly emerged independent state. Within a few years many would apply the same fiercely critical approach to developments in post-independence Africa. The 1960s saw new and talented writers follow the paths opened up by Achebe and Sembene and offer similarly powerful works of social criticism, among them Ngugi wa Thiong'o (beginning with *Weep Not Child* in 1964) in Kenya and Ayi Kwei Armah (with *The Beautyful* [*sic*] *Ones Are Not Yet Born* in 1969) in Ghana. Much of this writing was couched in the form of socially realist novels more reminiscent of the nineteenth-century European tradition than of contemporary experiments in narrative writing in the West, but there were some writers who sought experimentation as well as social relevance. Kateb Yacine's formally innovative *Nedjma*, for example, is widely considered a masterpiece and has been described as 'the greatest French-language work to come out of North Africa'.[11] A similar high reputation attaches to the English-language drama established in the 1960s by the Nigerian playwrights Wole Soyinka and John Pepper Clark, and striking poetic fusions of African and European elements were achieved by Christopher Okigbo in Nigeria, Okot p'Bitek (as with his *Song of Lawino: a lament*) in Uganda and Kofi Awoonor in Ghana.

Questioned about their use of French or English as the medium of their writing, most of these writers would be forced to agree with Chinua Achebe, who wrote: 'For me there is no other choice. I have been given this language and I intend to use it. . . . I feel that the English language will be able to carry the weight of my African experience.'[12] For Achebe, writing in 1964, the necessary distinction was between a national literature and an ethnic one:

> A national literature is one that takes the whole nation for its province and has a realised or potential audience throughout its territory. In other words a literature that is written in the *national* language. An ethnic literature is one which is available only to one ethnic group within the nation. If you take Nigeria as an example, the national literature, as I see it, is the literature written in English; and the ethnic literatures are in Hausa, Ibo, Yoruba, Efik, Edo, Ijaw, etc., etc.[13]

The difficulty with Achebe's formulation is the necessary qualification 'realised *or potential* audience'. Not only is the bulk of Nigeria's population destined to remain illiterate in English for the foreseeable future, the language of this elite writing is often such as to close it off even from those with basic reading skills. As Barber has noted, the language of Wole Soyinka's plays makes them inaccessible to a mass readership:

> They are not only in English, but in a superb high style of English that few even of the best educated English speakers would claim to comprehend fully; they are not just structured according to the

conventions of modern western theatre, but they explore the limits of these conventions in a way that bespeaks total mastery.[14]

Despite such reservations, the achievement of the 'national' writers was recognized universally in the 1980s, as is shown by the admission of Léopold Sédar Senghor to the Académie française and the award of the Nobel Prize for Literature to Wole Soyinka.

It might seem paradoxical to describe African elite literature as an official literature, in view of the oppositional stance adopted by so many of the writers who have, as a result, suffered imprisonment and exile. Individual works have undoubtedly caused offence to governments, as for example, the novel *Dramouss*, which earned Camara Laye a sentence of death *in absentia* from the Guinean authorities.[15] But at the same time, the existence of a modern literature in a European language can be seen partially to meet the state's need to present itself as a modernizing force in a context in which – to adapt an observation by Harold Rosenberg – to fall behind in the 'process of technique' in the arts would be equivalent to falling behind in electronics: a nation that did so would be making a public confession of backwardness.[16]

As early as the 1960s some writers were beginning to question their elite status and the limitations it placed on the reception of their work. In 1969 Okot p'Bitek was forced to conclude: 'At the moment Ngugi's *A Grain of Wheat* and my *Song of Lawino* are as irrelevant as the freak rains that fall during droughts, because they do not reach the millions of Africans for whom they are intended.'[17] A few writers consciously abandoned both their elite status and their acquired language. The Algerian Kateb Yacine moved from the radical French-language literary experimentation of *Nedjma* to novels and plays in Arabic and in an idiom 'akin to that of guerrilla street theatre and the political cartoon'.[18] Similarly Ngugi wa Thiong'o, who had begun his career as James Ngugi writing in English, first Africanized his name and then began to write drama and fiction in Gikuyu. For him the political experience of being able to reach an African peasant audience had a crucial impact on his literary approach. Now living in exile, he writes in Gikuyu and works for the establishment of a multilingual national culture in which indigenous languages play their full role.

The 1980s have seen a number of African literary critics follow a similar path and attack the equation of elite literature in European languages with African literature as a whole, on the grounds that, in the words of the Nigerian critic Chinweizu, this 'confounds a part with the whole, passing off a small grove of young trees grown from transplanted, hybrid saplings as the entirety of a vast and ancient forest'.[19] Pointing out that 'African literature (i.e. literature written by Africans, for African readers, in African languages) is at least as old as the Pyramid

Texts of Pharaonic Egypt' and thus 'older than European literature by some 2,000 years',[20] Chinweizu contrasts the social application of elite literature – 'a sideshow that is brought into the African's life mainly for classroom purposes' – with that of the popular traditional folktale, which forms an integral part of African personal and social life, at work and play, in family ceremonies and religious rites.[21] The irony of the situation, for Chinweizu, is that:

> [I]t is academic literature, with all its Euro-assimilationist characteristics, which has been given official status, and which dominates the curricula of African schools and universities, whereas Afrocentric, popular literature languishes in the shadows, a barely noticed outcast from where it ought to reign.[22]

The starting point for most post-independence Arab and African film-makers is very similar to that of the writers of European-language African literature. Film-making demands close contacts with Europe for aspiring film-makers virtually everywhere outside Egypt (and even there many of the leading directors have close European ties: both Yusuf Chahine and Tewfik Saleh graduated from the English-language Victoria College in Alexandria, Shadi Abdel Salam studied at Oxford, Hussein Kamal at the Institut des hautes études cinématographiques (IDHEC) in Paris, Galal Charkawi at the Centro sperimentale in Rome, etc.). Feature films are not made by people coming directly from remote rural villages, since the successful realization of a film involves both mastery of a Western-originated technology and understanding (if not imitation) of Western systems of audiovisual narrative. Self-taught film-makers such as Omar Khleifi from Tunisia or Moustapha Alassane and Oumarou Ganda from Niger are comparatively rare. A period of study in Europe has been customary for most actors who have turned to directing, such as Philippe Mory (Gabon), Daniel Kamwa (Cameroon) and Med Hondo (Mauritania), the only notable exceptions being the Yoruba theatre directors from Nigeria, such as Hubert Ogunde and Ade Love.

More striking still is the roll call of graduates of the European film schools, who make up the bulk of today's film-makers in Africa and the Arab world. The veterans of Nigerian cinema (Edward B. Horatio Jones and Ola Balogun) as well as the three pioneers of Ivory Coast cinema (Bassori Timite, Désiré Ecare and Henri Duparc) all studied at the IDHEC in Paris, as did Paulin Soumanou Vieyra (Senegal), Ruy Guerra (Mozambique), Nacer Ktari and Abdellatif Ben Ammar (Tunisia), Moumen Smihi and Hamid Benani (Morocco), Maroun Baghdadi (Lebanon) and Pierre-Marie Dong (Gabon). Also in Paris, the CICF (Conservatoire indépendant du cinéma français) has trained a number of African film-makers: Mahama Johnson Traore and Thierno Faty Sow (Senegal), Jean Pierre Dikongue-Pipa and Jules Takam (Cameroon), Moustapha Diop (Niger) and Gnoan M'Bala (Ivory Coast), and other graduates include the Syrian documentarist Omar Amiralay. Borhan Alawiya (Lebanon) graduated from the Brussels film school, INSAS (Institut national supérieur des arts du spectacle et techniques de diffusion), in the early 1970s and since then many of the key figures in the new Arab cinema have also been trained there: Michel Khleifi (Palestine), Ahmed al-Maanouni (Morocco), Brahim Tsaki (Algeria), Mahmoud Ben Mahmoud and Nouri Bouzid (Tunisia). Ababacar Samb-Makharam (Senegal) and Souheil Ben Barka (Morocco) both graduated at the Centro sperimentale in Rome, while Idriss Hassan Dirie (Somalia) and Adamu Halilu (Nigeria) studied in London. Several key pioneer figures of African cinema – Ousmane Sembene (Senegal), Sarah Maldoror (Angola) and Souleymane Cisse (Mali) – studied in Moscow, as did some of the younger film-makers in Mali (Djibril Kouyate and Kalifa Dienta) and Syria (Samir Zikra and Mohamed Malass). King Ampaw (Ghana) studied in West Germany, Falaba Issa Traore (Mali) in East Berlin, Nabil al-Maleh (Syria) in Prague. . . . The list is long and, with the exception of the Egyptians trained in Cairo, only Khalid al-Siddiq (Kuwait) lacks a European connection, since he graduated from the Indian Film Institute in Pune.

A lengthy period of study in Europe can have enormously beneficial effects on a film-maker but it inevitably weakens the direct links with both traditional and popular culture, and at times there is a sense that film-makers are returning almost as tourists to their own countries. Certainly the issue of language was generally ignored to begin with by film-makers in Francophone black Africa, who used commentaries and dialogue in French. Ousmane Sembene has admitted his surprise at being asked by villagers to whom he had shown some of his early documentaries why, if the films were for them, he had made them 'in his own language', that is to say, in French.[23] Subsequently Sembene pioneered the use of African languages, making a version of *The Money Order/Mandabi* in Wolof, even though this was not at the time a written language. With the adoption of indigenous languages or local dialect variants of Arabic, an important distinction emerges between the elite writer and the film-maker, even if the latter still has to seek facilities for editing and post-production work in Europe. Whereas the writer, working at his desk in a foreign language, is inevitably cut off from the immediate reality around him, the shooting of a film brings the director into direct contact with local actors and extras in indigenous towns, villages and landscapes. Since there is no need to use a European language, a direct relationship with at least the immediate popular audience can be maintained, even if the particular language employed is only one of many used within the national borders. At the same time, subtitles make the film universally accessible to a wider literate audience than that able to cope with elite literature.

Film and popular music

If one way of defining the cultural context of film-making is in comparison with the elite literatures in European languages which are as characteristic of the Maghreb as of sub-Saharan Africa, another is in relation to contemporary developments in popular music. The record industry was selling its products in Africa and the Arab world as early as the years between World Wars One and Two and the consumption of records and tapes – the bulk of them imported – has continued to grow. The transformation of local musical production through electric guitars, amplification and electric recording generally occurred in the years immediately preceding independence; the growth of a new popular music parallels the development of an elite African literature.

But with popular music we find both a direct contact between performers and the urban masses and a general freedom from state interference and control, though the early years of independence did see some unlikely state initiatives. In Guinea, for example, as a part of Sékou Touré's cultural initiative, a national recording company was set up and the all-female dance band Les Amazones was formed in 1961, all its members being serving officers in the *gendarmerie*. Similarly in neighbouring Mali there has been government support for local bands and the Rail Band of the Buffet of the Hôtel de la Gare de Bamako was actually founded under the sponsorship of the Ministry of Information in 1971. In addition, some presidents have shown a close personal interest, among them Kwame Nkrumah (who took bands like E. K. Nyame and the Uhuru Dance Band on some of his trips outside Ghana).[24] Generally, however, the music industry is in private hands. While much of the record market is still controlled by multinationals – particularly in countries like Kenya and the Ivory Coast – there have been many successful local initiatives, and indigenization decrees have allowed leading musicians in Nigeria and Zaire, for example, to become millionaires. Though by 1974 some 7 million records were being imported into Nigeria, 3 million records were also sold that had been produced by the Nigerian industry, which had three major record companies, twelve recording studios, two major indigenous labels, two pressing plants and over fifty small local labels.[25]

The former colonial capitals of Paris, London and Brussels remain magnets for musicians seeking international reputations, and fascinating cross-fertilizations have been made in Europe, such as *zouk*, with its hi-tech fusion of African and Antillean rhythms, in Paris. But basically the new popular music is rooted in the multitude of local musical traditions. Though the popular music of sub-Saharan Africa has achieved the greater international exposure, there have been similar developments in the Arab world. The death of Oum Kelthoum in 1975 can be seen to symbolize the ending of Egyptian dominance over Arab popular music, as the 1970s and 1980s saw the emergence of new styles with local roots, particularly in North Africa. Examples of the new sound of Arab popular music are the 'folk revival' groups such as Nass al-Ghiwane in Morocco and Jil Jilala in Tunisia or such Algerian *rai* singers as Cheb Khaled or Chaba Fadela. Ahmed al-Maanouni's 1981 feature-length documentary *Trances* gives a fascinating portrait of the styles and sources of the popular Nass al-Ghiwane musical group. One factor uniting the diversity of styles is the fact that all the music is a product of urbanization, which has led to the reworking of traditional rural music for new audiences and its fusion with imported styles and new instrumentation. The roots of many of the major styles – highlife in Ghana and Nigeria, juju and the soukous of Zaire – can be traced back fifty years or more, even before the bringing of recording to Africa. But the modern sound is very much a reflection of the Western technologies first available in the mid-1950s: amplification, the electric guitar, the tape recording studio and the long-playing record.

Latin American records imported after World War Two are universally acknowledged to have had a decisive impact (see chapter 1), as have radio and the migrations of the musicians themselves – such as the movement of Zairean pop groups into Central and East Africa during the 1960s civil war or the continuing lure of Abidjan for musicians from the poorer countries of Francophone Africa (prompting Manu Dibango to claim that the Ivory Coast has many good musicians but no music).[26] But equally striking is the way in which the new developments in popular music reflect the new consciousness of the emergent independent nations and the desire to assert Africa's place in world music. While some of this music may be as bland as Western pop, there are strong currents of social comment in many of the songs, such as those of the prolific Zairean Franco, who has released over 100 albums and whose sometimes uneasy relationship with the Zaire government was reflected in 1978 when he was both imprisoned because of two of his songs and also decorated by President Mobutu for his services to music. Even more sharply critical of the military is the Nigerian musical star Fela Anikulapo Kuti, whose verbal and musical attacks led to many clashes including the burning down of his home by soldiers in 1977 and a five-year prison sentence (of which he served two years) on currency smuggling charges in 1984.

Common to all these African musicians is the concern to rework traditional rhythms for electric instruments and the recording studio, so that tradition and modernity become inextricably entwined. Some of the musicians have solid traditional backgrounds. Mory Kante, the Guinean player of the kora (or Mandinka harp-lute), is descended from a family of musicians and *griots* (praise-singers) and had a traditional education. At 15, however, he was singing with the Rail Band in Bamako, before moving first to Abidjan and then to Paris. In his work he has developed a very distinctive style, 'a virtually new language for the kora, creating a sound that would blend with electro-funk, reggae and soul'.[27] Similarly the Senegalese singer and drummer Youssou N'Dour was the son of a traditional musician who trained him in Wolof music. After making his public debut at 12, N'Dour was singing with the leading Senegalese group, the Star Band de Dakar, while still in his teens. It was the Star Band which had marked the transition from Latin American dance music to African sounds and rhythms in Dakar. In his own work N'Dour takes a Wolof percussion rhythm, the *mbalax*, and adds to it 'a range of modern instruments: a base of rolling, almost flamenco-like guitars, from which the talking drum explodes, along with fuzz-box guitar solos, inspired perhaps by the excesses of Western rock'.[28]

Other African musicians have had Western musical educations and approach the traditional from a very different angle. Fela Anikulapo Kuti studied at Trinity College of Music in London, but his Afrobeat sound was a conscious reaction against Nigerian imitators of Western pop music. Manu Dibango studied classical piano in Paris and played jazz in Brussels but made his reputation with a modern version of a traditional Cameroonian rhythm, the *makossa*. His current eclectic style sets out 'to get out of the "ethnic music" label, to let people know that there is an electric Africa too'.[29] The African musical scene is one of constant change and movement: new fashions in sound spread across national boundaries, local musicians link up in new groups only to split again in rivalry, a breakthrough to the international market seems to be assured and then the foothold is lost, Western pop stars seem to offer support but turn out to be interested only in self-promotion. Only the advent in the 1980s of the audiocassette, which allows both the piracy of original local compositions and the flooding of the market with cheap bootlegged imports, threatens the economic basis of an industry which over twenty years or more has grown rich and diversified without losing its popular base.

Film-makers are far from possessing the market strength of the African or Arab musician, which has allowed, for example, the Zairean musicians Franco and Tabu Ley to record thousands of songs and release a hundred or more LPs. There are no millionaires among the ranks of the film-makers, and outside the commercial film industry of

Egypt even a sustained rhythm of a feature film every four or five years is comparatively rare. Film is potentially a popular art like music, but the level of investment required for each individual production normally makes access to a wide distribution market in Africa and/or the Arab world, as well as abroad, imperative. The only national production entity which operates on a truly international scale – the Egyptian film industry – is customarily attacked for its triviality and indulgence in melodramatic excess. But any consideration of its output over seventy or so years shows that it has genuine popular appeal throughout the Arab world and the work within the mainstream of such film-makers as Salah Abou Seif, Yusuf Chahine and Tewfik Saleh shows clearly that it offers to those film-makers willing and able to work within its confines as much scope as any other commercial film industry elsewhere in the world.[30]

Outside Egypt, the sole body of genuinely popular cinema reaching a mass audience is that in the Yoruba-speaking region of Western Nigeria, where cinema is heir to decades of theatrical performance and has a potential audience of some 10 million. There can be arguments about the cinematic specificity of the adaptations of their stage successes organized on film by Hubert Ogunde, Ade Love and Baba Sala, but none about the directness of their appeal to local popular audiences. Writing in 1987, Barber noted:

> Until a year or two ago, every Yoruba town showed American, Chinese, and Indian films. Now they are hard to find: they have been replaced by the rapidly expanding indigenous film industry which has already produced dozens of Yoruba-language films using the personnel, styles and themes of the well-established travelling popular theatre.[31]

Film and broadcasting

Because of the costs involved in the production of any film designed to reach an international as well as a local audience, the role of the state is crucial in any system of film production. But the development in the African and Arab worlds of those modern communication media which conform as closely to the priorities of the independent national state as they once did to those of the colonial administrators – an official press, for example, or a centralized, state-controlled radio transmission system – offer striking examples of the dangers of too great a state involvement. The lessons of the past are borne out by the post-independence development of television. At the very opposite extreme to the vibrant and ever-changing contemporary African and Arab music scene are the monolithic bureaucracies characteristic of the official broadcast media, of which television is the newest example.

In terms of access to the media, there is an enormous gulf between the tiny, oil-rich state of Qatar, with some 2,000 television sets per 1,000 inhabitants, and an impoverished West African state such as Burkina Faso, where the level is a mere 1.6 sets per 1,000. But a common factor is the difficulty of constructing an appropriate television programme schedule. Whereas virtually all states have been able to make useful applications of their existing radio systems – for such purposes as nation-building, education, minority-language services – few if any have been able to make a similarly positive use of television. In sub-Saharan Africa the cost factors involved – a ratio of 30 to 1 compared to radio[32] – inhibit both significant local production and even the extension of the television network to as much as 10 per cent of the population; 1983 levels were 8.8 per cent in Burkina Faso, 5 per cent in Niger, 0.5 per cent in Senegal.[33] At the other extreme, wealthy Qatar's tiny population makes it unable to support a significant level of local production. It is clear that Burkina Faso, which imports only programming offered free,[34] is unlikely to receive much which is locally relevant. But even a wealthy Arab state able to pay well for imported material is unable to obtain programming which does not convey values alien to the local community. In practice there are no exchanges between African television corporations,[35] and in the Arab world 'top-quality programmes, especially drama series . . . are subject to exchange only in exceptional circumstances'.[36]

Throughout Africa and the Arab world, therefore, material imported from the West – films, serials, major documentaries – makes up at least 40–60 per cent of the overall viewing time and fills most of the peak audience period. Local production tends to be centralized in the capital (marginalizing important sectors of the population) and subject to grave technical and manpower limitations. Usually it comprises little more than newsreels (with inordinate coverage of the daily public appearances of the head of state), sports programmes and studio discussions. The flavour is captured by a recent report on communications in the Arab states: 'recourse is frequently had to the simplest programme formats, such as placing guests face to face and launching them into an uninhibited round-table discussion' and 'most political programmes are overtly propagandistic, conveying only one point of view, and are hastily produced and naively presented'.[37] In this situation foreign assistance has generally worsened an already bad situation. Overseas staff training schemes, for example, have been described as 'an unconscionable abuse of foreign technical aid programmes', since the attachments siphon off key personnel, are regarded by those given them as a holiday and as a reward for seniority, and return the officials confused and dissatisfied to their old posts.[38]

There were occasional early attempts to set up private commercial television channels in the Arab world: in Morocco in 1954 (an experiment which failed within two years), in Lebanon in 1956 and 1962 (the two competing stations, which both needed foreign capital investment, were merged by the government in 1978), in Kuwait in 1961 and Bahrain in 1972. But by 1978 only Dubai, where television broadcasting began in 1972, had a purely commercial television system.[39] In 1956 state-run television systems were set up in colonial Algeria and British-dominated Iraq, but these were isolated instances, as uncharacteristic of the overall pattern as the fact that Libya had to wait until six years after independence for even a radio transmission system. Generally, in both Africa and the Arab world, radio was introduced under colonialism, but television came only after independence, as a result of state initiative and as an expression of emergent nationalism. In Egypt, for example, where the July 1952 revolution had already given a great impetus to radio, television was introduced on a grand scale in 1960; the eleven-studio complex built on the banks of the Nile in the midst of Cairo clearly signified the Nasser government's intention to take the same dominant role in television that it already occupied in Arab radio, cinema and the music industry.

The Egyptian system was installed under a contract with the Radio Corporation of America, which also gave Egypt the capacity to manufacture television sets; this was one of the first examples of US–Egyptian co-operation after the dispute over the Aswan dam.[40] Syria, which was linked at that time to Egypt, also bought from RCA, but generally the newly independent states built on their existing radio experience and turned to the former colonizing powers for technological assistance. Though the Belgians were characteristically uninterested in the administrative structures developed in Zaire and their other former colonies, both the British and the French were keen to export their particular institutional structures of broadcasting. Of the two models, the centralized French system proved better suited to African and Arab one-party states, whereas the British independent public corporation model needed rapid modification.[41] Zaire and Nigeria have developed both national systems based in the capital and strong regionally based production centres. Indeed, in Nigeria the Western Nigeria regional government managed to get its television broadcasting installed and operating by 1959, in advance of the central government. But elsewhere, with only minor exceptions – such as Gabon's second channel under President Omar Bongo's direct personal control – television is centralized, government-controlled and operated under the Ministry of Information. The key role that broadcasting is seen to occupy is exemplified by the fact that the seizure of the broadcasting station has become as important as that of the airport or the presidential palace in any political coup.[42]

The situation of the film-maker is generally more favourable than that of the state television employee, since normal film production systems allow space for individuality and personal creativity – if within the strict confines of an agreed and usually very limited budget. In many countries film production (apart from newsreel and informational documentary) is recognized as being the responsibility of the Ministry of Culture, and this enhances the status of the feature film maker. But at the same time the very distinctions which permit a degree of freedom deny any possibility of real interaction between cinema and television. With rare exceptions, such as that of Niger at the beginning of the 1980s, television services have not funded feature film making, and there has never been any equivalent to the sustained and fruitful interplay of film and television instigated, for example, by Channel 4 in Britain. Moreover the general low level of independent creativity and innovation in television broadcasting shows clearly the dangers of a system held too tightly under bureaucratic control and provides a warning to those who seek too great an involvement of the state in film production. Where state organizations exist, film censorship tends to be tightest, as in Syria, where film-makers are forbidden to attack government policy, to question the socialist line, official morality or tradition, to criticize friendly countries or to fail to show respect for religion.[43] Such examples of constraint have not, however, prevented film-makers from recognizing the crucial importance of state support for the development of cinema.

Film and the state

It is obviously impracticable – and ultimately unilluminating – to trace every facet of African or Arab governments' involvement in the various sectors of the film industry: each of the sixty or so states offers its own particular juridical status to film and in most cases the organizational structures for handling film production, distribution, exhibition and import have varied over twenty or thirty years. But we can at least follow the general thinking of the film-makers themselves. In 1970 the African film-makers established their own professional organization, FEPACI (Fédération pan-africaine des cinéastes), which unites film-makers from both the Arab North and sub-Saharan Africa and has observer status at the Organization of African Unity. Though formal meetings of FEPACI have been rare, the organization has continued to be an active force thanks to the efforts of individual members. Since the late 1960s these have been aided by the existence of a number of regular forums for discussion: the thirteen biennial meetings of the JCC (Journées

cinématographiques de Carthage) in Tunis between 1966 and 1990, and
the twelve meetings of FESPACO (Festival panafricain du cinéma de
Ouagadougou) in the capital of Burkina Faso between 1969 and 1991.
There was also briefly a third festival, this time in Anglophone East
Africa, MOGPAFIS (Mogadishu Pan-African Film Symposium),
which held meetings in the capital of Somalia in 1981 and 1983, as well as
a number of one-off events, such as the colloquium held in Niamey in
1982. Ferid Boughedir, Tunisian film-maker and indefatigable conference-
goer, has traced the evolution of the strategies proposed by film-makers
in a paper presented at the JCC in 1984 and subsequently reprinted.[44]

Taking as his starting point the definition of distribution as the key
sector of the film industry made by Tahar Cheriaa, the founder of the
Carthage Film Festival, in 1967,[45] Boughedir looks back at the African
and Arab film-makers' initial cry for total nationalization. Seeing the
crucial problems as foreign control of distribution, national markets too
small to support a national cinema and the failure to return money taken
from cinema in taxation to foster production, film-makers of the late
1960s and early 1970s placed their reliance on state control. This seemed
to meet the priorities of many of the states themselves. In Egypt at the
beginning of the 1960s, the Nasser government, which had already used
radio as 'a vital means of welding the new country together into a
coherent nation and making its influence felt as a vital force throughout
the Middle East'[46] and had launched television on a massive scale in
1960, turned its attention to the film industry. State involvement, which
culminated in the setting up of the General Organization of Egyptian
Cinema in 1961, took place in the context of Nasser's concern with the
implementation of Arab socialism, which found its full expression in the
1962 Charter of National Action. This called for public ownership of
much of the economy, control of all import trade and of three-quarters
of the export trade.[47] The first state-produced Egyptian films appeared
in 1963 and, as Farid notes, 'the public sector produced all the films of
any importance during the period 1963–1971'.[48] Though Egyptian state
production petered out in the early 1970s as a result of the persistant
losses made by the General Organization and an economy reoriented to
the private sector, later Egyptian film-makers were to look back on the
1960s as 'a golden age of nationalized, protected cinema' and as 'one
dedicated to Egypt and the Arabs in the name of land, and to solidarity
and integrity in the name of the family'.[49]

Before the eventual commercial failure in Egypt became apparent,
similar state organizations were set up in Syria and Iraq. Both began
producing feature films towards the end of the 1960s in a context of
expanding privately funded production, but their chosen paths diverged
sharply. In Iraq, where the one or two state-funded films produced
annually came to constitute the only Iraqi output after 1977, the General

Organization for Film and Theatre specialized in superproductions aimed at the wider Arab market. Though talented directors were employed and given massive resources – the veteran Egyptians Tewfik Saleh (*The Long Days/Al-ayyam al-tawila*, 1981) and Salah Abou Seif (*Al-Qadisiyya*, 1980), and the most gifted of the younger Iraqi filmmakers, Mohamed Chukry Jamil (*Clash of Loyalties/Al-masala al-kubra*, 1983) – successful foreign distribution was never achieved. In contrast, the Syrian General Organization for Cinema, which had produced some two dozen features by the end of the 1980s, specialized in low-budget, smaller-scale projects, achieving particular success with the first films by a pair of talented, Moscow-trained directors, Samir Zikra (*The Half-metre Incident/Hadith al-nasf metr*, 1983, and *Events of the Coming Year/Waqai' al-'am al-muqbil*, 1986) and Mohamed Malass (*Dreams of the City/Ahlam al-madina*, 1984).

There are state organizations too in the Maghreb, but these vary widely in their structures and effectiveness. In Morocco the privately owned infrastructure is favourable: it comprises a flourishing distribution sector (the number of cinemas rose from 79 in 1945 to some 250 in the 1970s) and three studios (Souissi, Ain-Chok and Casablanca). But the state organization, the Centre cinématographique marocain (CCM), remained virtually unchanged after it was set up in 1945 under the French protectorate; it largely limited itself to newsreel and documentary production and offered no support to Morocco's struggling feature film makers until the 1980s. In Tunisia, SATPEC has taken a more forceful role, controlling the import of films and participating in the production of a considerable number of features (including some disastrous French co-productions), though throughout its early years it was burdened with debts stemming from a costly but initially underequipped studio complex at Gammarth. Algeria adopted a more radical approach, recognizing the value of film, which had been used during the long struggle for liberation. All sectors of the industry – importing, distribution and exhibition as well as production – were nationalized through the Office national pour le commerce et l'industrie cinématographique (ONCIC). This organization was able both to maintain a constant flow of production (four or five features a year) and to exercise control over the choice of subjects – the cycles of films on the liberation struggle following Mohamed Lakhdar-Hamina's *Wind of the Aures/Rih al-Awras* (1966) in the 1960s and those on the agrarian reforms in the 1970s, in the wake of Mohamed Bouamari's *The Charcoal Burner/Al-fahham* (1972). More recently, the scope has been widened in terms of both subject and approach, as is exemplified by the films of Merzak Allouache.

In sub-Saharan Africa, in most of the territories that had been colonized by the British, the national production structures after independence largely retained the role (previously filled by the colonial film units) of making educational and instructional documentaries while totally ignoring the fictional feature film. In Ghana and Nigeria all the impetus for feature film making has had to come from the private sector, and Anglophone East Africa remains a virtual desert as far as fiction film making is concerned.

But the approach is very different in those West African states which inherited from the French a very different view of film's cultural role. The French themselves continued funding a large amount of low-budget African film-making – through a scheme devised by the French Ministry of Co-operation – until 1980 when the experiment was discontinued at the request of the African governments. In the fourteen newly independent states of what had once been French West and French Equatorial Africa, national film corporations charged with fostering production were set up: SNC in Senegal, SONAVOCI in Upper Volta (later Burkina Faso), OCINAM in Mali, FODIC in Cameroon, ONC in Congo, SIC in the Ivory Coast etc. These corporations were inevitably underfunded and with a few notable exceptions – particularly SONAVOCI in Burkina Faso – film-makers found them to be unadventurous and overbureaucratic. None was able to sustain a flow of films over a decade, and in certain cases when the corporation was given a monopoly of production, it actually brought the output of films to a halt (as in Dahomey when the country was transformed into socialist Benin). Following the example of Algeria, which had to survive a five-year boycott by the Motion Picture Export Association of America when it chose to exercise what might seem a normal national right to control the import of films into the country, several other African states tried to confront the interests of the handful of multinational corporations which control the worldwide flow of films. None was successful and, though apparently amicable negotiation has now replaced the earlier threats and boycotts, little has changed in the film fare which African filmgoers are offered, namely the cheapest and shoddiest imported films which are available.

The difficulties faced by African film-makers in dealing with the international situation are graphically illustrated by one of the more ambitious schemes to create film common markets linking regional groups of countries. In 1981 the CIDC (Consortium interafricain de distribution cinématographique) came into operation after years of patient effort, taking into African hands for the first time the import and distribution of films in the fourteen states of Francophone black Africa, where control had previously been exercised by a succession of French-owned companies. The aim was to create a system which would both allow the commercial showing of African films to the African mass audience and, with the profits from the screenings of foreign films, support a parallel production organization, CIPRO Films (Centre interafricain de production de films).

But as Boughedir has pointed out,[50] things did not go smoothly. Most states did not reform their tax structures to allow the common market to come fully into operation, nor did they pay their contributions to CIDC. Many national cinema organizations saw distribution purely as a commercial operation and were uninterested in the cultural role of finding an audience for African films. At the same time many local exhibitors refused to show African films – though some of those which were properly distributed (most notably Souleymane Cisse's *The Wind/Finye* and Kramo-Lancine Fadika's *Djeli*) achieved remarkable commercial success. Internally the lack of national ticketing systems prevented the monitoring and control of the market; externally there was just no other source of supply than the companies which had serviced the old French combines. By 1984 the CIDC, which in any case had only 59 African films among the 1,200 it distributed (that is, barely 4 per cent) had lost the confidence of African film-makers and its operations had virtually come to a halt. Once more the market was vulnerable to US films, distributed this time through a Swiss-registered company, SOCOPRINT, which has shown no interest in handling films made by Africans.

Because of the difficulties experienced by state organizations in Africa and the Arab world in sustaining film production and ensuring adequate distribution for those films which are made, the 1980s have seen a number of contradictory developments, but two new key concerns seem to be privatization and internationalism. Some of the old state monopolies have been broken up. ONCIC in Algeria was split in the mid-1980s into a distribution arm (ENADEC) and a production arm (ENAPROC). Many of the state-owned cinemas are being sold off to private investors and at the same time film-makers are being allowed to set up their own companies to co-produce their work.[51] In Iraq an attempt to relaunch private funding for films involved the setting up of the Babel company, a mixed enterprise owned 60 per cent by public and 40 per cent by private capital.[52] Morocco finally gave state aid to individual film-makers in the early 1980s, which led to a surge of productions not all of which have been able to find distribution. Tunisia revised its laws governing film production to encourage privately funded output, but simultaneously gave up control of the import of films, thereby making it more difficult for local films to recover costs.

Internationalism of all kinds is also currently favoured. Some schemes have had excellent results – as when the state corporations of Burkina Faso, Algeria and Tunisia combined their efforts to produce Ousmane Sembene and Thierno Faty Sow's *Camp de Thiaroye* (1988). Med Hondo turned to the French ministries of Culture and Foreign

Relations, as well as to the Burkina Faso government, for the funding of *Sarraounia* (1986). The film, an excellent anti-colonial epic, was completed, but despite its French finance it received only the briefest of screenings in Paris, where it stood its best chance of recovering its costs. In the desperate search for the necessary foreign outlets for their work, Arab film-makers have also used internationalism of a more questionable kind. A striking example here is the Tunisian Ridha Behi, best known in the West for his first film *Hyena's Sun/Shams al-diba* (1977). Having used Egyptian stars and dialect in his 1984 Tunisia-set film *Angels/Al-malaika* (and still failed to get distribution in Egypt), Behi has since used the French language and European stars playing Arab roles in *Scarlet Memory/La mémoire écarlate* (1986). Others have followed similar paths, and with the growing diversification and internationalism of the film market, pressures on other African and Arab film-makers to do likewise are bound to increase.

Contexts of production

It is impossible to generalize about the situation facing individual Arab and African film-makers, since circumstances vary widely and there are a number of models of production, varying from the industrial context of film-making in Egypt to the independent resourcing forced upon film-makers in, say, Ghana, Morocco or Senegal.

In Egypt, film-making follows its own pattern, quite unlike that elsewhere in the Arab world. Film-makers can receive their training locally, at the Higher Cinema Institute in Cairo, so that they evolve in close relationship with Egyptian film-making traditions, with none of the alienation involved in foreign technical training. Cinema was industrialized in Egypt in the 1930s and output has been sustained at around forty to fifty films a year for decades. This means that the new film-makers of the post-Nasser era are working within a conventional film industry structure of genres and stars, and their films are likely to achieve distribution both in Egypt and in a wider pan-Arab market. The pressures under which they work are real, but they are those faced by workers in virtually any film industry outside Hollywood or Bombay, where local production is uniquely sufficient to dominate and control the domestic market. Elsewhere, whether in London or Cairo, difficulties stem from the economic fact that in order to sustain a film production sector with an output of, say, fifty films a year, a distribution and exhibition infrastructure of considerable dimensions is required, one which demands not just fifty films but several hundred a year to sustain its commercial viability. This opens up a gap in interests between producers and distributors, since the latter derive the bulk of their profits from handling imported films and therefore have a stake in an open import system, even if this may be harmful to local production (by pushing down costs, for example, or determining dependence on a handful of key box office stars).

In the late 1960s a New Cinema Group emerged in Egypt which might, potentially, have offered a parallel to the new cinemas emerging in the Maghreb and sub-Saharan Africa. But little came of their efforts, the sole truly innovative film of the period being Shadi Abdel Salam's *The Night of the Counting of the Years/Al-mumia* (1968). The 1970s are generally recognized as one of the low points of Egyptian film-making. The three established veterans of Egyptian cinema all experienced difficulties: Chahine made his three late 1970s features in collaboration with ONCIC, the Algerian state production company, Tewfik Saleh made *The Dupes/Al-makhdu'un* (1972) in Syria and Salah Abou Seif made *Al-Qadisiyya* (1980) in Iraq. Films of even limited interest – such as Ali Abdel Khalek's *Song on the Road/Ughniya 'alal-mamarr* (1973) – are rare in the 1970s.

But the 1980s have seen a fascinating renewal. Whilst two of the veterans have returned to the Cairo studios to make films which, admittedly in very different ways, echo the traditions of Egyptian cinema – Yusuf Chahine with *The Sixth Day/Al-yawm al-sadis* (1987) and Salah Abou Seif with *The Beginning/Al-bidaya* (1986) – the younger film-makers have adopted a new approach. Faced with the crumbling infrastructure of the Egyptian film industry (disused studios, poor technical facilities) a number of them have come together to collaborate in a new way: 'they work together, exchange ideas, share technicians, and even take turns at being scriptwriter, director or actor for each other's films.'[53] The informal grouping – which includes Mohamed Khan, Atef al-Tayyeb, Bechir al-Dik, Khairy Beshara and Daoud Abdel Sayed – is of film-makers steeped in the traditions of Egyptian cinema and working within its production structures and constraints. But instead of echoing the past, they rework the genre conventions, invert the clichés and offer radically new roles to the popular stars of the day. For the time being at least, the strategy of these film-makers, dubbed by a Lebanese critic 'the children of Abou Seif, the streets and Coca Cola',[54] has paid off in both commercial and artistic terms.

Outside Egypt film-makers throughout the Arab world and sub-Saharan Africa work in a very different context, since film output is everywhere too low to constitute an industry as such. Lebanon and Syria, where production began tentatively in the silent days, are the only two countries that have produced over a hundred feature films. None of the new cinemas of the post-independence era has reached this figure in twenty or thirty years, indeed only Algeria, Iraq and Morocco have a total output of over fifty films. Three further countries – Senegal,

Nigeria and Tunisia – have produced between twenty-five and fifty, but otherwise barely a handful have an output running into double figures. Detailed statistics are difficult to arrive at, since many films announced as completed are never shown, some get festival screenings abroad but no domestic release, while some are limited to a purely local market, and so on. But it can be estimated that, in all, between 700 and 800 features have been produced in some 35 countries of Africa and the Arab world outside Egypt. Though books exist on cinema in Gabon and Mali,[55] barely a dozen features have been produced in either country and we can scarcely consider that such a tiny output constitutes a national cinema.

African cinema has grown up largely separate from developments in literature. The French-language novels of North Africa are more likely to be adapted to the screen by French film-makers than by Algerian, Tunisian or Moroccan directors. One interesting, if tentative, exception to this general rule is to be found in Angola. There, as in Mozambique, the liberation movement which fought for freedom from Portuguese rule until the mid-1970s attached great importance to the cinema and, as in Algeria or Cuba, the cinematographic institutions developed immediately after independence reflected the form of socialism adopted in the liberation struggle. The roots of the new approach lie in a committed documentary style of film-making, adopted in Mozambique as well as in Angola, which is the antithesis of the apparently neutral, informational style adopted throughout Anglophone Africa. *Mueda, Memory and Massacre/Mueda, memória e massacre* (1979), made by Ruy Guerra (who was born in Mozambique but has made his career largely in Brazil) exemplifies this trend. The film, shot on a very low budget in just two days, achieves great force and authority from its combination of interviews with survivors of the 1960 Mueda massacre with a record of the re-enactment of it staged annually by the local inhabitants.

The links in Angola between the liberation struggle, literature and film first became apparent in the early 1970s with two films adapted from stories by Luandino Vieira, Angola's leading novelist, who in 1977 became head of the newly established film institute, IAC. Directed by the Moscow-trained Guadeloupean film-maker Sarah Maldoror, the short *Monangambee* shot in Algeria in 1970 and the feature-length *Sambizanga* made in the Republic of Congo in 1972 emerged as generalized statements of Third World struggle, somewhat marred by an inappropriate Hollywood-style gloss.

Film-making in Angola during the 1980s has been very limited but two films shown internationally in 1984 – the documentary *Memory of a Day/Memória de um dia* directed by Orlando Fortunato and the fictional *Nelisita* directed by Ruy Duarte de Carvalho – give a fuller expression of the Angolan experience. Both films base their structures on the patterns and rhythms of oral storytelling techniques so as to reach a popular audience for whom a cinema of social and political awareness is inevitably quite novel after the long years of colonial rule. Duarte – like Vieira a poet and novelist born in Portugal but raised in Angola and now a naturalized Angolan citizen – is no doubt aided by the fact that both literature and film-making use the national language, Portuguese. But *Nelisita* remains a remarkable achievement showing the full potential of a fictional style that creates a synthesis of documentary practice and literary-based exploration of narrative structure in the context of a redefinition of the social function of cinema within an emerging African society.

If Angola is unusual in the close links existing between its literature and its film-making, Nigeria is certainly unique in offering an example of a genuinely popular ethnic cinema in the Yoruba-language region of Western Nigeria.[56] Sporadic attempts at film-making, mostly in English, were made in Nigeria from the 1970s and indeed the IDHEC-trained Ola Balogun emerged as Africa's most prolific feature film-maker with ten features between *Alpha*, made in 1972, and *Money Power* which was completed a decade later. Balogun pioneered Yoruba-language production with *Ajani-Ogun* in 1975 and then went on to make initial feature films with three of the leading figures of the Yoruba travelling theatre: *Ija Ominira* (1977) with Ade Folayan (Ade Love), *Aiye* (1979) with Chief Hubert Ogunde and *Orun Mooru* (1982) with Moses Olaiya Adejumo (Baba Sala).

The latter film is the most elaborate of the series, mixing folklore and rural comedy, traditional songs and dances, satire on the modern rich and elaborate trick effects (for a ghostly dream sequence) in a setting from which all hint of the colonial era is absent. This kind of interplay between cinema and popular local dance and drama has the potential to be highly fruitful, since it offers a model of film-making which is not derivative of Western models. To date, however, the resources of film have been used to do little more than record performances already elaborated in stage terms. This is particularly the case when the three leading actor-managers have ignored their own total lack of training in film-making technique and proceeded to direct their own work: Ade Love directing *Kadara* (1980), *Ija Orogun* (1982) and *Taxi Driver* (1983), Hubert Ogunde co-directing *Jaiyesinmi* (1981) and *Aropin 'N'tenia* (1982), and Baba Sala making *Aare Agbaiye* (1983). The same theatricality also characterizes *Efunsetan Oniwura* (1981), made by Balogun's former assistant Bankole Bello, with members of a fourth troupe, that of Ishola Ogunsola.

This burst of production activity in the early 1980s, which was rooted in a thriving forty-year-old style of popular theatre, shows great vitality and direct popular appeal. The films' mode of production is unique in that the companies operate as polygamous family units, with all the actresses married to the actor-manager. The films exist too outside the normal film distribution circuits, and in a very real sense Yoruba film production is a cottage industry, with the actor/film-maker taking the sole copy of the film on tour on the informal theatrical circuit in a manner reminiscent of the fairground exhibitors of early European or Indian cinema. When screenings occur, the star presents his work directly to the public and the actresses take on other roles: projectionists, usherettes, sellers of programmes and records. These films are not shown at foreign film festivals, and the only European screenings occur on occasions like that, in July 1983, when Hubert Ogunde hired the Porchester Hall in London to show two of his films. While other African films may find success with art house audiences abroad and may prove extremely attractive to those African audiences they are able to reach (festival screenings at the 1989 FESPACO in Ouagadougou attracted an estimated half-million spectators), none has the particular hybrid qualities which mark off this Yoruba film-making as a genuine expression of popular culture. For each of the theatre companies, film-making represents only part of their annual output. While each remains an individual competitive small business, the breadth of expression takes in the whole spectrum of the modern entertainment media:

> A typical Yoruba theatre company . . . will be involved in the production not only of stage plays but also of television and radio serials, films, photoplay magazines, and records. Some theatre companies are also involved in neo-traditional oral performance and in publishing.[57]

The individual film-maker

Though some governments, most notably the changing regimes in Burkina Faso, give support to film-makers, the kind of potentially fruitful contexts provided in Angola and the Yoruba region of Nigeria are rare. Looking at African and Arab film-making outside Egypt we are usually concerned with the output of individuals, often working in some isolation and in a sharply competitive world of limited resources. Whereas Egyptian film-makers can be sure of finding spectators familiar with the genre conventions they employ (or subvert) and the Yoruba film-makers are guaranteed filmgoers intrigued by a retelling in movie terms of a well-known play, other African and Arab film-makers are in constant, often desperate search for their audience.

Perhaps the most striking instance of the frustrations of separation from a mass audience was that suffered in the late 1960s and 1970s by film-makers in the newly independent states formed from the former French colonies of West and Equatorial Africa. For almost twenty years until 1980 – when the scheme was discontinued at the request of African governments – the French Ministry of Co-operation in Paris developed a programme of aid and technical assistance for black African film-makers. Finance was provided through the purchase at an inflated price of the non-commercial rights for distribution in France and French cultural centres and the result was a curiously self-contradictory cinema: an expression of African culture conceived and completed in Paris, contained in films /most readily available through the ministry's excellent archive in Paris and viewable in Africa only at French cultural centres. Whilst production activities were fostered by French government policies, distribution possibilities for the films produced were nonexistent in Africa, as the films were systematically excluded from the screens in Africa's commercial film theatres by the power of French-based international film distribution companies.

The French input undoubtedly stimulated interest in film-making among young African intellectuals and an awareness of the cultural role of film on the part of some governments, but it also set a pattern of separation between film-maker and audience which often persists to this day. Because of the constraints of budget and the difficulties of distribution, most African and Arab films today are personal creations in a way that films can never be once film production is fully industrialized. The film-makers tend to come from a fairly circumscribed, educated background and most, as we have seen, have studied in Europe, often in one of the major film schools. They are mainly men, since few African or Arab women have made feature films: Safi Faye in Senegal, Assia Djebbar in Algeria, Selma Baccar and Nejia Ben Mabrouk in Tunisia, and Heiny Srour in Lebanon are among the rare exceptions. They will usually be concerned with every aspect of production, beginning with the raising of the money from state or private sources, the negotiation of co-production deals, contacts with foreign funding sources and so on. This often means writing one's own script as a way of controlling the production, and in some cases appearing as one of the leading players as well.

Even if there is a state-run co-producer, the actual shooting will be organized through the film-maker's personal production company: Newin Productions for Ridha Behi and Latif Films for Abdellatif Ben Ammar in Tunisia, Domirev Films for Ousmane Sembene in Senegal, DK7 Films for Daniel Kamwa in Cameroon, Afrocult Foundation for Ola Balogun in Nigeria etc. New legislation in Algeria has led to Mohamed Lakhdar-Hamina and Ahmed Rachedi founding their own production companies there, and the same system applies to film-makers living in exile: Marisa Films for the Palestinian Michel Khleifi in

Brussels and Les Films Soleil O for the Mauretanian Med Hondo in Paris, for example. Often the film-makers have to take a direct hand in arranging local distribution and if the film is lucky enough to achieve screenings abroad, the film-maker will have to travel as the work's sole publicist, moving from festival to festival, doing deals with representatives of European distributors and television companies.

It may be argued that this is the fate of any independent film-maker working outside the system in any part of the world. But in much of Africa and the Arab world there is quite literally no system to work outside. Film-makers operate in a context where there is no pre-existing tradition of film-making, no standard procedure for organizing production or conventional source of film finance, no pool of experienced technical or acting talent, and virtually no appropriate models for a film's dramaturgy or visual style. Most Arab and African films therefore represent an awesome personal effort on the part of their makers, whose rewards will be strictly limited. They and their backers will probably have to wait years to recover their investment (if at all). The local market will probably be so unregulated that the film producers never actually recover the appropriate proportion of the box office takings, and foreign commercial screenings – in Africa, the Arab world or elsewhere – will be rare.

The result of these circumstances is that a large proportion of Arab, and especially African, films of the past twenty-five years are first features, since many newcomers of real talent never get the chance to make a second feature. In Burkina Faso, admittedly an extreme example, nine directors have made first feature films over a period of seventeen years, but only two of these, Gaston Kabore and Idrissa Ouedraogo have gone on to make a second. The gap before the appearance of a second feature can be enormously long: six years (followed by a further eight years of silence) for the Moroccan Moumen Smihi, author of *El Chergui* (1975) and *Forty-four, or Bedtime Stories/Quarante-quatre, ou les récits de la nuit* (1982), seven years for the Ghanaian Kwah Ansah (*Love Brewed in the African Pot*, 1981, and *Heritage . . . Africa*, 1988), eight years for the Lebanese director Borhan Alawiya (*Kafr Kassem*, 1974, and *Beirut, the Meeting/Beirut, al-liqa*, 1982), ten years for the Senegalese Ababacar Samb-Makharam (*Kodou* in 1972 and *Jom* in 1982) and no less than fifteen years for Désiré Ecaré from the Ivory Coast (*It's Up To Us, France/A nous deux, France* in 1970 and *Women's Faces/Visages de femmes* in 1985). Apart from the unique example of the Nigerian Ola Balogun, who completed ten features between 1972 and 1982, the realization of half a dozen feature-length films before the end of the 1980s is a remarkable achievement even for directors with an international reputation whose careers began in the 1960s. The forceful Algerian director Mohamed Lakhdar-

Hamina, winner of the Palme d'Or at Cannes in 1975, managed this feat, as did the novelist and veteran of Senegalese cinema Ousmane Sembene, but the Iraqi Mohamed Chukry Jamil managed just five, as did the Mauretanian-born exile Med Hondo.

All these independent film-makers share one thing in common: film-making is an extremely risky business. The Moroccan film-maker Moumen Smihi puts this very well:

> Being a freelance worker in a Third World country means walking the high wire without a safety net. There is no social protection, no unemployment benefit, no social security, no right to a pension. A bohemian life of a kind long forgotten in the West. An artist's life, absolute risk, total dependence on the patron, the prince (that is, today, the state).[58]

But along with this awareness of vulnerability there is – even for an artist like Smihi who is not in any way given to making direct social statements in a readily accessible realist style – a sense of commitment to deal with the national culture:

> To be a film director in Morocco, for me, is to demonstrate the total or general act of living, filming, thinking life, society, history, cinema.[59]

What supports this conviction – for Smihi and a great many of his Arab and African contemporaries – is a fundamental certainty:

> A country without images or a nation which does not produce images is like a country or a nation which does not produce its own food supply. . . . If the Arab image were to fail, to be lacking, to disappear, if it could not be constituted and perpetuated, all human culture would be amputated.[60]

Part Two
Arab Film

Brahim Babai,
And Tomorrow? / *Wa ghadan?*
(Tunisia, 1972)

Mohamed Lakhdar-Hamina,
Chronicle of the Years of Ashes / Waqai' sinin al-jamar
(Algeria 1975)

Yusuf Chahine,
The Sparrow / Al-usfour
(Egypt, 1972)

New Tunisian Theatre Collective,
The Wedding / Al-'urs
(Tunisia, 1978)

Ahmed Yashfin,
The Nightmare / Al-kabus
(Morocco, 1984)

Beshir al-Dik,
The Journey's Road / Sikka Safar
(Egypt, 1986)

Mohammed Khan,
The Wife of an Important Man / Zauja rajul muhimm
(Egypt, 1987)

Samir Zikra,
Events of the Coming Year / Waqai' al-'am al-muqbil
(Syria, 1986)

Khairy Beshara,
The Necklace and the Bracelet / al-tauq wal-aswirra
(Egypt, 1987)

Shadi Abdel Salam,
The Night of the Counting of the Years / *Al-mumia*
(Egypt, 1968)

Assia Djebar,
The Nouba of the Women of Mount Chenoua / *Nouba nisa
al-jebal Shnua*
(Algeria, 1978)

Mohammed Khan,
Dreams of Hind and Camelia / Ahlam hind wa Camelia
(Egypt, 1988)

Khairy Beshara,
Bitter Day, Sweet Day / yawm murr, yawm hulw
(Egypt, 1989)

Mohamed Khan,
Return of a Citizen / *'awda muwatin*
(Egypt, 1976)

Ahmed al-Maanouni,
Oh the Days, the Days / *Al-ayyam, al-ayyam*
(Morocco, 1978)

Jean-Pierre Bledo,
Empire of Dreams / *Mamlakat al-ahlam*
(Algeria, 1981)

Yusuf Chahine,
Alexandria, Why? / *Iskanderliya, leeh?*
(Egypt, 1978)

3. The Epic

Heroes

With its lone rider galloping off into the sunset to the strains of stirring music, *The Outlaws/Al-kharijun 'an al-qanun* might look like the perfect (Algerian) cowboy film. Actually, though set before the war with the French, this is the perfect Algerian Revolution film.

But are the two so different? The cowboy story usually tells of an outsider who, by espousing a just cause, takes on the fight of others and becomes a hero, an insider. Directed in 1969 by Tewfik Farès, *The Outlaws* does the same. As an Algerian sharpshooter in the French colonial army, the hero at first looks like a bad boy, being gratuitously troublesome. But after he flees back to his family and witnesses the death of his father, his new sense of responsibility leads him to such determined revolt that he lands in jail. But there with his cellmates he learns something about solidarity with other Algerians, with his countrymen and, when free again, he combs the countryside in search of help against the oppressive French and their local collaborators, the rich landlords. He becomes the medium of a collective cause, an agent of virtue.

To say that he is involved in holy war (*jihad*) might, however, be going a bit far. 'Political combat has suffered too much by being confused with *jihad*,' writes the Tunisian Mohsen Toumi, in connection with the discourse of the North African state. He continues, 'Bringing ideology into metaphysics is a confusion.'[1]

Because of Algeria's brutalizing struggle against the French, however, it was almost inevitable that this confusion happened there. When, in the early sixties, after the war, Algerian film-makers obtained their own cameras and set about showing the population at large what the fight had been all about, they did so largely in terms of a heroic quest, a voyage towards what might be expressed as a kind of Holy Grail, the victory which history, in fact, had given them: hence, lyricism and the happy end.

But lyricism did not always mean sunsets and panoramic scenery.

Abdellatif Ben Ammar's 1973 Tunisian version of the heroic quest, *Sejnane*, is shot in muted tones, in a middle-class urban household. The voyage of the young student from ignorance to knowledge via participation in group struggle is similar to that in *The Outlaws*. Also, just as the battle in the countryside was simultaneously against the French and the rich landlords, here it is both against the French and the bosses of industry. Moreover in *Sejnane* the catalyst for the boy's action is the death of his father, just as in the Algerian film, and with the death of the real, good father the fight with the surrogate, bad father begins.

If in these North African films, the bad father is local bosses and the French, in Mohamed Mounir Fanari's 1986 Iraqi film *The Lover/Al-'ashiq* the bad father is local bosses and the British. Though the hero is seduced for a while by the arguments of collaborators, the rape of the young girl he loves sends him off in fury on his white horse, over the horizon. It is on that horizon, on the white horse, that he reappears at the film's end. As the living hero or as an image of the dead one, it does not much matter: he is the vision of a victimized community's hopes, the apotheosis of a budding nation.

Another implication of this temporary visual 'ellipsis' of the hero is that after a long struggle throughout the film to get over the horizon, he will be back as saviour. Thus one does not even have to know that the hero in Tewfik Saleh's 1981 Iraqi film *The Long Days/Al-ayyam al-tawila* is Saddam Hussein, the leader of Iraq. One could guess from his disappearance into the sunset that he would be back again.

The form is so pervasive that in Faisal al-Yassiri's 1977 Iraqi film *The River/Al-nahr* it is varied by offering up, at least for a while, two heroes. After following the film's main character (hero?) for a while one notices that, though well-intentioned, he is weak. Sure enough, a less weak man then turns up and this is the one to follow, as he goes off over the horizon.

The problem is that watching a perfect hero throughout the length of a film might lead to a degree of boredom. But then, when was a hero ever a highly personalized figure? As André Jolles writes, in connection with a form he calls legend, the hero 'does not give the impression of existing by himself and for himself but by the community and for the community'. Moreover, 'the community does not see in him a man like any other but the means of seeing virtue actualized'.[2]

Admittedly, Jolles is writing here about the Christian saint as one version of the legendary hero, but the same saintliness can often be found in Arab film heroes. As the Algerian critic Abdelghani Megherbi writes, films on the liberation war often 'propose, in an explicit way, the myth of the hero who is invincible and allergic to fear and anguish'.[3] Mohamed Chouikh's Algerian film *Rupture/Al-inqita'*, made in 1984 with some insight into the audience's eventual boredom with these exemplary heroes, is an interesting attempt to break down the monolith. In it there is a tripartite splitting up of the hero's instrumentality: one man is a reformed bandit using his guns, another a political activist using his brains, and the third a poet, using his emotional outpourings to rouse the masses.

But actually, this is another perennial form; if the heroic quality is not split into three this way, there will be three friends, three paths, three destinies, and so on; this form is often used in films about nationalist struggles. In the Egyptian Salah Abou Seif's 1966 film *Cairo '30/Al-Qahira thalathin*, for instance, there are three university students, united in their friendship and in their disapproval of British imperialism and corrupt local officials. Life and circumstances force them apart and eventually only one takes the correct, that is, revolutionary, path. But at the film's end, he is seen distributing tracts to indifferent crowds, and then to the wind, with no certainty that his will be the winning side.

But where do the heroes go after the nationalist struggle has been won? Granted, colonialism is over, but what next? Do the heroes follow the same patterns, but in some other war? Concerned after independence that equality had not yet dawned for all, the Algerian authorities encouraged films on the next revolution: agrarian reform. But in Sid Ali Mazif's 1975 *The Nomads/Masirat al-ru'ah* the saviour, the agricultural co-operative, stands out stolidly as an insentient monolith, even less arousing than a saint. So it takes three poor, nomad brothers a long time before they finally join this common cause and thus avoid being bought out by the rich local nomads.

It seems that no matter what one does, revolution or no revolution, the bad and the rich creep back in again. Is this necessarily so? To answer this and to check up on the new revolution's progress a young media team of three are sent out into the countryside in Ammar Laskri's 1979 Algerian film *The Beneficial/Al-moufid*. From what they see, it is clear that the wily rich, once dispossessed, are indeed back in possession of communal properties. So, joining the cause of the poor, the three young people begin the struggle again.

In fact, you cannot keep 'bad people' out of stories about 'good people', and so often a film's action seesaws back and forth between the quests of the one and the plots of the other. Or, like in Mohamed Radi's 1974 Egyptian film *Sons of Silence/Abna al-samt*, the good and the bad trade places in the film's foreground. At one point, the screen is dominated by a group of young Egyptian soldiers at the war front, at another by the corrupt editor back in Cairo, controlling people, plot and, implicitly, the future of Egypt, more effectively than can its heroic soldiers.

Even more interesting, it sometimes appears that the current villain, even if unseen, is in fact a past hero. In Ali Badrakhan's 1975 Egyptian film *Al-Karnak* the heroes (and heroine), again university students, are repeatedly arrested, tortured, released and rearrested. The first charge is that they belong to the Muslim Brotherhood (none do), the next that they are communists (one is). The charges hardly matter, what does is their brutal encounter with authority, with the bad father in their own country. As the film ends, another lot go off to prison, this time the officials themselves; as if in vindication of revelations about the previous Nasser era, this film was screened annually on television under Sadat. Badrakhan insists, however, that 'the film is against the excesses of all authority, whether in the time of Nasser, Sadat, or Mubarak'.[4]

An Algerian variation on this theme of the ex-hero as villain is Ahmed Rachedi's 1984 *The Mill of M. Fabré/Tahunat al-sayyid Fabré*. In a small town about to be visited by the 'great man' from the capital, some sign of post-independence progress must be shown, a nationalized property, for instance. Considering all the pressing local problems, this is quite beside the point, but the town authorities go through the motions, nationalizing M. Fabré's tiny mill, stunned when this Frenchman who not only fought with the Algerians but is a confirmed socialist is delighted by the honour! However, the reluctance of the mayor, army officer and party official, as local representatives, to bow and scrape for meaningless ceremony is noted from afar. As local heroes, they are picked off, one by one, and made to disappear by the bigger 'hero' in the capital.

According to Mohsen Toumi, it is the Manichaeism of the discourse of the state, which bases itself on a heroic rhetoric, which leads to this kind of situation. The post-independence leader, dragonkiller of colonialism, sees himself as 'accomplishing ideal historic mediation as actor/hero of an edifying narrative'.[5] Not only that, but since the discourse is a closed circuit forever enunciated, even by the opposition, in the same terms, the risk is that 'a providential and paternalist state might replace another providential and paternalist state'.[6]

Marginals

But even before such replacement and its game of musical chairs, what of the initial aim of the heroic quest and its implementation of the common cause? In other words, what of the new nation and its people? The problem, Toumi points out, is that 'the people' is a constantly recurring theme, eating up its own reality. Since, in the edifying narrative, the leader is considered the image of a collective ideal, 'the people' is then an abstraction, indivisible, all differentiations (and potential conflicts) are to be blurred. What is 'heterogeneous is homogenized'[7] writes Toumi, so the supposedly miniscule number of people who do not fit in are marginals.

One of the problems with being called a marginal is that it is not a positive term, more like a tag around one's neck. This is especially true for those in a newly independent country who are still so poor that they must go abroad to find work. In fact, in the Tunisian Nacer Ktari's 1974 film *The Ambassadors/Al-sufara* it is clear that this is just a displacement of their marginal status. Though the communal trials of poverty and racism undergone by a group of North Africans in Paris creates some sense of extra-national solidarity among them, by the film's end they have advanced only as far as crying out that they do have an identity, that they are 'immigrant workers'. But this rallying cry, though in unison, is made in a French police station.

How melancholy, after all the struggle against the French to be back under French authority again, and again as nobody. Even before the war of independence, some Algerian workers in France ended up outside, and crushed, by steamrolling groups. This rarely told story turns up in Touita Okacha's 1982 Algerian film *The Sacrificed/Al-dahaya*. Caught, sometimes even literally, between the crossfire of anti-French *and* internecine Algerian battles, the young worker simply cracks up. The bells that ring out for the Algerian victory at the film's end re-trigger a cacophony within his tortured head, and he is clearly on the margin, alienated from everyone, everywhere.

The man who is marginal at home usually does not even get a chance to go abroad to look for a better living. But in the Tunisian Brahim Babaï's 1972 film *And Tomorrow/Wa ghadan* the young peasant roars through the film, making a desperate attempt to get out, to go somewhere, running from his parched olive groves, where the water is controlled by the local boss, to the city, where papers and exit visas are controlled by an urban boss, the bureaucratic despot. By the film's end, the hero staggers around a bar; his voyage has taken him nowhere except from the category of rural poor to that of urban destitute, and into crime.

As for the hero of the Moroccan Mohamed Reggab's 1982 *Barber of the Poor Quarter/Hallaq darb al-fuqara*, he is edged out and edged out, from the centre to the periphery. Eased out of his shop, his flat, and his marriage too, and last seen stumbling backwards in a true wasteland, he wails and rages, alone. This is all the more striking because it is not just the 'bad' father figure, the ex-collaborator merchant who pushes him out; it is done with the connivance of the local people, the neighbours, a homogeneous lot when it comes to ostracizing the marginal.

One of the barber's problems is that there is no real language for him to fight back with, no positive terms to express his difference. He is merely unsuccessful. And how about the term 'juvenile'? It does not just designate a generation gap; usually it is also paired with 'delinquency' as in Mohamed Ifticene's 1980 Algerian film *The Left-handed One/Jalti*. Here again one sees the marginals move from centre to periphery, in this case a voyage from family home, to cardboard boxes, out to a shack in a vacant lot. There, several rejected young people get together and try to reconstitute some cohesion of their own, some home. But it is striking and ironic that only when they are acting out a hero story, playing out a mock cowboys and Indians adventure, is there ever any real sense of purpose among them.

But if the young people's shack seems marginal, what of a house in the City of the Dead, or to be more precise, what about *Furnished Tombs for Rent/Madafin mafrusha lil-ijar*, the title of Ali Abdel Khalek's 1987 Egyptian film? Here again there is a spatial transition from the nice flat commandeered from a young family by a rich merchant, to a sleazy transit hotel, out to the tombs. The father is a solid professional at the film's start but he becomes so demoralized that he loses his job and slides from being one of society's insiders to being one of its outsiders. He starts to smoke hashish, to giggle, and to close his eyes to his responsibilities.

Heroines

In *Furnished Tombs for Rent*, who keeps the family going, or not just going but in some relationship to society? The wife does. As the sociologist Hans Günter Semsek puts it:

> Female power, not male power, organizes daily public behaviour and social action in the cemetery. The norm of segregation, which means a total division according to gender . . . is not merely inverted in the marginalized world of the cemetery. Here, women dominate both: they act in the public realm as well as in the private.[8]

So, in this film, the terrain changes the wife. Initially a gentle and fastidious middle-class woman, she learns to hit out, to kick and even to threaten with a knife. Is this new? Back in 1954 Niazi Mustapha made a swashbuckling romp *The Black Knight/Al-faris al-aswad*, which featured his wife, Kooka, bent on righting a wrong, with sword in hand or barefisted. She was, however, disguised as a man for most of the film; such heroics, and especially fighting for a cause, were still considered men's business.

When it comes to causes, women in Arab films do not have to go off on quests, they are already there. Or they are the quest, the cause. The suffering mother in the Algerian hovel is invariably the Algerian earth, the Algerian nation, waiting for the return of the son/saviour. This symbolism is so prevalent that even in a film as wordly as Ghaleb Chaath's 1972 Egyptian *Shadows on the Other Shore/Dhilalun 'ala al-janib al-akhar* about university students on a houseboat in the Nile, the Palestinian boy scarcely conveys anything about his country. What does convey the plight of Palestine are the images in the background: photos of anguished refugees in one room, paintings of victimized women in another, and in the foreground the story of a girl buffeted around by all, through malevolence by one and negligence by most.

When it is a matter of the nation and its integrity, there have been a few active heroines, a few flashes of assertiveness. It may just be in a cry, but a loud one, as when in Yusuf Chahine's 1973 Egyptian film *The Sparrow/Al-'usfur* the woman who ties together all the strands of the story finally rejects the cant that conceals the disappointments around her and goes out into the streets to shout her disapproval and rouse the crowds.

But rousing the crowds can be done quietly too, just by setting an example, as Abdelaziz Tolbi shows in his 1972 Algerian film *Noua*. About a young peasant heroine of the same name at the time of the outbreak of Algeria's revolt against the French, it traces her voyage from ignorance and dependence on collaborationist relatives to a flight from home and active aid to the guerrillas in their growing community. In fact, images of women like her, uneducated but politically committed, fill the background in many films of the Algerian Revolution, enshrouded figures carrying guns in their bread baskets.

Ironically, it is in an Egyptian film that the Algerian woman as central character is most fully developed and she is shown on a voyage from ignorance to awareness, from a life centred around individual activities to one given over to collective struggle. Despite its flimsy surface of Egyptian romance, a strong image comes across in Yusuf Chahine's 1958 tribute to the Algerian partisans *Jamila/Jamila al-jazairiya*. A cute and innocent teenager at the film's beginning, by its end Jamila is the spitting image of Joan of Arc, and as her tortured face and shaved head are superimposed on images of the Algerian masses, they march out together from the countryside to confront the French.

Since the film is against French colonialism, the Joan of Arc image is nicely sardonic. Still, it is also the nation and the suffering woman, together again as a single entity. So what happens to the heroine when a film is not about national struggle, when the concerns are domestic, in all senses of the word? In melodrama, women again suffer, mostly in silence, occasionally with a final word of protest in court (see chapter 5). In Egyptian films, however, there is often a lively female character, a rather florid woman of the people, who does not take things lying down. She usually has a 'heart of gold', and always a loud mouth. She is always subsidiary, however, even when, as in *The Bully* (see chapter 5) or

Third Class (below) she is the hero's wife.

Where a woman character is more subdued and sensitive, there seems to be a new tendency to allow her frustrations to explode on the screen. She might have been driven mad by injustice, as is the heroine of Ashraf Fahmy's 1987 Egyptian film *For Lack of Sufficient Proof/Li 'adam kifayat al-adilla*. Despite the help and support of a woman lawyer, her husband's lies have deprived her of her child and the law is a spiral of Catch 22s, with, for example, papers requiring the signature of the very person she is accusing. On temporary release from a mental hospital, she sees her husband and simply batters him to death with his own wrench. End of film.

This is not just gratuitous violence or the aberration of an uneducated peasant girl. In Atef al-Tayyeb's 1984 Egyptian film *The Clink/Al-takhshiba*, it is a woman doctor who is victim of the law. Reporting to a police station in connection with a minor traffic accident, she is at first harassed and narrowly escapes being locked up in the clink overnight. But when that is cleared up, it is noticed that her description tallies with that of a woman accused of robbery. On the basis, again, of lack of sufficient proof to the contrary, and in the face of people like her husband who fear any social contagion, be it only from supposition, she is considered guilty and so she takes off to plot, plan and obtain the confession of the person really responsible. This means, however, torturing a man. Here again, no happy end.

Pent-up violence on the part of women is not always directed only at the inequities of the law. Raafat al-Mihi's 1986 Egyptian film *A Last Love Story/Lil-hubb qissa akhira* extends the heroine's frustrations with her husband's fluctuating health, lack of family support and sudden death on to her repugnance of superstition. Going to the deserted shrine where a local saint had been so fanatically adulated that, before her husband's death, even the two of them had been caught up in a pilgrimage there, she smashes his throne, this saintly relic, to smithereens.

This act of desecration takes place in a film which is in every other way a celebration of a sane, life-glorifying attitude, and set in a multi-religious community on a Nile island. This community is probably much like the vision of Egypt which the heroine of Atef al-Tayyeb's 1988 Egyptian film *The World on the Wing of a Dove/Al-dunya 'ala janah yamama* brings back to Cairo after many years abroad. With that vision, she stuns everyone. Her dream is to take her three million dollars and put it into (not take it out of) Egypt, and not just Egypt but the Egyptian national bank. 'Not into houses or cars or furs or jewels?' cries the constantly chewing, swallowing taxi driver who is her pugnacious but kindly guide. 'No,' she says, but for her plan to work, she needs the help of her girlhood beau, now supposedly mad and incarcerated in an insane asylum. She and the taxi driver must rescue him.

Rescue by a woman? Well, this is a new heroine, she not only speaks out, not only takes action, but she has a vision, a kind of Jimmy Stewart 'dream'. But note: for this dream to come true, she needs a man, not just the rough-and-tumble taxi driver, but the beau, the educated thinker also. So, in a sense, just like Kooka in 1954 jumping off walls, sword in hand, but disguised as a man, the 1988 heroine, armed with her vision, also needs the disguise of a man's presence. Any positive change in a situation must still come from a man's hand or through a man's eyes.

Violence

Unfortunately, the word 'positive' is used very loosely these days. It often refers to action films, full of smoking guns and dead bodies. The destruction technology of foreign films has made an awesome impression, though perhaps Sahib Haddad can be excused for trying it out in his 1986 Iraqi film *Flaming Borders/Al-hudud al-multahiba*. After all, this is a film about a real war, the Iran–Iraq war, and the screen's pyrotechnics, with fragmented bodies flying all over the screen, is maybe a chilling reflection of reality.

Mostly, though, the reflection seems to be of other films, the Bruce Lee type from the East, the Charles Bronson type from the West. Action is swift, solutions are simple and, above all, the guns are big. Police or gangs, it does not matter, what does matter is that there be a shoot-out or, one could even say, a tried and tested shoot-out, because what is the second part of Samir Seif's 1988 Egyptian film *The Tiger and the Female/Al-nimr wal-untha* but a derivation of the police-versus-gang gun battle made famous in *The French Connection*?

Some films borrow all the Western big guns, over-the-wall invasions and ghastly, graphic liquidations and then try to cover it all with an Arab cloak, with symbolism, for instance. In films like Hisham Aboul Nasr's 1986 Egyptian *The Gang/Al-'isaba* 'action' means big guns for rescue, but rescue means rescue of the fair damsel and the fair damsel means, of course, Egypt. This is crystal clear, because, crystal clear too, 'the gang' is Israel and the USA.

So, US-type action solves problems in an anti-US film, though the irony is probably not meant to be perceived by the audience. Occasionally, a film-maker may indicate what all the borrowing adds up to, as Mohamed Khan does in his 1980 Egyptian film *Vengeance/Al-thar*, very consciously opening and closing the film's action with the Bruce Lee posters stuck up all over Cairo. It is about one man's revenge for his wife's abduction and rape, and not only does it acknowledge its foreign prototypes, it doubles back on them, showing how misguided the husband's self-appointed mission is. He manages to kill the members of the gang, but it is the wrong gang.

In other words, there is nothing very positive about such violent and individual solutions, and it is notable that action films mostly come from Egypt, not from other Arab countries. For one thing, massive destruction on screen is expensive. Even one car crashing through a plate glass window costs money, too much money. For another, some state-supported cinemas fear the whole idea of proposing crude, and lone, violence as a solution to anything. As the Algerian critic Megherbi writes, 'The image permits terribly real projections and identifications, when one has to do with subjects which have no political or social conscience, nor even national conscience.'[9]

Subject to censorship but not vulnerable to state support, Egypt's largely speculative cinema industry gives the free-enterprise excuse: popular demand. This accounts, perhaps, for such hodgepodge films as 'Abdel 'Alim's 1988 *Policewomen/Al-bulis al-nisai*, whose only notable feature is a few slow-motion karate chops, lunges and plunges, by women. As the Egyptian actor Farid Chauqi points out, however, popular demand is what you make it. Having bashed his way with his fists through aeons of Egyptian films, he is distressed by all the big guns now on screen and says that Turkey, worried about the same thing, is trying to distract its audiences by upgrading another genre they love. Copying some great Egyptian classics, they are providing plenty of good melodrama![10]

Sport

So, if the Arab hero does not, or cannot, have the biggest gun or the best technology in town, where can he go and be positive? Into another contest, perhaps?

> Football above all. Invested since the first hours of the revolution by the notables, the chief officers, the rectors of universities, the round ball is the most equally shared piece of national culture, the only, since with the death of Nasser, Oum Kelthoum, Abdel Halim Hafez, and some 'famous actors', consensus is no longer possible on expression, the 'mise en scène' of life, food, clothes, or lodging.[11]

So writes an Egyptian sociologist. Jolles too, reflecting on what in the world could be legendary these days, comes to the same conclusion. Sports heroes, he says 'are not the objectivation of a virtue but the place where a force becomes activated in which we transpose our own force and which admits us in it; they are models.'[12]

This may be an obvious road to take but, in film, few Arabs are on it. In Mohamed Mahfoudh's 1986 Tunisian film *The Cup/Al-kas*, the background, shot at the time of a real match in Tunis, seethes with yelling fans, flying pennants, fun and festivity, but in the foreground we see the desultory winding-up of a friendship among some spectators. Like some minor version of the US director Cassavetes's *Husbands*, four men off on a spree cannot keep the glee going, and each wanders off, alone.

In Mohamed Khan's 1983 Egyptian film *The Streetplayer/Al-harrif*, there is a hero who trains and plays in the neighbourhood, on the asphalt. While he would like to concentrate on this challenge and on his athletic skills, he is constantly distracted by domestic problems. Moreover, he cannot deal with the men who set up the local games, and who also set up the gambling on the games. Dwarfed by the larger systems of family on one side and graft on the other, he and his sport appear small beer, asphalt marginals.

Looking at the larger game, Sharif Arafa's 1988 Egyptian film *Third Class/Al-daragat al-thalitha* puts the spotlight on the politics of it all. Dressed as if in uniforms and crouching in a huddle, the football club owners discuss strategy. But this game strategy is to keep the 'third class', the fans, in their place, sweltering and dying in the stands. When a 'hero' is named to represent this class, he is made to echo the harangue of the club owner out on the balcony, chastizing the crowd like Mussolini, and then making them feel grateful for raised entrance fees. Politics as sport, sport as politics, a constant swapping of images, makes this film sharp, parodic and stylized.

There is one exhilarating athletic feat shown in *Third Class*. Holding the championship cup aloft, the hero races in a marathon across the whole country, passing the trophy from the peasant on his tractor to the worker on his conveyor belt to the head of the belly dancer! Fantasy, of course, but a glimpse of ecstasy, an ebullience of released energies almost never felt by frustrated fans.

Anti-hero/ine

This thrill of a simple but grand physical feat could still surface in films about sport, and has an important literary precedent, though it is from long ago, in pre-Islamic poetry. The hero of the ode (*qasida*) glories in his prowess, dominating nature and his own limitations. Death exists only to highlight life, and the exploit is its own reward. In Arab films so far, though, this seemingly gratuitous tempting of fate occurs only when the hero steps outside all communal norms of behaviour and is willing to go it alone. In most films this process is doomed, and only disaster can follow; hence 'men's melodrama' (see chapter 5). If successful, it would be a kind of Faustian journey, that of the sinner, the perpetual outlaw, the anti-hero.

Or the anti-heroine, because one of the films which best fits this description is Nadir Galal's 1988 Egyptian film *The File on Samia Sharqawi/Malaff Samia Sharqawi* about an up-and-coming woman whose methods are unprincipled. Granted, there have been films about villains in the past, but they are always on one half of the seesaw, with a hero or heroine at the other end, virtue there to show up vice. Here, Samia is the centre of all attention, and like the immigrant boys in Sergio Leone's *Once Upon a Time in America* she knows that if she plays straight she will remain marginal all her life. What is more, as in the case of the immigrant boys, no family intrudes on the screen, so no Freudian problems are provided as excuse for her behaviour. She simply understands the system, attaches herself to successful men and moves up through them. Her final victory, as she sends a man off with the wrong suitcase and she pulls the right one (full of money) out from under her bed, drew a choke of disbelief as well as shock from one Arab observer: 'Oh people, oh heavens!! Thus, with all ease, a woman wins out over a man of powerful position . . . .'[13]

True, she is a mere woman, and she does not have the 'made in USA' PhD of another current anti-hero, Hatem of Mohamed al-Naggar's 1987 Egyptian film *The Time of Hatem Zahran/Zaman Hatem Zahran*. Bristling with as much brashness as Samia, Hatem breezes back to Egypt with grand plans. Eyes glistening with the thrill of his own initiative, he describes his expertise and pushes his project through: a cosmetics factory will be built in the jasmine groves no matter how many peasant homes have to be destroyed.

Needless to say, by the end of the film, he has lost his best friend, his wife and his female soulmate, though he instantly shows them how replaceable they are. What cannot be replaced is his brother, or rather, he cannot take his brother's place in his father's heart. While Hatem was away studying, his brother, a considerate and community-minded man, was killed in war for Egypt. Not only that, but he left a son, and the only discomposure one ever sees in the glib Hatem is when he finds out that he himself is sterile.

Of course, on another level, his patter is sterile too. It is directed implicitly against his brother's self-sacrifice, and explicitly against the precepts of his father, a noted economist of the previous, socialist, school. The father watches Hatem's manoeuvrings in dismay, his health fails, and the Oedipal struggle becomes more and more clear. This film is actually not about a lone (anti)hero defying fate for the thrill of it. It is not the struggle of the saint versus the bad father, but that of the sinner versus the good father. It is, in other words, still the discourse of hero–leader, which runs through all the films mentioned so far, only reversed.

Anti-epic

There is something very compulsive about this discourse, like a ride on a rollercoaster: up–down, good–bad, hero–villain, and above all, round and round. In the epic narrative of 'the good, the bad, and the ugly', or its political equivalent the North African discourse on leader, opposition and marginals, the hero's goal is to remain within the system, not to transform it.

The system, what system? one could say. But some Arab films, instead of focusing on the face of the handsome hero walking upstairs, actually focus on the stairs themselves – the system – both rotten boards and red carpet. In Samir Zikra's 1983 Syrian film *The Half Metre Incident/Hadith al-nasf metr*[14] for instance, the hero sits glumly in his government office listening to the boards creak: he is listening, in other words, to the gossiping and grovelling of his fellow workers. Most of them know this is the way upstairs. But his thoughts lie elsewhere: the pretty girl on the bus, where does she come from, will he see her again, will she go somewhere with him? When she finally does, and he makes her pregnant, his daydreams change. They are now focused on the red carpet and, leaving her aside, he gets on it by stepping out of the office and joining a newly formed national guard. It is a film about steps, all the little ones that take you sideways, and all the others that take you up.

So precise are the steps up in fact, that they can operate on all stairways, front stairs, back stairs, in the law and out of it. In Ashraf Fahmy's 1972 Egyptian film *Night and Bars/Layl wa qudhban* the steps are the same inside the warders' world and inside the jail. If you do favours, you get privileges. The problem is that one can be caught straddling the two stairways. On call to repair the recurrently and, ostensibly, failing electricity in the chief warder's house, the hero is actually consoling the warder's beautiful wife. His crossing back and forth shows up a larger system – hypocrisy buttressing privilege and hierarchy – and when he is killed at the film's end it is for the bogus crime of escape, not the real one of adultery.

Such iniquity initially shocks the hero of Tewfik Saleh's 1966 Egyptian film *The Rebels/Al-mutamarridun*. As a doctor himself, he is classed among the well-off patients in a tuberculosis sanatorium and treated with all due privilege. But his concern for suffering leads him eventually to identify himself with the other patients, the poor patients dying of thirst in the sanatorium's godforsaken wasteland. Aha! Back to the standard hero story: the identification of one with the cause of the many! But it is not that simple here, this is a film of drama and of analysis, analysis of economics as well as politics. So as soon as the hero rouses the mob and takes over, he discovers two things. One is that though in control now of their own sanatorium, they are still dependent on the world beyond it. They must choose public assistance or private aid, the blundering bureaucrat or the officious society matron. They cannot have both, and of course each has sticky strings attached. What the doctor also discovers is that in order to have maximum bargaining power with the outside, he cannot risk any dissension inside. He can no longer listen to the case of the unwilling or minister to the needs of the incapable. He must push, push and punish. What kind of ruler has he become, and what mass does he rule over?

This must be asked quietly, not out loud. Only a man who truly feels himself alone would whisper that to himself, and, as is clear from the films on marginals discussed above, the situation of isolation is rarely given any dignity in Arab cinema. Northrop Frye writes: 'the center of tragedy lies in the hero's isolation, not in a villain's betrayal', and he goes on, as if he were actually describing *The Rebels*, this is true 'even when the villain is, as he often is, a part of the hero himself'.[15]

In his isolation, the tragic hero himself vacillates, he is not constant. But that should not be surprising, as what he is up against is a system; it has nothing of the human, of the good or the bad about it. When Frye writes, 'In its most elementary form, the vision of law . . . operates as . . . revenge. The hero provokes enmity, or inherits a situation of enmity, and the return of the avenger constitutes the catastrophe',[16] he could be describing Sa'id Marzuq's 1988 Egyptian film *Days of Terror/Ayyam al-ru'b*. Threatened with revenge as a child, a young man from Upper Egypt has settled in Cairo, fallen in love and is about to lead a normal life. But the avenger returns and much of the rest of the film shows the hero's paranoia, his increasingly morbid imaginings about his own future murder. This is in spite of himself: he has studied Egyptian history and as he never ceases to tell his friends, the country's paralysis is largely due to its age-old fear of the inevitability of the man with the gun, of the inescapable verdict (*hukm*) of the man with the gun.

So, unlike the bewildered marginals of films cited above, Sa'id Marzuq's hero understands what is happening, he has a language for it; it gives him dignity, it gives him tragic recognition, but it gives him no reprieve. In fact, impersonal systems like economic dependencies, or fate and revenge, operate as efficiently as they do partly because one is simply duped by the words. A word like 'leader' or 'verdict' marks out its own road, and like a sleepwalker, one just follows along. What does 'enemy of the state' mean, for instance, to a poor simple-minded peasant commandeered into the army? Well, it means that if the 'enemy of the state' tries to escape from the prison camp that the soldier is guarding, he must be restrained at all costs, even killed. Here, with the soldier's subsequent commendation as 'hero', is where things stand about halfway through Atef al-Tayyeb's 1986 Egyptian film *The Innocent/Al-bari*. But then the village intellectual, the soldier's boyhood friend and protector, arrives among the next lot of 'enemies of the state', and the soldier's safe world of religious jingles and nationalist slogans splits open: words on one side, realities on the other, and the bloodbath follows.

But, after all, it was with words that the Arab poet of the pre-Islamic ode made himself into a hero, shaping his words and forming his world and slipping himself in as mediator between life and death. It is in a film which emphasizes just this kind of lucidity, and an ingenuous authorial voice, that young Arab audiences for many years saw their most positive hero: in the Omar of Merzak Allouache's 1976 Algerian film *Omar Gatlato*. Ironically, the title is known to be an abbreviation of 'Omar, whose machismo killed him' (*Omar, qatalatu al-rujula*).

Sample film: *Omar Gatlato*

The great voyage of Omar is across the street. Or it would be across the street, if he ever managed it. As in a cowboy film, it is only at the end, after many delays, that the final shoot-out, or at least confrontation, takes place. On Omar's side of the street are all his friends, men, while on the other side is someone foreign, a woman. Friend or foe?

In Omar's male world, or as his uncle tells it, in his generation, a man knew his enemy (the French) and went out and did battle against him. Narrating to camera, Omar tells the audience that he takes this with a pinch of salt, and it would seem that the camera does too, as the latest version of these tall tales is told by the uncle while the rest of the family around him are oblivious, hooked into an Egyptian melodrama on the television.

Omar's power is much more awesome than his uncle's old grenades: it is not just a matter of Omar's asides to us during his uncle's ramblings, Omar controls both narration and representation. In fact, under cover of the most natural seeming reportage, the film oscillates back and forth between such poles, between various oppositions, seemingly presided over by Omar's authorial prescience. If, at work in his government office for instance, Omar tells the camera the nicknames of his colleagues, explaining that they are due to a particular tic, constantly recurring behaviour, he then shows us the colleague, saying, 'Now he will do X,' and lo and behold, he does do X!

So as the film loops back and forth from the one-off event we see to the daily habits Omar knows, oppositions simply seesaw. Where does machismo (*rujula/rejla*) end and honour (*sharaf*) begin, for instance, when at one point Omar struts in front of his housing estate to warn off an encroaching Lothario and at the next stoops to tie his shoelace in order to glance up surreptitiously at a woman in her window?

Even though Omar's flat is crowded with sisters, aunts and cousins, for a young unmarried Algerian male the female world is a far-off mystery and all romance is vicarious. From the thrill of a Hindi musical film to the ecstasy of local (*sha'bi*) songs on his cassette, displacement follows displacement and the more absent the subject, the more present the allure.

This, Omar tells us, is the common experience of all his friends, of his whole generation. But then, suddenly this quasi-documentary, this general survey, is interrupted by the particular experience. Testing a new cassette, a supposedly virgin tape, Omar is shocked to hear a foreign voice, a girl's voice. She says only a few words, sadly describing her banal and dreary world: the four walls around her, the need to paint them. It is the most moving thing Omar has ever heard and he listens every night, over and over. He must meet her, he tells us.

But meeting her is not easy. If the film so far has allowed event to slide back and forth into habit, or cliché into context, and let the particular represent the general, the public and private spheres of Algerian life merge less easily, and seemingly the male and female worlds mix hardly at all. But she is Selma, a work colleague of one of his friends, and she agrees by phone to meet him. She waits across the street. On his side are his friends, calling out to him not to cross over, not to leave their male world. Omar hesitates and does not cross. But who knows, in the last words of the film, Omar says, 'In a little while I will call Selma. . . .'

Is Omar lucid or self-deceiving? Is everything he has told us about Algiers and his generation accurate, true reportage? Or even, how mixed up with the eye of the camera is the 'I' of Omar's voice? The film subtly sets up these oppositions but chooses none, tagging none as good or bad. None will win in some final shoot-out.

But Omar is a hero because he has been telling it like it is to a heroic degree and, since it is never really told, telling it in total irony. In fact, it is above all in the film's language that Algerians identified most closely with Omar and his voyage across the street, his voyage towards consciousness. Dialogues are casual repartee, monologues are in bantering slang, it is an evanescent speech, sure to be rephrased or replaced tomorrow but for today allowing an epic slide through, around, out or above the hegemonic heroic discourse.

Conclusion

Omar Gatlato represents the final, ironic modulation in films I have loosely classed under 'the epic'. For most of the chapter, its most primary, heroic quest form is like what Northrop Frye calls 'romance' or what is included in Giles Deleuze's *'grande forme'*. In relation to cowboy films, for instance, Deleuze writes, 'it is as representative of the community that the hero becomes capable of an action which makes him equal to his milieu'.[17] But as articulated in the hero's journey in *The Outlaws*, there is a model even closer to home for Arab cinema. What is the outlaw's journey if not one from precepts based on blood ties (*hilm*) to those based on shared belief (*'ilm*), from battles for plunder (*ayyam al-'arab*) to those for a good/holy cause (*ayyam allah*): in other words, a close analogy to the famous journey of the Arab nation into the community of Islam?

Because all these heroic forms resemble each other so closely one is tempted to see them as archetypal, as eternal and universal. None the less, there are slight mutations, back and forth over time and in space. As Frye writes, 'The high mimetic period brings in a society more strongly established around the court and capital city, and a centripetal perspective replaces the centrifugal one of romance. The distant goals of the quest, the Holy Grail or the City of God, modulate into symbols of convergence, the emblem of the prince, nation and national faith.'[18] These changes have their counterpart in Arab literary tradition: the centrifugal journey of the lone hero in the pre-Islamic poetic form, the *qasida*, turns into the centripetal Islamic form of the panegyric (*madih*) as the hero makes his way from the disorder of nature into the order of the perfect ruler,[19] into Toumi's discourse of the state.

But as is clear from the films cited above, this prince, this father figure, can be a bad parent, a foreign colonialist, a local boss, in which case there will be an Oedipal encounter and a killing. Or if this encounter with the patriarch is that of a heroine, its terms will be less personal, she will 'kill' the bad law or the bad religion. Good or bad, one father figure stands for all his children, an exemplary image for the community itself perhaps, but thus static and unmoving.

Because of this stasis, any voyage toward the Grail or the prince must take the form of a linear series of highly motivated acts, whose intent is clearly marked, for good or for bad. As the voyage implies progress, its goal is inevitably salvation of some sort. To reinforce this, history is often dragged in as proof of resolution or, failing that, news stories of relief or rescue. But because in narrative terms none of this provides many surprises, sometimes for drama the resolute plans of the good are contrasted with the dastardly plots of the bad. Another strategy is for the narrative's straight line to be broken up by delays or temporary disappearances. Or, it can fragment the unitary voice by momentarily diffusing decision among several characters. Current devices for adding more narrative punch seem in action films to be to keep the life-and-death struggles as full of bullets as possible, or in reverse, to turn the saint into a sinner and the story from hagiography into heresiography.

These resolutions or salvation oriented devices produce an oppressive, even paternalistic discourse. But in films such as Marzuq's *Days of Terror* or Allouache's *Omar Gatlato* life is breathed back into the epic as an alternative discourse comes in to cross swords with it. The heroic encounter may lead, for instance, to tragedy, with salvation or linear history up against a cyclical world. In other words, it may be that the hero's centripetal voyage in from chaos to cosmos does not suffice, and that chaos may rise up to face him, over and over again. Or the encounter may lead to irony, as faced with the obdurate structures of society's language, the hero may just pick them up, ride away from the centre and rearrange them in ambiguity and insolence.

4.   The Comic

Comedies in the Arab world are treated like bread in Europe, regularly consumed but rarely discussed. European critics classify most of them as farce and go on to grander things.[1] Among the Arabs involved, directors complain of the lack of good scripts, and writers of the absence of competent directors.[2] Yet people continue to see the films and probably think the attraction lies in performance. Is not 'Adel Imam, a little man with a large grin, not simply Egypt's top comic but the Arab world's highest-paid star? Not only that, but he has by now moved comfortably into some serious dramatic roles. Will he abandon comedy because it is not considered serious?

Gags

Certainly, in contrast to the will and purpose implicit in the hero stories discussed in chapter 3, some Arab comedies would seem no more than aimless meanderings or a series of haphazard incidents. A good example is the 1980 Tunisian film *Two Thieves in Madness/Farda wa liqat ukhtaha*[3] made by Ali Mansour, which chronicles the comings and goings, slippings, slidings and fallings of two country idiots. Using them as innocents abroad within their own country to point up the foreignness of the tourists they encounter, this counterpoint does not work for the good reason that, even down on the farm, at the film's beginning, the heroes could not cope. But even though theatre actors go through a series of visual gags with ladders, buckets, blankets, the film does not evoke Laurel and Hardy. What seems to be missing is a sense of the obdurate nature of things, matched by a relentless, if misguided, intent on the part of the heroes to confront them on comedy's level of 'ontological equality', in what Stanley Cavell calls 'the heroism of momentary survival'.[4]

Momentarily surviving, but as who? That is the question in a different version of slapstick, in Abdel Hadi al-Rawi's 1986 film *Love in Baghdad/Al-hubb fi Baghdad*. Having fallen on his head and lost his memory, the hero is pursued from village to city, back and forth, by people who claim to know only too well who he is. The film probably gives a good overview of contemporary Iraq and some of its more savoury social and political jokes,[5] but the Keystone Kops type chases somehow lack tension. Perhaps the hero's schizophrenia disperses the narrative line to so great an extent that since no clear direction takes hold, no interference does either. If anything, comedy based on pace and timing, whether of the super-slow *Two Thieves in Madness* or super-fast *Love in Baghdad* type, has to be even more tightly constructed than dramatic narratives. The rubber band effect is funny only if the rubber band snaps back and into place.

Of course, perhaps it helps if the hero's face has something of the flexibility of a rubber band. Egypt's Isma'il Yasin not only had such a face, but he was squat and dark and, like many other famous comedians, could so transform himself as to look almost simian! But he looked human too, and in all his films was so demonstrably good, solid and reliable . . . so human. But as he flails around and seems to do everything wrong, does one identify with him or not? The suspense lies there, rather than in the occasional chase. Actually, by the time the chase comes, one is clearly with him, out to get the lovely lady and outflank the wicked rich; he is the noble 'little man'. But there is another variation on this theme of ambiguous identification: the child/man. In his films directed by Fatin Abdel Wahhab he was always within some institution: *Isma'il Yasin in the Army* (1955)/*Police* (1955)/*Navy* (1958); *Isma'il Yasin MP* (1958). He is always up against orders and commands, and as a sort of Egyptian Jerry Lewis, he can never seem to get these straight. But turning left instead of right or vice versa as he trains for the navy, on a peaceful Spring day, does not seem to matter. The meanings of commands slip gently out from under the words, signifier and signified quietly part company.

Ambivalence of identification and ambiguity of signification are at the base of many of the best Arab comedies. There is often a little man with whom one almost identifies, but not quite. He goes along separating words from their meanings like a child delighting in oral/aural games, or perhaps like a man of common sense appalled by the cant surrounding him. Because of a long tradition of jokes (*nukat*), witticisms (*zurafa*) and even political cartoons, Arab comedy is probably stronger here than in comedy based on pace and timing, and can be light-hearted but pungent.

Take, for example, a film from the Algerian series of *Inspector Tahar* films, *Inspector Tahar on Vacation/'Utla al-mufattish Tahar* directed by Moussa Haddad. Made in 1973 after only about ten years of Algerian independence, the film is a series of gags built around the question of identity, and not simply the identity of the crooks to be apprehended, or of the inspector and his sidekick in disguise, but the identity of Algeria itself. Asked to investigate a crime in a 'foreign territory', like the Hope and Crosby of the *Road to . . .* films, they must put on funny clothes and try to learn the customs and lingo of the natives. Only, in the beginning of this film 'foreign territory' means a hotel for tourists well within Algeria itself, and in its second part, it is an adjacent Arab nation. Both are territories on which the heroes are totally disoriented and out of control: so much for slogans of national sovereignty, or even of pan-Arab identity.

The instability of the slogans surrounding the hero is balanced by his recurrent appearance in film after film as a little man, a site of stability in himself. Not only did Inspector Tahar, played by the same actor, appear both on Algerian television and in the cinema, but there were also several *Hassan* films, always with Algeria's Rouiched as both actor and author. In the first of these, *Hassan Terro*, directed in 1968 by Mohamed Lakhdar-Hamina, Rouiched plays a meek little man at the time of the Algerian Revolution who just wants to keep his hands clean and not join any side, let alone what looks like the most dangerous one. But driven by events, and despite his reluctance, he finally takes on the stature of the person he had been mistaken for: an Algerian terrorist/freedom-fighter.

This reluctance to join up, or join in, remains a hallmark of the character and in Hassan's latest appearance, in Slim Riad's 1987 *Hassan Taxi*, an added bite is given to the film as it knowingly plays on its own genealogy and asks 'What ever happened to . . . (X?) . . . (Algeria?) . . .?' Not just reluctantly but grudgingly taxi driver Hassan helps his passengers out of trouble, and in his conversations with them it becomes clear that he, like his passengers, and 25 years after that first film, is still a little man; the benefits of the Revolution have gone to those who were absent at the time, or even to foreigners since enticed in. In a film that is a series of gags more than a developed story, there is none the less a clear theme: where has it all gone? or, worse still, what was it all for? If in the 1968 *Hassan Terro* the reluctant hero finally joined the system, in the 1987 *Hassan Taxi* he remains resolutely outside all systems. In fact, in comedies like this which compare the pure and the corrupt, the winners and the losers, the very format of verbal commentary increases the hero's isolation. He has to stand apart in order to speak.

When commentary is effected through visual as well as verbal means the result is a little different: a little man who wanders among the big ones and is consistently shunted aside, one who is part of the gag, not outside it. The images used by the Syrian actor–director Doreid Lahham and his usual scriptwriter Mohamed Maghout are often not simply visual gags, but a kind of symbolic figuration. What, for instance, is more graphic in its presentation of the Palestine problem than the sight of Lahham, as a driver who has lost his passport between borders, stripping down his now useless car to use the bits for a Robinson Crusoe house? This 1984 film *Borders/Al-hudud* operates through a series of advances and retreats as the hero tries to cope not only with the inconveniences of life in the middle of nowhere, but with the intractable forces that keep him out of society, out of nations.

One might think that the hero of Lahham's subsequent, 1986, film *The Report/Al-taqrir* would be better able to deal with blind forces; after all, he was once part of government himself. The irony is that as a bureaucrat dismissed for an unpleasing report, he cannot, as a bureaucrat, stop issuing reports, now more and more critical: on the situation of the PhD taxi driver, on the restaurant that will serve only tourists, on apartments built only for speculation, and so on. It is not just a matter of rhythms here: this figure pushes and pulls at issues as if they were things, with the stubborn relentlessness of a Keaton.

Or, one could say, he pushes with the stubborn naivety of a Candide, because what happens in these comedies which are based both on overt social criticism and on the little man's interference is that if the hero does not, at some point, retreat to his garden, the system will mow him down. At the end of *Borders* Lahham tries to run for it against the guns, and in *The Report* he is trampled underfoot by two oblivious and warring football teams.

These are very definite dead ends and perhaps, despite the gags, not what comes to mind when one says 'comic'. But the form is built around balancing the dead ends with a kind of perpetual resurrection, a series of open ends. Not only are the gags arranged in series, with situations opening up all the time and everywhere for comment, but in Algeria Hassan is always the reluctant little man played by Rouiched, and in Syria, in the Lahham films, though the hero's name changes it is always Lahham who plays him in the same ingenuous style. Both these actors also go back and forth between stage and cinema in corresponding roles, so that it seems as if this constant resurrection of the candid little man is evidence that this comedy/criticism can and will continue.[6]

Another way of viewing this is that the appearances and disappearances are necessary to cover an equally recurrent void at the end of each gag. Certainly the Moroccans seem to be aware of some kind of hiatus in this area of comic but overt social criticism. Despite their theatrical backgrounds, both Tayyeb Saddiki in his 1984 *Zift* and Nabyl Lahlou in his *Brahim Yach* of the same year have gone beyond the verbal gags of a Hassan or the metaphorical substantiations of Lahham and created whole cinematic visions of nightmare. In these films, the little man is wandering and out of place because the world around him is itself out of joint, much like in the British comedy *Brazil*. Though the films criticize society and politics, one is back in the realm of quasi-ontological duels. Things themselves take on inordinate importance. The poor, uprooted peasant of *Zift* is not just shocked at the strange collusion between the modernizers of the state's infrastructure and religious charlatans. His eyes are also dazzled by the brilliant new motorway which goes nowhere but through his ancestral lands and then carefully bypasses the glossy shrine of a brand-new holy man. As for the Brahim Yach of that film's title, he runs around like a scared rabbit looking for the papers that will prove his identity not just in the entrails of a multinational company but in the womb of a theatre director's lurid imagination, and it is in the film's visions that the hyperbole lies, not in my words.

Using all the techniques of cinema, especially the close-up, to disorient the spectator and confuse him about what he is actually looking at, *Zift* is still not as bizarre as *Brahim Yach*, which sews fantasy into the real and then unravels both. But watching both films, the spectator's feeling of unease is similar, as what he senses is a vacuum, some lack of norm, of the everyday world. Though the caustic criticism of these films and their gags have to do with society and politics, one cannot help feeling that this time the little man has wandered right through ontology; battles here are not with solid weapons but obdurate systems; he has levitated above the realm of physics into the realm of metaphysics.

Situations

Most comedies are anything but metaphysical, their whole concern being the here and now and one's place in it. If the Moroccan films close off all their own exits by ferocious pictures of a world in which no compromise can or should be made, most comedies on the contrary are about finding one's, momentarily lost, place in the sun. According to the literary critic Northrop Frye, 'The theme of the comic is the integration of society, which usually takes the form of incorporating a central character into it.'[7] This discrepancy between the stormy Moroccan comedies and the sunnier types that Frye is referring to is actually just a matter of focus. In Arab cinema, there are at least two versions of comedy, depending on whether the subject is society or whether it is the character who desires integration into that society. Both versions pit identity against error. In the films of social concern, the word collides with its willed misreading. Because in these films society is a problematical aggregate of commonsense beliefs and rabid slogans, it is through language and the images it proposes that this is played out. From 'left' and 'right' for Isma'il Yasin, through 'foreign territory' for Inspector Tahar, to 'the national interest' in *Zift*, the little man wanders around, wondering what all this verbiage really means.

In another version of comedy, the situation comedy, mistake intrudes into the life of the central character. Somehow he himself is out of place, and to get back in he must voyage from an extreme position outside society to a warm, secure one at the other extreme, inside. But just seeking one of the cosy firesides of society, and not having a very critical approach to it, he cannot move very well on his own. His voyage has to be effected by circumstantial mistakes: by being in the wrong place, or arriving at the wrong time, or having his identity mixed up.

Usually this identity is some kind of stereotype, which is not surprising if society is assumed to be a stable structure with only one or two people briefly out of the right slot. One version is sometimes articulated in terms of nationalities, or in terms of the dichotomy between city cousin and country cousin. In Hassan al-Saifi's 1954 *Country Girl/Bint al-balad*, for instance, the question is whether the rich and simple Egyptians adrift in Paris among the wily and rapacious French can hold on to their cash box. Though the film's features seem an almost endless accumulation of what might now be seen as racist caricatures, the necessary comic resolution is reached by a reversal of situations: the supposedly simple Egyptians outwit the supposedly wily French, and in the process the real problem is solved. Now worldly wise, the Egyptian boy snaps back into his proper place – Egypt – into the arms of his Egyptian sweetheart.

But stereotypes and exaggerated behaviour need not be employed only along national lines. Just as the US Shirley Temple films pitted her against the adult world, so too Niazi Mustapha's 1966 Egyptian film *Too Young for Love/Saghira 'ala al-hubb* also has his child heroine lecturing adults. Only this time, she is really a young woman who has disguised herself as a little girl in order to get a singing job. Predictably she also falls in love with the show's director, who neglects his fiancée because he is charmed by the 'little girl', and so on. All behaviour is determined by supposed age and what might have been an interesting investigation of roles turns into an endless series of hurried costume changes, entrances, exits, with more and more people to be fooled until, in the happy end, the correct reshuffling of fiancées takes place.

Obviously such films are fairly glib but what most bothers critics of Arab cinema is what they perceive as these films' cloning of Hollywood, their derivative quality, for instance in terms of décor. This means the luxury hotels and nightclubs of *Country Girl*, and what then passed for an exotic locale, the broadcasting studio of *Too Young for Love*. Henri Barakat's 1977 *Mouths and Rabbits/Afwah wa aranib*, though resolutely set in the Egyptian countryside, is no less glib and dependent on stereotype, in this case stereotypes of class. The extremes in this film are still situated topographically: the heroine must voyage from her poor, overcrowded, overbreeding ('rabbits') home in a village to the lonely country estate of a solitary young gentleman. There she uses her native cunning to raise herself up the ladder, becoming not only an irreplaceable housekeeper-cum-secretary but also the kind of bourgeois lady the gentleman can (and will) marry – because marriage is usually what these comedies are all about. As in the US director Woody Allen's *Hannah and Her Sisters*, the heroine's main problem is to find the 'right' person, who then ensures her 'right' place in society, stabilizes her wandering and, incidentally, ends the film.

What is interesting in these films and what constitutes the game is how to provide movement at all between stereotypes, because almost by definition the stereotype does not move, he accepts his place in society, and initiates no change. So forget events directed by intent and substitute coincidence, events triggered by mistakes, by muddled times, muddled places; and if the stereotype has no will to change, someone else has to get his identity wrong and force him to adjust. So, the game is here: just as stereotypes structure society, so coincidences and mistakes destructure it. For instance, only after a false marriage to a villager puts the heroine's virtue in question in *Mouths and Rabbits* is she able to move into another slot and be claimed by her gentleman.

But in this kind of comedy it is not only the hero and heroine who are important: the comings and goings of the people around them are usually what push them towards each other. If this society is static, it is also hierarchical. But nuances can appear precisely through that hierarchy, and inevitably the hero has a sidekick who can move into areas forbidden to him because of his status. The sidekick is a 'helper', like fairy tale helpers described by Propp;[8] his silly/wise remarks allow the hero to think the unthinkable or do the undoable. Sometimes the helper is a kind of neuter, unattached and unattachable; he can be like Edward Everett Horton was in many American comedies but more often in Arab films he is someone with rather 'goggly' eyes peering over the shoulder of the more elegant hero at the sidekick of the heroine across the way, as Abdel Mun'im Ibrahim did in many Egyptian situation comedies. In which case, and in many such comedies, the film ended with a double wedding.

Two different organizations of comedy, using mistaken identity (or: mistake/identity) as a basic problematic, have been outlined so far. Those films based on a series of gags put everything in question using words to subvert other words, and thus to undermine society's slogans. In situation comedies, on the contrary, society's slogans are seemingly reasserted as people scramble around to get into the most attractive social position, though not without these characters, or stereotypes themselves being put in question. What is not in question in this form, however, is the character's dependence on society, the forlorn state of a part when not integrated into the whole.

Analogies

Some Arab comedies use various devices to subvert the difference between part and whole. One of these devices is to use the comic analogy, the 'mistake'; for instance, something concrete may stand in for something abstract. The Egyptian director Salah Abou Seif uses this to very funny and trenchant effect in *Case 68/Qadiya 68*, which was made in 1968 and seethes with the unrest felt all over the world at that time. This is a film in which everyone has a little story, a little problem; eventually they all clash in a courtroom, while at home the building they lived in collapses. The building was lopsided anyway, just like the motto about justice above the judge's head. Most of the film had been taken up with showing the debates of the building's inhabitants: repair, no repair, how to repair, does the law even permit repair, can one go against the law? But as the debate goes on, life goes on too and all eyes are on the girl who keeps losing her shoe under the table around which they debate. And all the buildings and by analogy all the institutions are shaky, unsteady and crumbling.

This kind of substitution, a building for an institution, is often loosely called 'metaphor'[9] and is said to be frequently used in Arab cinema to avoid censorship. But another device used in Arab comedy is both closer to real metaphor and to the joke: it is a twinning of two very unlikely things with the intention of bringing about a new understanding, or at least, a new vision of an old object. This device appears in even such an old comedy as Niazi Mustapha's 1937 *Sallama is Fine/Sallama fi khair*, which on the face of it is a pretty glib comedy with its fair share of stereotypes. In fact, because of its luxury hotel setting and the high society foreigners who drift in and out, this film might also appear to be an Egyptian pseudo-Hollywood film. Conversely, the hotel could also be seen as a kind of neutral ground, home to neither of the main characters, a smooth surface on which identities can slide around and be exchanged. The main character is Sallama, the poor porter of a large department store, adrift because of circumstances. Then there is a visiting foreign prince who, in order to be free to pursue the beautiful young girl, changes identities with Sallama. Sallama goes off on official princely visits and listens to the complaints of all and sundry. In addition to being a nice twist on the Arab theme of the prince going in disguise to listen to the people, this identity switch is a mechanism which associates Sallama with that other implicit presence in the film, namely Egypt. Egypt appears as not just a place of culture, where the prince (the foreigner) had formerly come for his education, but as a place where the common sense of the pauper (the Egyptian) Sallama can resolve some princely problems. With this initiation behind him, Sallama goes back to where the film began, to the department store. There, though he had been the boss's right-hand man, he had never had the status appropriate to this function, and just as Egypt at the time of the film's making was still dominated by the British, so the store, Hindawi's (meaning: of the Indian), is clearly controlled by a foreigner. As Sallama demands justice and the proper rank for his responsibilities, it is to be understood that Egypt should (and would) do the same.

Derision

In what is superficially, at least, a simple film these scramblings of identity have the complexity of metaphor: an analogy, Sallama–Egypt, is added to a joke, prince/pauper; similarity intersects with dissimilarity. These equations and their logical conclusion, however, are pretty clear from the beginning of the film. More suspense arises from the use of another tradition in Arab humour, that form of derision called *hija*. This is a kind of satire and is probably best known as one of the early, pre-Islamic, poetic styles. In it, the poet likens his enemy to something laughable, if not actually degrading, a monkey for instance.[10] The progress of the poem depends on the various things that are said about this monkey and how well the epithets can be made to stick to the enemy. Unlike the joke (*nukta*) or even metaphor, which makes an immediate association between things, *hija* draws the issue out.

This process has been most clearly articulated in some recent Egyptian films, in which, despite the presence of various jokes along the way, the narrative itself seems to follow along the lines of *hija*, in other words, it is a long voyage of disbelief between opposites, between, as it were, man and monkey. A particularly good example is Ali Abdel Khalek's 1987 comedy *Four on an Official Mission/Arba'a fi mahimma rasmiyya*. One of the four is a Sa'idi, that is, a man from Egypt's South, such men being the common butt of Northern or Cairene jokes just as the Irish and Poles were in the UK and US respectively. Of the other three, one is a goat, one an ass, and the other a monkey. How the hero, the Sa'idi, proceeds from this situation of ignominy to that of spokesman for the common man in Egypt is the voyage of the film and, as comic example, will be discussed below.

What is clear already is that the better new comedies are using a different kind of pacing. Jokes or puns are not just one-off serial events but are integrated into the film's problematic. Also, analogy is not being used in such a static way as previously: Sallama for Egypt, buildings for institutions. In some of the newer films, things move, or even lurch, back and forth from one term to another, from mistake to identity to mistake again, in a whole new category.

In *The Gentlemen/Al-sadat al-rijal* the move is actually from one sex to another. This film was made in 1987 by Raafat al-Mihi, one of whose previous films, *The Advocate/Al-avocato*, was a muckraking series of jokes on law and equity and involved him and his star, 'Adel Imam, in a lot of legal troubles. It is not surprising then that *The Gentlemen*, which is about a harassed working mother who changes sex to enjoy the benefits of a male society, raps sharply on the knuckles of that male society: its compromising lawyers, posterity-seeking doctors and double-talking politicians. As the visiting official says every time he arrives in a new place, 'We criticize, we condemn and we support.' In such an upsidedown world, why not really turn the tables, make a mother into a father and, 'for the child', at the end of the film, a father into a mother? Physically, that is, no analogies here, and much like the transformation of a white man into a black man in *The Watermelon Man*, it is this physical substantiation that gives the film its bite. This is because *The Gentlemen* uses very conventional Egyptian film codes the better to subvert them. The joke of the sex change can shock precisely because the standard courtship scenes, with their ubiquitous coyness, tears and the furtive kiss, are played out between two women (one 'changed', one not). How well do the labels 'man' and 'woman' stick, or, more important with regard to cinema, who is the hero and who the heroine?

In some of these newer comedies, then, through an initial and ostensible mistaken identity, such as man/monkey, or man/woman, like any good metaphor the derisive narrative eventually proposes a new vision, a third form. By the end of *The Gentlemen*, for sex change read cinema change, or for identity change, read change of codes.

Sample comedy: *Four on an Important Mission*

One of the major mistakes that structure this film right from the beginning is that the hero does not seem to know who he is. As if he were a repugnant beast who needs camouflage, he douses himself with strong perfumes which make all flee from him. He also allows himself to be passed off as a high official, though he is really a minor bureaucrat.

The next mistake is that from the start of the film we see him tracking the wrong kind of women, foreign tourists, humming little 'I love you's' in English, and under his breath, to absolute strangers, and making dates to meet at the swimming pool of a flashy hotel where he most certainly does not live.

The third mistake is that his 'important mission' is simply to hand over some animals as government property. The last thing in the world he wants to do is to accompany three animals to Cairo but he has leave to go on holiday abroad afterwards, and like the good official he is he will accomplish this mission for the state.

So, wrong man, wrong women, wrong job: despite all these muddled directions, it is clear that, as in an ordinary situation comedy, there will be some kind of narrative which, at the very least, will find him a girl and get the animals off his back.

Literally off his back, which is where one of the animals, a female chimpanzee, likes to hang. As he has acted rather like a monkey himself with regard to the tourists, this close association may not be surprising. But things are not what they seem: because of the chimpanzee's initial coquetry, he not only names her Dalal (coquetry) but also with erudite sensitivity he recites the relevant classical Arabic poetry, provoking astonishment among his colleagues.

Not only that, but the chimpanzee will also take him to the right girl, again eliciting the best in him. Having arrived late at the government offices through humane concern for the monkey's burned hand, he is forced to stay with the animals at a kind of manger–hotel. That is where the girl is, and she is coquettish, and like him, Egyptian and fatherless. There is no reason why she should not find him attractive. Unperfumed now that he is away from the tourists, this is not an actor with a rubber face, like Isma'il Yasin, but the handsome Ahmed Zaki. All the comic play in this film is in the acting, not in the physiognomy.

Association with the chimpanzee, or rather trying to get rid of it properly, is what clears up the third mistake, the mission: he has to run through empty corridors, find forgotten certificates and have them stamped by absentee officials. Time and place never coincide, and even numbers change as the waiting animals either disappear or their progeny multiply. All this allows him to turn from a slightly ridiculous minor official into an articulate and assertive spokesman for the Egyptian common man.

He is up against government as dumb monolith, a theme so common in Egyptian film these days that to avoid scenes in bureaucracy's offices looking indistinguishable from film to film they are often given a cinematic polish and individuality absent from the remainder of the otherwise banal stories they are part of. In *Four on an Important Mission*, however, cameraman Sa'id Shimi shoots the film as a voyage from one absurdity to another. The hero is first seen mumbling his inanities among the colossi of ancient Egypt shot from deep angles as towering ruins, and later he will be filmed as a lucid and vociferous force kicking his way through the debris and detritus of state, shot in foreshortened distortion.

The point is that in this kind of comedy, in derision, the ambivalence is not resolved by a simple switch of words, roles or positions at the film's end. Also, despite confusions, coincidences and even a sidekick helper (the lorry driver, who among other things helps get him into the manger–hotel) this is not situation comedy. Instead, as the opposition and similitude between man and monkey play themselves out, a third term materializes, intervenes and insinuates itself between them. The film ends with replacement: from man/monkey to government/monkey.

Conclusion

By the end of *Four on an Official Mission*, comedy has accomplished its own mission. Through its insolent category mistake, the question is no longer 'Who is the monkey?', but instead 'What is more apish, the monkey or the cage?' As for *The Gentlemen*, it highlights the fact that as a film it is operating within at least two sets of codes: those of comedy and those of society. The base code is society, static and hierarchical, the parasitical code is comedy, dynamic and anarchic. In other words, comedy's narrative allows one or two elements in the social picture to come unstuck, drift about, go into disguises, get into muddles, stray off too far in one direction or another, and either pop back up sempiternally, settle into a more comfortable place, or even take on a new form. Moreover, what I have loosely termed 'elements' can range from words detached from their meanings, stereotypes detached from their social positions, or matter floating freely from abstraction to abstraction. All are versions of comedy's brash 'mistakes'.

This does not exhaust the ways in which Arab comedy can be seen, as long as what is kept in mind is that this comedy is a question of dynamics, of one thing being set off against its opposite. In connection with the little man, for instance, the void created each time a gag is enunciated, the abyss that opens when it seems an issue has been dealt with once and for all, is countered by a breathtaking fluidity, a constant escape and resurrection of both man and gag, that is reminiscent of the battles between the US cartoon characters Tom and Jerry.[11] As for situation comedies, in these society is shown as so inflexible and stereotypes so immovable that only magic works. It is only through the graciousness of chance and the fairy godfather's wand that, in a wild swing from stereotype to stereotype, the ugly duckling does indeed turn into the swan. Finally, in films seemingly very down-to-earth or at least contemporary, unmixables are mixed and a hybrid threatens to look out from the mirror.[12] What can eventually emerge is a new man, or a new form.

Then again, the mirror may reflect things people would rather not see, and comedy is one of only two genres in Arab cinema that take on the beast in man. Not a grisly beast, but a creature who disputes the automatic equations of language, conventions always socially determined. The only other genre which really dares consider the beast is, of course, melodrama, with its disturbing detours around the dry, well-trodden path of the socially acceptable.

Finally, there is still another way of looking at comedy. This is that it offers another vision of society itself because it is a form in which the signifier is detached from what it is supposed to signify, with the result that there is much free flow and free exchange of meaning between things. This is not simply anarchy, it is, for Arab cinema, one of the most interesting ways of positing a more pluralist society.

5. The Dramatic

Melodrama . . .

At the end of Atef al-Tayyeb's 1986 Egyptian film *On File for Morals/Malaff fil-adaab* the heroine cries out that though finally found innocent by the court, she has already been found guilty by the press. The same cry could be heard from Arab melodrama itself; its press is bad, but of what is it guilty?

Derivation from Hollywood forms is one of the accusations, and in the words of the Egyptian critic Kamal Ramzi, this means, for instance, concern with 'events which occur in closed rooms and the problems of individuals'.[1]

Certainly this is an accurate description of some of the older melodramas, such as Niazi Mustapha's 1955 *A Cigarette, a Glass/Sigara wa kas*. Through jealousy, the heroine drags out her life in an alcoholic daze and her dropped cigarette almost sets fire to her child's bedroom. The heroine in Yusuf Chahine's 1952 *The Lady on the Train/Sayyidat al-qitar*, on the other hand, is an ultra-virtuous woman who, to support her debt-ridden husband, allows him to collect her life insurance and lock her up in an abandoned house, away from her child, for years.

Though opposite personality types, both these women are heroines of melodrama, meaning that they will stagger and suffer through much film footage. What did they do to deserve this? Both singing stars, wives and also mothers, in the eyes of society they would seem to have too much in their lives. Not only do they have excess wealth but they also have excess options, too many possible roles. The social instability this creates acts like a narrative trigger, causing suffering first, choices next. The heroine of *A Cigarette, a Glass* gives up her career in favour of her family, and the heroine of *The Lady on the Train* accepts being hidden away for so long that she has no career left to go back to.

But narratives are triggered just as often from an instability arising from lack. And in both these films, the male figure ambles around in the film's perimeter, liable to initiate lack or loss by walking out of it. Both women here clearly make their decisions in order to retain him, be he father or husband. In fact, probably one of the reasons opulent milieux are so popular in melodrama is that problems of excess and lack can alternate, disorienting, disconcerting and delighting their audiences in turn.

But if, in films about life upstairs, the threat of family deficiency is often muffled by wealth, in films about life downstairs it is all too shrill. In Atef al-Tayyeb's 1987 *The Basement/Al-badrun*, the story actually begins with that primordial narrative device: loss of the father. By falling to his death in the lift shaft of a large block of flats, a janitor leaves his family not only with little material support but also basically unstable. From now on, all its members will try to scramble up, out from under the stairs, and the camera will go with them, lurching up the flimsy steps, to the lift itself and the grand stairway to the flats above. Getting up and into one of these flats becomes the main desire of both daughters in the film. The younger one will have to repudiate her mother, the building's charwoman, in order to pass off a borrowed flat as her own. The elder one will accept a flat (in which to 'entertain' him) from an older married man, the flat camouflaging the prostitution.

The hovel below stairs, the luxurious flats above, these topographic extremes mark the melodrama as visual indicators of economic highs and moral lows. 'As subsequently criticized in "Marxist–positivist" terms', writes the Moroccan scholar Abdallah Laroui, 'this is also the topography and structure of the frustrated petit bourgeois world depicted in Egyptian post-war "realist" literature.'

> Ascension in this structure can only be achieved at a loss: either one keeps one's integrity and loses one's life, or else one succeeds, to realize that one has lost, en route, one's own values, hence the insistent, obsessional problem of prostitution.[2]

In many films based on the books Laroui describes, girls forced to find their own place in society lose both their integrity and their life. Lies and cheating must be paid for, but then Egyptian melodrama has always been fairly flamboyant (unless otherwise indicated, all films mentioned in this chapter are Egyptian). But what of a girl who does not lie, and is not trying to claw her way up, a girl such as the heroine of Jilali Ferhati's 1981 Moroccan film *Reed Dolls/'Arais min qasab*? As the film opens, small boys are playing freely out in the street but the young girl at her window is told to shut it and attend to her work inside. She is restricted, maybe, but she is indoors in safety, in her aunt's house where she will soon be happily married to her cousin. But panning across a family photograph on the wall, past what Roger Garcia calls 'the static state, the happy family photograph',[3] the film makes its transition from happy past to uncertain future. Because of the husband's sudden death, the absence of the man in the picture, the heroine must now go outside to earn a living for herself and her children. But outside is a place of temptations. Eventually made pregnant, she candidly confesses to her mother-in-law who with compassion says, 'May God forgive us, for we are only women.' But a court judges the heroine as too weak to maintain custody of her children, and at the film's end she might as well be dead, thrown back on to a labour market glutted with indigent women.

Compared to Egyptian melodramas, this Moroccan one has a sedate pace and a gentler tone, but the signals and landmarks are the same: emotional extremes are inevitably accompanied by topographic extremes: upstairs–downstairs in Egypt, inside–outside in Morocco. But what about strong women, or at least self-sufficient women? Independence does not matter; as far as melodrama is concerned it is still a woman's place that counts. Even inside, if it is not a family home, is a dubious place for her to be. Any woman living on her own must be a kept woman, as she is in Hussein Kamal's 1985 *Licit Days/Ayyam fil-halal*. Unfortunately, this kind of opinion reflects back on women like the heroine in Sa'id Marzuq's 1974 *I Want a Solution/Uridu hallan*, who has simply moved out on her brutish husband, in hopes of divorce. Going to a man's home is deemed questionable too. Though the heroine of Sa'id Marzuq's 1985 *Save What We Can/Inqadh ma yumkin inqadhuhu* has only visited the hero to talk with him, the staff living in the basement are not convinced. But what of such a totally innocuous situation as the heroine going over to a prospective fiancé's flat duly chaperoned by her friends from work? In Atef al-Tayyeb's *On File for Morals* this is no good either, and when the morals squad come rushing in to round up the friends sitting there quietly, eating fish, the state feels it has a case.

But a case based on what? The friends sitting there at the table are three men and three women, in other words, three potential couples, that is, it is appearances that count. We are back, full circle, to Ramzi's criticism of melodrama's preoccupation with 'events in closed rooms', with the additional qualification that not only is it where a woman is situated which counts, but what that seems to indicate. Just seeming or really being? This is one of the main areas of titillation in melodrama. If melodrama otherwise seems a genre of extremes, of ups and downs, ins and outs, economic highs and moral lows, this, the play between appearance and essence is one of the areas obscured by a fog, it is where ambiguity balances out extremes.

Appearances, in fact, are of prime importance. However innocent she may be, alone in a room with a man a woman appears available. Even alone on a public bus, as in Ashraf Fahmy's 1987 *For Lack of Sufficient Proof/Li 'adam kifayat al-adilla* the naive country girl can be surreptitiously pawed by a frustrated bureaucrat. This particular scene is funny as the male director implies what is happening by intercutting shots of the bus driver shifting gears, metaphor being a common method of avoiding the explicit in sexual matters. More dubious than the treatment of such an event with humour, however, is the surprising prurience with which some female directors have portrayed woman and her appearance as available object, the most flagrant and recent example being the 1987 *Woman and the Law/Al-mara wal qanun* directed by Nadia Hamza. Though the shocking subject of the film is that a girl is actually judged guilty in court of her own rape because she had been alone with her attacker, the film had pandered throughout its tedious length to the male and even included a long, lascivious dance sequence.

Granted, the dance is to be taken as existing only in her attacker's mind, but what does she herself feel? For most of the film, we see the heroine looking blank, like a startled gazelle. Such women do not command specular relations. They do not gaze, they are gazed at. As the Moroccan literary critic Abdelfattah Kilito writes in connection with traditional Arab courtly love poetry (*'udhri*), it is man's desire which is expressed and 'as object of the amorous discourse, she [woman] cannot be its subject'.[4] An object of desire, in other words, is not capable of expressing its own desire.

Or is it? What acts do these women initiate? Is the blank look, prevalent in more films than just this one, to be taken for lack of desire? A disturbing ambiguity covers this area also. If one of the daughters in *The Basement* gives herself to a man for a flat and the other disclaims her family for social status, the woman in *Reed Dolls* gives in to adultery because, simply, of a lack. With the husband or the father gone, these are insecure women, who are often the support of other family members, and there is usually a very understandable reason for what they do. In other words, it is very rarely a question of their own desire.

At least, it is never avowed to be desire. In fact, avowing anything is rare. With their blank looks and ambiguous acts, what thoughts can be attributed to these women? Of course, a lot of weeping and wailing goes on in these films, but it involves them, their female relatives and their female neighbours, and so on. In other words, these are formulaic lamentations, the social marking of death, disappearance and failure. No secrets are exchanged. The expression of a woman's feelings and desires happens elsewhere, behind an outward silence.

It happens, often, in interior monologue, a device which otherwise is rarely used in Arab cinema, perhaps precisely because of its strong associations with melodrama. 'Should I, shouldn't I . . . ?' Here, behind the numb look, there is at least a voice, and the audience can become involved in the choices. Not all films use this device however, whilst Egypt's Henri Barakat uses it so much that it begins to seem his signature. But in one of his more recent films, the 1984 *The Night of the Arrest of Fatma/Lailat al-qabd 'ala Fatma* Barakat turns the tables. He has his heroine recount, out loud, and to all her friends and neighbours, the years of her self-sacrifice as sole support of her orphaned brothers and sisters, only in the end to be grossly mistreated and martyred by the one she had protected most. The hitherto pent-up voice has broken free and Barakat makes it clear that not only is this a reformulation of melodrama's formal devices, but that he intends it to be taken metaphorically: that, like Fatma, a maltreated Egypt should 'tell all'.

Not all melodrama's devices are reformulated here though. Meant to explain all as well as tell all, Fatma summons up the past via flashback, another device rarely seen in Arab cinema outside the context of melodrama. In fact, like true desire which has no real object but is just a constantly displaced unease, melodrama relentlessly shifts the ground of its evidence: onscreen, offscreen, visual, aural, from the dubious position to the blank look to the ambiguous act to an interior monologue to pictures from the past. In what Deleuze calls the 'false piety' of the flashback,[5] the glance creeps sideways to some evidence offscreen.

Because piety, or, at least, innocence asserted, is what this is all about. Asked in connection with his 1974 film *Progressive Slides of Pleasure/Glissements progressifs du plaisir* why one recounts one's memories, the French director Alain Robbe-Grillet said that it was 'to establish one's innocence',[6] and in this film of his, the man trying to cope with women's memories is a judge, submerged beneath teetering volumes of words, looking for innocence in books slipping and sliding away from him. Just so, in many Arab melodramas about women, by three quarters of the way through the film, if not before, the issue has come to court.

Some may say that this is simply a reflection of reality, that a woman's inferior status in society and law in many Arab countries means that sooner or later a heroine will appear before a judge. But it can also be argued, as does Robbe-Grillet, that this is one of the conflictual organizations of narrative, that the slide of events, events which seem just to happen, in a downward progress and a process of dissolution, needs to be blocked, blocked by some law, some ordering, some narrative syntax in which motive is followed by act, act followed by guilt.

In fact, call it law or call it narrative, in melodrama this structure has not only to block the slide of events but to integrate repetitions. Summoning up the past, over and over, never seems to release these women from their predicament; not only do they seem to have a tenuous hold over the present but they seem doomed to repeat the same mistakes in the future. Or to reappear over and over again in the same film: sometimes the same actress plays both mother and daughter, as in Chahine's 1952 *Lady on a Train* and as recently as in Khairy Beshara's 1987 *The Necklace and the Bracelet/Al-tauq wal-aswira*.

This device in the first film makes it appear inevitable that both mother and daughter will be victims of the gambling husband/father and, in the second film, just as inevitable that both mother and daughter will, one after the other, suffer the same absence of the brother/uncle. Another version of repetition is to have one actress play the same role over and over, in film after film. Her fate may not be inevitable but, set above and beyond time, her presence is. Faten Hamama has for so long played the long-suffering Egyptian woman that when people call her 'the lady of the screen' (*sayyidat al-shasha*) it is not clear if this refers to her acting ability or to her embodiment of an ideal. In ancient Arab poetry, according to Kilito, the consequence of various poets citing the same ideal woman over and over by the same name (namely, Layla) is that 'the proper name must then be considered a common noun'.[7]

Futuwwa

Is melodrama, then, a recurrent cinematic type, or a lived reality? From Henri Barakat's 1959 *Call of the Curlew/Du'a al-karawan* to Khairy Beshara's 1989 *Bitter Day, Sweet Day/Yawm murr, yawm hulw* if Faten Hamama has been doing nothing over the years but express the forlorn status of women in the Arab world, what then about men's melodrama? Hardly acknowledged, certainly not called thus, and surely not contained in the formulation 'events in closed rooms', there is none the less such a genre, even though in a man's world one cannot look blank and slide offscreen even if on a slippery slope. A man must be seen to act. Or, at least, 'if you can't fight them, join them'. The fighting option was discussed in chapter 3, in connection with heroes, but here in melodrama is the joining option, and in Arab cinema this is particularly well articulated in the *futuwwa* films.[8]

The word *futuwwa* in the Middle Ages and in religious contexts generally designated ideals of chivalry and brotherhood. By now, in Egypt at least, its meaning has degenerated so that it denotes a kind of bully system, a sort of marketplace Mafia, in which any boss who loses his iron grip on his followers will rapidly be replaced by the next toughest aspirant around. Like the women in melodrama who seem just to drift into bad situations, the central character of the *futuwwa* films usually starts out with pure intentions. In one of the best of the genre, Salah Abou Seif's 1956 *The Bully/Al-futuwwa* the hero is a simple country man who comes up to the city, sees the injustice of the local boss and plots with others to get around the system through fair competition. When elbowed out by the boss's rough tactics, the hero takes another tack and pretends to go along with him, becoming the boss's trusted aide. As a result however, he begins to see greener pastures and seemingly endless possibilities for his own aggrandizement, never mind those who will be left behind, his former partners or even his wife.

The process has begun, the process of corruption, rise, downfall and replacement that is the basis of all the *futuwwa* films. Going nowhere but round in a circle, the process is similar to the inexorable repetitions in women's melodrama. For men, there are only two possibilities, either the feeble hope voiced by the hero near the end of *The Bully* that he himself will rise up again, or the more real possibility that a new man will come up from the country, become involved and replace him, as shown in fact at the very end of the film. This revitalizes but only repeats a rise-and-fall pattern. Not just a theory of power, this is also a theory of history, first traced out in Arab literature by the fourteenth-century Arab thinker Ibn Khaldun. Societies, he wrote, live a life not unlike that of a man, with youth, vigour and success followed, through necessary organic laws, by corruption and decay, leading only to replacement in the same cycle by different men.[9]

But the circularity in these films, the inevitability of everything starting all over again and following the same pattern, is in constant dynamic play with a linear narrative of initiation, a step-by-step 'how to' – how to get to the top. Never mind if the hero goes too high and must fall, there is fascination in the mechanics. Usually the mechanics are those of the capitalist system, hence the market as the main setting for most of these films, and all the details about withholding produce and inflating prices.

But a film's emphasis on these economic and public operations risks blurring its more political and private basis, the bully system. So some films, such as Samir Seif's 1984 *Streets of Fire/Shawari' min nar* are set in more shadowy recesses of society. In this case, a previously good and honest policeman rises to replace and become, in his turn, a top nightclub operator and pimp. In addition to showing how the policeman gets there, the film flaunts the décors he strides through. As in women's melodramas, furnishings do not simply surround the characters but instead indicate the direction of the narrative, and act as visual manifestations of whatever point has been reached, up or down.

Dissolution

But what about a man's outward appearance? Can he actually *look* weak and corruptible, open to enrichment but vulnerable also to moral dissolution? In the *futuwwa* films, if a man lost his integrity by joining a bully system, his inner disintegration would be marked by an increasingly rough exterior, to be excused, perhaps, by his position *vis-à-vis* potential adversaries. But what about solitary ascent up the economic ladder, with only social vengeance as its motivating force? In Ahmed Yahya's 1984 *So That the Smoke Does Not Blow Away/Hatta la yatir al-dukhan*, for example, as the hero enriches himself in a milieu he despises, his expressions become more and more pained. Since he dies at the moment all his desires are achieved, one can only assume that his malignant soul has corroded his body.

Compared to the terms in which most men's melodramas are expressed, however, this outward manifestation of an inner decay is somewhat elliptical. A more usual and popular form is for the hero's dissolution to be blamed on some outside corrupting force. Ali Abdel Khalek uses drugs, for instance, in his 1986 film *Hashish/Al-kayf*. The easygoing musician hero simply cannot abandon the habit and, when he is deprived of drugs, his agonized weeping and wailing, when added to those of his previously upright but now 'hooked' brother, equals in decibels a whole neighbourhood of mourning women.

The same effect is achieved in another recent film by Ali Abdel Khalek, his 1987 *The Run of the Beasts/Jary al-wuhush*. The outside malevolent force is again 'devilishly scientific', but biological, not chemical. Having reaped a fortune by agreeing to bizarre surgery, the hero staggers around possessed by the brain cells of another, in incoherent and dishevelled lament. Clearly, a very blatant male exculpation is at work here and this highlights two main differences between men's and women's melodrama. First, if a woman staggers around in public emotional displays similar to those of the men described above, she is assumed to be in a state of terminal disarray rather than temporarily unhinged. Secondly, the blame for this disarray will be attributed not to some neutral, outside force such as scientific experiment but rather laid sanctimoniously on her own doorstep, on her inability to stay at home, or to find her proper place in society.

Usually, however, she is not in her proper place because of the absence of a male. But given a heroine's sense of decorum, this dependence is often expressed by her distantly focused look, a kind of wavering, double focus, never clear whether it is directed at someone or something, here or there, in the past or in the present. This ambivalence also occurs in men's melodrama, demonstrating that heroes are no more integrated and self-sufficient than are their female counterparts. But it is expressed quite differently: at the hero's side, very much present throughout the film's action, is an *alter ego*, be he buddy or enemy, the brother of *Hashish*, or the other contender of *The Run of the Beasts*.

And if the ambivalence in women's melodramas allows the implicit to be glimpsed, in men's melodrama it allows the explicit to be acted out. It is a narrative device for argument about the bad and the good. This is true even in *futuwwa* films in which the relations between two men are not of amity but of enmity. These moral choices are emblematic at the film's beginning as the good underdog and the bad bully, but the *futuwwa* genre pushes the heroes out of oversimplified categories and into a closed system of initiation and imitation where one figure actually merges into the other. In many other films, the reverse direction is favoured: two friends become enemies. In Daoud Abdel Sayed's 1984 *The Bums/ Al-sa'alik* the buddies are not just good friends: one is just as much a tramp as the other. In this story of two down-and-outs who successfully make their way up through all the loopholes of a new *laissez-faire* economy, the stakes become so high that when one will no longer go along with the other, his friend simply shoots him. Or, he shoots his conscience, because in many films about corruption, the hero and his complement are constantly flailing around, each visibly and audibly attempting to pull the other down.

Solution

Their attempts are extremely audible: indeed the dialogue in these films often eats up a good deal of the narrative, to the detriment of action. But what used to be a fairly clear contrast – monologue in women's melodrama, dialogue in men's – is nowadays often blurred by general discussions carried on by either sex. In Ashraf Fahmy's 1987 film *For Lack of Sufficient Proof* (see pages 72 and 98), for instance, it even seems as if the talks between various women – a villager, a lawyer, and the lawyer's colleague – work through a series of *alter egos* as in men's melodramas, and that changing opportunities for women are changing the more classic forms of melodrama.

But can one slide out of melodrama that easily? In the Fahmy film and others like it, the women's discussions are not revelations of frustration and desire but talk of situations and circumstances. And in Arabic the word for 'circumstances', *zuruf*, is a catch-all, blame-all. Used more and more in these films in connection with hints of eventual disclosures or future (offscreen) solutions, the word becomes impersonal and invalidates both the past that the women are looking back to and the present that the men are stumbling through. In fact, the word represents a double displacement: individual responsibilities are first to be dissolved by *zuruf*, then afterwards by words: discussion of these *zuruf*. Actually, the words change nothing, they only block the narrative vehicle, the events; they do not transcend the genre and move the film out of melodrama.

Another attempt to get around melodrama these days is to challenge its predictability, particularly the inbuilt circularity of the *futuwwa* type. Thus, at the end of Ali Badrakhan's 1986 *Hunger/Al-ju'* the conventional narrative in which a strong brother supplants the local bully and becomes a boss in his turn is suddenly aborted. His weaker brother leads the mobs against him, not to supplant him, not for the usual replacement, but to allow the people to take their own future into their own hands, and be bossed by no one.

In this film it is not a matter of words pretending to erase acts; instead a whole new series of acts, a new mentality to break the cycle, is proposed. In Badrakhan's film, the Cairo mobs who tear branches off their trees in order to charge victoriously into their own future are seen by the Egyptian critic, Samir Farid, as analogous to the Palestinians fighting in the *intifada* with rocks from their streets. Moreover, he claims, the image repudiates the individual-centred, Robin Hood-type saviour myth.[10]

The political solution might be easier to propose than the change in narrative form. The film's ending repudiates everything in it up to that point. It negates itself, its own form, as well as individualist myths. Melodrama is not only self-consciously centred on the individual but in Arab cinema it is one of the few forms in which desire is acknowledged. This means desire not just as an individual urge for possession, but as a constantly displaced unease, vaguely oriented offscreen. Ironically, *Hunger*, by providing a solution at the end, kills off desire just as surely as the older melodramas did through their formulae of death or surrender.

In the older films, if the individual deviated too far from legal or social norms, he would have to die; if he was not too far gone, surrender lay in accommodation to the norms. Usually the solution was to redirect desire from an unacceptable object to an acceptable one. Proper family equations were particularly favoured. In Salah Abou Seif's wonderful 1956 *A Woman's Youth/Shabab imra*, for instance, the dissolution and decay of a young student commandeered by his middle-aged landlady to spend all his time in her bed is blocked not only by the self-sacrifice of a surrogate father but by the arrival of his real mother and the love of a true sweetheart. Until then, the landlady had very competently been assuming all these roles.

Abou Seif was playing melodrama off against comedy in this film on a grand scale, but many lesser directors fudged the genres at the end of their films so that, after much anguish and disintegration, all characters would slide into the proper slots. In many cases, such solutions were too glib. Another route to resolution lay through symbols. Yusuf Chahine, in his 1964 *Dawn of a New Day/Fajr yawm jadid*, mixed symbols enough that this film about an unhappily married woman and her young lover could also be seen as a commentary on old and new Egypt, conservative and liberal options, culture and energy. None the less, the proper solution employed at the film's end is to give the woman a real child, an orphan, to take care of, one whose hand she must take after letting go forever that of her lover.

Symbols, however, are just a refiguration of the same object, they do not move the object. Not only by opting for the appropriate ending but also by using symbolism Chahine's story stays within the rules of melodrama: it posits a dynamic individual at odds with a static society. Melodrama thus enunciates its stories in the vocabulary of law and society. The titles of many of the films concerned with women mentioned in this chapter imply the illegal (using such words as morals, licit, proof, law, arrest) and many of those concerned with men imply the asocial (bully, smoke, hashish, beasts, bums).

All but one of the films discussed in this chapter are Egyptian. Why? Partial attempts to answer this are made in chapter 6 (in terms of Egyptian social cohesion) and chapter 7 (in a discussion of how anguish is expressed). But various strategies of melodrama seem linked to general articulations in Islam, and in Arab literature. Consider, for instance, the spatial parameters within Islamic law, with its notion of basic limits (*hudud*). Then, in classical literature, to express the sliding and stumbling within or beyond these limits, there are the displacements of desire in the poetry of longing (*hanin*) and the comradeship of wine song (*khamriyya*). But wordly wisdom (*hikma*) indicates that the corruption (*fasad*) of one entails the downfall (*inhidam*) of all, so one must finally arrive at the prosaic resolutions of the socially acceptable (*adaab*).

. . . And beyond

If, in melodrama, society's rules are always given priority over individual desires, what form does drama take if that society is not stable, or even orderly, in itself? What if society too has a lack, an internal flaw, and is an amorphous series of arrangements, of temporary accommodations with desire, of transient adaptations to law? If, in other words, it is not simply a matter of desire versus law, but of desire as a continual displacement within law?

Some of Arab cinema's most impressive dramas, from the quiet and subtle to the shattering and discordant, operate through these displacements. Although little known, even in Algeria, one of that country's best war films is Jacques Charby's *Such a Young Peace/Salam hadith al-'ahd*. Made in 1964, immediately after independence, the film begins as a mob of war orphans moves into an imposing old estate, now a surrogate parent system, an orphanage, an adult system. This system operates within society's rules of hierarchy and territory, and any fierce feelings left by the war, whether anarchic or partisan, are to be coached out of the boys. They are allowed to play games; but games, organized sports, lead to the idea of teams, of taking sides. So, with childlike seriousness and concentration, the boys set about playing games, organizing themselves into warring sides, and the film ends as the first bullet is fired. Masters and boys had made strenuous efforts to avoid this, but the film leaves all questions open. Are teachers parents, are orphans really children, when is a game not a game, whose system is war, anyway? Screened again in 1987 in the context of a children's film festival as part of Algeria's celebrations of twenty-five years of independence, the impact of this old black-and-white film was shattering. It was the only significant Algerian or, indeed, Arab film dealing with children.

But because of its complexity *Such a Young Peace* cannot simply be labelled 'about children' any more than Abdellatif Ben Ammar's 1980 Tunisian film *Aziza* could be labelled 'about women'. Like Charby, Ben Ammar dissolves so many categories that no labelling is possible; there is constant movement, of dispersion and of recentring. As the film opens, various pieces of old-fashioned furniture are being quietly moved offscreen, away from the crumbling walls of the old city, later to be stacked up in a bland white box in a new workers' suburb. But this extension into space and the supposedly good things in life is also marked by a diminution of traditional male roles. The old uncle, for instance, cannot accustom himself to riding into the city on a bus to do his errands, and must be accompanied by his niece Aziza, who used to stay at home. Aziza's swaggering cousin makes the logical move and acquires a car, beginning his extension into an entrepreneurial life he cannot sustain, and which will eventually force him back within the flimsy new walls. Only Aziza copes, gradually, with the new space and, with the death of her uncle and the collapse of her cousin will, anyway, have to go out – to work. In melodrama, as noted, this move out would be the precise point where insecurity and downfall would begin. Not so here: the ground is shifting under everyone's feet in this film. The scenes with neighbours, for instance, are a matter of constant territorial victories and defeats. This is not just a film about Tunisia in the 1980s, or just about women, but a film about constant reconfigurations.

Many would probably label Tewfik Saleh's 1972 *The Dupes/Al-makhdu'un* a film 'about Palestine'. But taken by this Egyptian director from a story by the assassinated Palestinian writer Ghassan Kanafani and produced for Syria, the film sets up its elements against each other in defiance of all labels. Extending out into space, the camera takes three men off to an El Dorado in the Gulf. But through reversals and annulments, as the film takes them from a deadend, landless, life in refugee camps in fact it takes them nowhere, across lands to no land. Totally invisible, frontiers are the most palpable presence in the film. Moreover, despite using the device of three men of different ages and varied backgrounds, this extension over time and across experience is a mirage. Castrated by his situation just as surely as the driver of the truck was in battle, the triple 'hero' is barely one man: the Palestinian. Also, if the camera seems to open up space by panning over it, or to delve into time by flashing back into it, these extensions are illusory, all played off against a reduction of options. In this, one of Arab cinema's best (and rare) dramas of real suspense, individuals and a people, the world and time, desire and the law all flicker off and on and finally consume each other.

In shots of the progressive dissolution and alcoholic disarray of the hero in Hussein Kamal's 1968 *The Postman/Al-bustagi*, it is clear that the road leads downhill, only. Why then not include this film among the male melodramas of the corruption type? It is because the system within which the postman is falling apart, the civil service, is only one of many vying for authority in the film. So, criteria for behaviour in it are very mixed; it cannot be called a film 'about rural problems' either, though an urban–rural struggle carries the storyline. As the film begins, the postman arrives to implement the city's ideas of an objective and unaffiliated public service. But immediately up against a countryside bonded by blood, he is shunted aside as irrelevant. More and more isolated, more and more turning to alcohol, he tries at least to sustain one modern code: that of romantic love. To do the good – to help a young girl – he does the bad: he tinkers with the mail. As for the girl's father, to do the good – to uphold family honour – he does the bad: he kills his daughter. Writing on women in Arab film, the Egyptian critic Samir Farid points out that this is a country code, not an Islamic code: the father is anyway a Copt.[11] True, but the point is not really there. By raping his maid, the father had already brought women's honour into conflict with man's desire, and using desire as well as codes, affiliations and systems, the film is not simply about blind subordination to one of these, but about all the shifting subordinations among them and . . . flux.

Sample drama: *Cairo: Central Station*

The dramas outlined above indicate only some of the areas of ambiguity within social, economic or political systems which allow Arab film to go beyond melodrama. Because of its availability to the public outside Egypt, a good example to consider in some detail is Yusuf Chahine's 1958 *Cairo: Central Station/Bab al-hadid*, whose basic story is about a poor cripple, a macho porter and the woman they both love.

Though simple enough in itself, this storyline is embedded in a tangle of desires and power plays whose different resolutions suggest some of the film's density. First, there is the love story of a young girl who waits all day at the station to see off her boyfriend. But he arrives surrounded by his family, who would forbid any such social mismatch, so the couple can do little more than say a furtive goodbye and then wave. If there is any resolution here, it can only be said to be a negative one. Next, there are the struggles of the woman soft-drinks vendor, the woman desired by both cripple and porter. In constant conflict with the authorities, she is chased by the police for selling without a permit, and hounded by the stall operator for taking his business. As the film ends, this conflict is still ongoing, with no resolution even in sight. Finally, the porter is trying to woo not just the woman but also the other porters whom he hopes to attract away from the traditional boss and into a fledgling trade union sponsored by the young post-revolutionary government. He succeeds, but his swagger suggests that this is a mini *futuwwa* situation, and that union laws may not stop him from becoming a boss in his turn. So although this is a positive resolution, it also falls within potentially cyclical limits.

All these options, these varying resolutions and convolutions pull on the central story of the cripple's love for the vendor, associating it with any or all: as a social mismatch, a problem of economic disadvantage, or a crude power struggle. She is healthy, he is a cripple. Her fiancé the porter is an up-and-coming man, the cripple is impoverished. The porter is also rough and strong, the cripple is less than vigorous. But Chahine, who himself takes the role of the cripple, does not play it for tears, though one aches for him in a courtship scene in the square outside the station. In pathetic contrast to the mammoth statue of Ramses II behind him, this little orphan figure tries to seduce the vendor with images of rural quiet, children and cows. She is enticed by the necklace he offers, but it is clearly 'no' to cows and villages as she laughs and chatters about what she likes: noise, people, movement. But at this point one's empathy is withdrawn, as the film's visual pulsations implicate the cripple in more pathological directions. His desire for this woman, all women perhaps, as well as for the beauty of a healthy body, is seen in his hungry glances, at legs particularly. And we see him cut out pin-ups, newspaper photos of women, and eventually not only cut them out, but cut them up, mutilating them every which way.

The pace changes, the focus switches, and what might have been melodrama – one man's desire against all society's norms – is caught in a swirl of other scenes. Trains come and go, relationships are truncated, and words and acts are cut away from their meanings. Thus, from one scene to the next the expression 'I take refuge in God from the Devil' (*a'udhu billah min al-shaitan*) shifts from suggesting overstated piety in face of dancing teenagers to suggesting understated shock at news of a trunk murder. In the same way, the phrase 'proof of the crime' applied to a bucket used to steal business is more than meaningless while people are looking for a real murderer. There are chases too, full of fun, games and coquetry when played out between the porter and the vendor, but full of terror when between the cripple and the vendor. Most grim, melancholy and fallacious, however, are the words 'groom', 'dowry', 'wedding suit', used at the end of the film to cajole and ensnare the cripple. Up until then they have been used seriously, but as the last phrases spoken in the film, they are not only an anti-resolution but a jab at the formulae of other films' glib endings.

Conclusion

There are many more fine Arab dramas than the few sketched here, and some are treated in other chapters in relation to scene, sound, sign, and so on. However, writing in 1975, the French critic Yves Thoraval stated that given the problems of censorship in Egypt, melodrama seemed to be the only drama possible in Egyptian cinema.[12] Certainly melodramas preponderate numerically in the country's film output, and seem to bloom perennially. So what of comments like Thoraval's, and melodrama's bad press? What is it criticized for, specifically?

For one thing, as Ramzi's reference to melodrama's concern with 'events which occur in closed rooms' implies, it is seen as concerned mainly with the rich or, at least, those able to hide their secrets behind closed doors; even in melodramas about the poor, the rich are very visible. But this is part of the equation, given melodrama's dialectic of up–down, in–out, this is part of the visual substantiation of that dialectic, especially important, as the desire of women must largely remain unspoken. Melodrama is also thought to represent a restrictive, highly coded society. So it does, but it also shows a cellular society, the basic cell being that of the family, and the death of the father representing the death of law itself, or the birth of narrative. Third, the sins depicted in melodrama are perhaps thought to reflect badly on Arab society. Yes, but, aside from the musical, melodrama is the only form in Arab cinema in which desire is acknowledged, and in which the conflict between being and appearing is cinematically expressed. Then there is the accusation that melodrama focuses on the individual; true, but it is the individual's collision with the barrier of legal and social norms which makes that barrier visible. Finally, there is the accusation of melodrama's too familiar, too formulaic resolutions. True again, but before one reaches a melodrama's end there are a whole series of Sindbad stories, stories of wealth found or lost, of how to or how not to, a map for treasure buried somewhere. . . .

Though this somewhere is almost by definition offscreen, it is probably the somewhere that most disturbs the critics. Most of their disapproval has to do with what the films show, it is not about the films themselves. As long as the world the melodramas show is disparaged, and melodrama as a genre is kept in some embarrassing closet, it will be hard to know why relatively few great Arab dramas come to the screen. Thoraval's explanation, that the reason is censorship, is just another version of the flirtation with the word 'circumstances' (*zuruf*). The obverse argument, perhaps thought by some but argued by few, is that melodrama is a form more innate to the Arab world than is drama. But in view of some of the superb films cited above under the heading '. . . And beyond', this will not stand up unless each director were considered so independent an *auteur* that his thought processes bore no relationship to the Arab world around him.

It might be more interesting to consider melodrama not just as a kind of juvenile, oversimplified drama, one that would never make it in the adult world, but as a different way of storytelling. Melodrama would be a narrative which, because it assumes a static and indivisible social order, tells its story in events related through co-ordination, by repeating, alternating, recycling, extending and, finally, reducing the options, all defined according to their ability to raise that person up, or out, into the coveted place in that social order. But if, as it appears on the other hand in the dramas described above, society is a kind of vacuum with free-floating roles, systems and codes as well as free-floating individuals, then narrative relationships could be those of exchange, dispersion, reversal, subordination and convolution.

Melodrama and drama would not only align their events differently, but would also declare them in different voices. In other words, because of melodrama's proclivity to histrionics, women weeping and men crumbling, it articulates itself through overstatement, through hyperbole. What is perhaps not so obvious is that this hyperbole, in order to work, has to be set against notable ambiguities and almost mute reticences. On the other hand, in the dramas cited above, no finger can be pointed to what exactly caused the disarray and from where disorder started, and therefore nothing very loud or precise can be declared. As one voice covers the other, contradicts it, intertwines with it, only in understatement, in a litotes, does one say 'and the film ends when the father kills the daughter'. In other words, in real dramas, 'telling the story' does not begin to tell anything at all.

6. Scene

Speaking in 1964, at a symposium on Arab cinema and culture held in Beirut, the Egyptian film archivist Farid al-Mazzaoui complained, 'We have always heard this refrain when art critics were talking about Egyptian films, or Arab films in general. They want us to produce more realist films.'[1]

Over twenty years later, the refrain is still heard: where are the Arab realist films? Moreover, it is still not clear what is meant by this term. There were hopes during these twenty years that a new kind of Arab cinema, a realist cinema, would materialize almost automatically from popular input, through the mechanism of public sector support. In Egypt in the 1960s, under the banner of 'cinema in the service of the people' independent companies were nationalized and the still extant Higher Cinema Institute was set up to ensure local training. As for Algeria, shortly after independence in 1962, the state proceeded to assume total control over cinema, although its training facility, the National Institute of Cinema at Bordj al-Bahri, existed only from 1964 to 1965.

Data

The Algerian state also reserved to itself the choice of subject matter, and in the name of its people began to produce a series of war films. After all, what was more strikingly real than the recent struggle for liberation against the French? But these films did not always seem very real. One of the main problems was probably the confusion of the terms 'people' and 'state'. A war film would tell the individual story of a hero and attempt a general one of his people. The two would run concurrently and were to dovetail in an image of the incipient state. Any screen image of mass is difficult, though, the problem here being resolved by recourse to newsreel footage. But in films like Ahmed Lallem's 1974 *Forbidden Zone/Al-mantiqa al-muharrama* this technique did not work. Concordance between the particular and the general is never really achieved and the story's texture is so fragmented by news inserts of Algerian masses that the hero's odyssey seems to disappear over the mountains.

Ideologically, this might be fine, if the people then seem to be real, but they do not. They are simply news material, hypostatized. One of the problems lies perhaps in a sense of stringency about historical sources. In Islam, the Prophetic tradition (*sunna*) has only been handed down through a strict system of credible transmission (*isnad*). On the other hand, in cinema, because of the basic inflation of the central character as hero in a revolutionary struggle, the abstraction of his exemplary conduct can perhaps be balanced only by another abstraction: the idea of objective document. What this means, writes the Algerian critic Reda Bensmaia, is that newsreels are inserted with 'the role of rendering believable that which the mode of narration keeps drawing into the "technicolour" (chromo)',[2] namely, the unbelievable.

But what if experience is all too believable, not high-flying heroics but a dreary and drab oppression, trivialized by its daily occurrence? In 1976, to explain oppression's base, the economic underpinning of colonialism, Lamine Merbah made *The Uprooted/Beni hendel*, setting out all the gimmicks, subtle and insidious, through which the French dispossessed the Algerian peasant. But is reality conveyed as the sum of its facts and figures? Unfortunately, despite the period costume and décor, the film's narrative moves stiffly from facts to figures, and the film's derivation from a thesis becomes as clear as the thesis itself. This uneasy alliance of fact and fiction is not unusual in Algerian cinema. Often, as the Algerian critic Abdou B. points out, 'One kills fiction by the documentary and one kills the documentary for fear of the immediate materialization of fiction.'[3]

Perhaps assuming that the two would mesh together better if employed elsewhere than on the overplayed subjects of war and colonialism, Mefti's 1981 *Marriage of Moussa/Zawaj Moussa* is set in the centre of contemporary Algiers as viewed by Moussa, a young Algerian returning from France. The device it uses to show what life is like for Algerians now is to have various characters come into Moussa's photographic shop, have their pictures taken and tell their stories. But, like lining up facts in a case against the French, lining up faces to represent today's problems results in a bland accumulation of scenes, in fragments unrelated to each other, as well as to the main narrative, the story of Moussa's marriage.

This kind of display of a country's ethnographic or sociological diversity has been a problem in Moroccan cinema also. The problem, in narrative terms, is a linear alternation of non-consequence. One has the impression that one is driving past a country, not into it. Even detached incidents can also be lined up for such folkloric appreciation, as they are in *Embers/Al-jamra*, made in 1984 by the Moroccan woman director Farida Bourquia. Static scenes of discussion between the members of an outcast family alternate with static scenes depicting the fury and frenzy of their enemies. Just when a limp plot rises up and begins to move, it is interrupted by scenes of Moroccan festival, circumcision and celebration, all unconnected with each other, or with the main plot.

The unwillingness to arrange and subordinate raw data, as if that would be some kind of aggression *vis-à-vis* life, can turn up in Egypt too. Occasionally mesmerized by facts, faces and phenomena, Egyptian films promote themselves as 'based on a real event', 'from the newspapers', and so on. What is often fragmentary here, though, is the film's introduction, like some tabloid headline, splattering 'the case' across the screen, whilst the film then proceeds with a quieter and sometimes unrelated story. For instance, after the lurid introductory scenes of sex, revenge and murder in Ahmed Fuad's 1987 *The Train/Al-qitar*, both men in the case die after only a few moments, and the film proceeds with stories of the runaway train's passengers.

The other extreme is to treat anything supposedly real in turgid, sentential fragments, shots of dialogue in which one chews the case over and over. Some say the recent rash of these discussion (*maqawalat*) films is partly due to reduced production and studio facilities, but clearly it also represents a rather naive idea about how to capture the real on screen.

Prescription/description

Despite these good intentions in the direction of objectivity, if not realism, most Egyptian films incorporate raw data back into the comfortable conventions of recognized genres, in other words, into what is already known to be commercially successful. But the mere mention of commercial criteria usually antagonizes the critics and leads them to declare that, *ipso facto*, such films could never be realist. The Tunisian critic Ferid Boughedir has always organized his film analysis within these axes.[4] Others, like the Egyptian critic Samir Farid read films in terms of a perceived historical development towards the ideal of realism. Writing in 1981, Farid argued that the pace of this development has always been slow because the first of the Arab cinemas, the Egyptian, got off to a bad start, with films 'made by the middle class for the middle class and which mainly revolve around the middle class'.[5] As for the French critic Yves Thoraval, in 1975 he considered that even in the most 'realist' films there is a ubiquity of clichés which can only be accounted for by a 'lack of precise ideology characteristic of even the best and most militant directors, bar one or two . . .'[6] Nowadays in

Egypt there exist a number of directors who are characterized as 'new realists', but writing in 1988 from Syria Mahdi Mohamed Ali commented that, 'All these artistic skills which film reality with precision are spent in vain or aimlessly, with neither a firm subject nor a specific deep content.'[7]

This is a brief sampling of a long, murky and ongoing polemic about where realism is in Arab cinema, or where it went if it was ever there. What seems to be the problem is that a message about reality is mixed up with cinematic realism, and since no one has suffered as much from this confusion as the Algerians, with administrative decrees coming down from on high to the film-makers declaring what the public should or should not see, let the last in this list be the words of an Algerian critic, Djamel Boukella, writing in 1987. 'Finally, everything takes place as if in Arab cinemas the existence and quality of a film proceeds from its disposition to translate a socio-political reality and to take a position on it, in a timid, prudent, nuanced, or official way.'[8]

In other words, prescription tends to take precedence over description, what one *should* see rather than what one *could* see. But the issue is not only relevant for the Arab world. Like Algeria, after its revolution Cuba was interested in a new social order and, like any nascent state, was anxious to project itself in an integral, if not overtly positive, image. 'But how,' writes the Cuban director Tomas Gutierrez Alea, 'can we *criticize* and at the same time *affirm* reality in which we are immersed?'[9] Not only does Alea cogently articulate this problem but also, on that of documentary inserts, he writes that if they are used adeptly in film, 'the relation between the protagonist's subjective and objective world has recourse to diverse levels of approximating reality'.[10]

In Mohamed Khan's 1987 Egyptian film *The Wife of an Important Man/Zauja rajul muhimm*, extraneous film clips are indeed used adeptly. In what might otherwise have been a thin melodrama, documents show exactly the subjective and objective worlds of the protagonist being played off against each other. Braiding newsreels of political events together with clips from old Egyptian musicals and weaving them into the story of a disintegrating marriage, the film explores not just the disparate emotional affiliations of the couple but the contradictions in some of Egypt's own visions. Here, the compounding of person, people and state works, but not because they float in loose co-ordination to each other. On the contrary, they swim up and down, in shifting subordinations and hierarchies and, surprisingly, the story looks all the more real for their interaction.

It may simply be that the concept of realism in Arab films is problematic, not its data. If used adeptly, even data such as 'faces in a landscape' can be made to fit into a story without either scarring their ethnographic integrity or blemishing the story. Take, for instance,

Mohamed Lakhdar-Hamina's 1966 Algerian film *Wind of the Aurès/Rih al-Awras*. As a widowed mother emerges from her hovel on the mountainside and makes her way down into the plain in search of her captured son, she meets more and more people on her way. Their faces are those of people who are active inside the story, confusing her, blocking her, talking to her and, in the case of some, helping her; everyone plays a role of some sort. By the film's end, her tiny, singular and very personal tragedy has bled out into the great gaping wound of a mass of others. Here the Algerian person joins the Algerian people, and makes up the Algerian nation.

This is a film about national consciousness arrived at through gradual rites of initiation. But in Borhan Alawiya's 1974 *Kafr Kassem*, blood joins history and national identity in one first, final and horrific blow. This Syrian film, made by a Lebanese, shows Palestinians, the inhabitants of Kafr Kassem, caught in unknowing infringement of an unexpectedly imposed curfew, gathered together and mown down by the guns of the Israeli army. Opening with an assessment of this act in an Israeli court and then flashing back to the village before the massacre, the film's impact does not lie in surprise, suspense, or even in sudden horror. It depends instead on its own internal dialectics. Historical and sociological data are not free-floating. Village trivia quiver in the air like butterflies and one grotesque act, the murder of all, is set up against so many little acts, so much gossiping, singing, swearing, sweating, that the scales seem overloaded with life. Death cannot come. In fact, by beginning his film with acknowledgement of the final massacre, Alawiya makes every little detail leading up to it seem inordinately significant. He constructs the perfect realist film, all details contained, wholly, within the context, and the context drawing its blood from all these little acts.

Or, to put it another way, one act is set up against many, and many lives up against one death. One reason these last three films, Egyptian, Algerian and Syro-Lebanese feel so real is that life's data – documents, faces, events – are not allowed to appear as they might in life, in random alternation or in haphazard, bland accumulation. A dialectic of contradiction and counterpoint is set up. Culture orders the data of nature and, ironically, the result feels real. It even feels natural, and that is because by now readers and audiences have become accustomed to this kind of construction, the pattern of the nineteenth-century novel or the classic Western film. But what is real for instance, about seeing a man running for his life on the screen but always held in a close-up frame, or about switching from a shot of stagecoach to Indians, to army fort, and back to stagecoach again?

As Christian Metz, the French expert on filmic signification, puts it, 'What demands to be understood is the fact that films are (actually) understood.'[11] Some might say, does a Moroccan peasant really see that way?[12] Of course not, no one actually sees that way, viewers simply are accustomed to conventions naturalized over time. Even in Arab popular literature there is an example of this kind of structure. The Egyptian adventures of Baibars are full of parallel events in space, flashbacks in time (in cowboy film terms, 'meanwhile back at the ranch . . .') and suspenseful delays over details followed by resumed speed through summing-up (in detective film terms, 'so now we know that X could not have . . .').

Metonymy and Metaphor

This, then, is the realist strategy: relating the detail to the plot, the part to the whole, it is a metonymic relationship. One of its manifestations in cinema is the point-of-view shot. A fragment of reality does not really register unless it is placed in the story, the diegesic context. Unless, in other words, one of the film's characters is known to be looking at it, giving it real existence within the film. Normally, this construction lies low, pretending to be natural, and so it usually seems. In Yusuf Chahine's *Cairo: Central Station* (see chapter 5), however, it is made flagrantly visible. The cripple's whole view of life is disintegrating, so visual fragmentation underlines blatant subjectivity, and with his particular view, the lame leaves the world of the hale, with their general one.

One could also say, the individual leaves society. It is maybe because of this implication that when it is a matter of tearing the seer away from the seen in Arab cinema, it is usually done very gingerly, in a style which attempts to cut and sew with the greatest naturalness, hiding its seams as fast as it can. Of course, it might be more acceptable if the seer is someone who has not yet really joined society, in other words, a child. Like Chahine's madman, a child cannot testify in law, he cannot 'say' anything. In terms of cinema, therefore, his is a privileged position from which to see. In Mohamed Malass's 1984 Syrian film *Dreams of the City/Ahlam al-madina*, the vibrancy of a whole city, of Damascus at a strategic point in its recent history, is brought together through the eyes of a young boy. All the little stories of the neighbourhood flicker on and off as he watches them day by day. The seams between his glance and what is going on are made fairly invisible, there is no real sense of fragmentation, but it is mainly through his vision that the episodic and anecdotal are bound together.

When the child finally does begin to participate in events around him, it is by banging his head so hard against a slammed door that blood runs down from his forehead, over his eyes. The child becomes part of the world not just by watching from outside but by pushing into, and sensing, the obdurate nature of things. Or, in the case of Nouri Bouzid's 1986 Tunisian film *Man of Ashes/Rih al-sadd*, the young boy's rite of passage is through his victimization, through his homosexual rape. Elliptically presented but explicit enough, as in *Kafr Kassem* it is not just the horrific that disturbs, but its counterpoint with its opposites, the delicate, tactile, sensual perceptions of the young carpenter hero. Not only does he caress the contours of the wood he works, but wind, fire and water come lashing into the film also. In the context of the old and formerly cultivated city of Sfax, the senses and the elements battle it out.

Like the explicit point of view, this battle is fairly rare in Arab cinema, which is not awash with the sensuality supposed by nineteenth-century Orientalism. Sensuality can be found only in small dark corners, like the place where the child hero of Hamid Benani's 1970 Moroccan film *Traces/Wechma* hides his box of treasured objects. There, with the kind of fetishism his adopted father shows to emblems of state and religion, the small boy sits in silence and caresses an egg, a feather. Again, though, this sensitivity is set off by violence, and again it is homosexual rape. In this case, the rape is implicit, only metaphorically presented, through the tussel between two birds in the branches above the two boys' heads.

The detour through metaphor here is not surprising, as it is not just a matter of sex or violence but of both together on a subject, homosexuality, treated charily by almost all cinemas. It can be argued, in any case, that violence on the screen is often most strikingly rendered through such analogies. Abdelaziz Tolbi's 1976 Algerian film *Noua* is a good example. Granted, it is shot in 16mm and blown up to 35mm, so its black-and-white images are silted up with a feeling of grit and grime rare in Arab cinema. Granted also, it was shot at a location still unchanged many years after the events it describes, namely the outbreak of resistance against the French. But the power of the film does not come from literal renditions or reconstitutions. In fact, it never even shows an Algerian fighting a Frenchman. Instead, aggression and resistance run all over the screen, as a peasant tries to fight off an invading tractor with stones, as chicken embryos in eggs dashed to the floor struggle in their shells, and as dogs with their throats slit no longer howl to guard the French farms.

As for sex, Arab cinema very definitely relies on a lot of metaphor, whether because of censorship or artistic construction. Certainly in comedy, with its subject substitution all about identities and mistakes, metaphor as a kind of gross category mistake is particularly appropriate. But when it comes to realism, metaphor is usually branded as a literary vestige or as a 'hiding behind symbols'.[13] Analogy, metaphor, and symbol become confused in these debates but what is being deplored is the 'one-off' image: for example, a coffee pot boiling over in the kitchen means passion in the bedroom. But prescription strides in again, with its prepackaged certainty: in realism things should be real, shown directly. But sex is still not shown in Arab films, and it is doubtful if it ever will, should, or could be. After all, what is more exciting, a glance from Bacall to Bogart, or a lot of sweating around in the sheets? The glance is that real fragment which, by the very fact that it withholds the whole, is in sensuous relationship to it.

If one wants to say that metaphor, by its displacement to another level, by its climb up to new connotations, is a rupture of the ongoing discourse, the ongoing story and so a flight from the real matter at hand, all right. But it should be recognized that the ongoing discourse, an apparently innocent line of denotation, is itself stitched out of otherwise arbitrary bits, occurring and reoccurring so that they not only begin to look natural but also take on significance. Take water and a chicken, for instance. Repeated over and over in different contexts in Lakhdar Hamina's *Wind of the Aures*, these two banal details are framed in such a way, with slight modifications over time, as to suggest the mother's gradual disorientation. By the end of the film, the water so freely available in her mountain home is imprisoned in taps, dribbled out at the whim of the French. As for her home-reared chicken, first so hopefully proffered in exchange for her captured son and so often shoved away, it is now a limp carcass. The cinematic means are simple and the message is clear and direct: real war changes the meaning of even everyday things. War as such, however, is not shown.

This ordering of detail, so that a whole picture seems palpable, concrete and real depends on occasional visual fragmentation. Aside from some very banal use of the explanatory close-up (often redundantly underlined by mood music) the visual space in Arab cinema is rarely cut up, and then often in connection with something distasteful. Take, for instance, the fragmentation of the human image in Omar Khlifi's 1972 Tunisian film *Screams/Surakh*. In the opening shots, there are strange, hesitant, or sudden movements of hands and feet, and one has the impression that the body they belong to is not quite right. Indeed, it is that of a young girl who has been raped. She has been looked at and attacked in part, as just so much flesh, and her conception of her total self, her integrity, has broken down and splinters, in its turn, the whole screen space.

Another striking example of this strategy is in the 1972 Kuwaiti film, Khalid al-Siddiq's *The Cruel Sea/Bas ya bahr*. The struggle and defeat of all the hopes of a young pearl diver is a symphony of cacophonous images; décor is dismembered as much as bodies, and walls, floors, ceilings, hands and fingers all spin around and flash on and off the screen. This last effect is due to a very vibrant montage, as one fragment is set off against another, whilst any whole, stabilizing, reassuring context is withheld for as long as possible.

This also is rare in Arab cinema and it could be thought that these two techniques, dating back to an older type of cinema, that of the silent screen, and that trend influenced by the theories of Eisenstein, are no longer acceptable to most Arab film-makers, if, indeed, they ever were. Certainly, the association in Arab cinema of visual fragmentation with the dubious or insalubrious seems to be maintained by the way in which Egypt's 'new realists' are using the close-up shot. Cutting up the body itself, or rather gazing at one part or the other in detail, might conceivably be seen as fetishism.

In Khairy Beshara's 1987 Egyptian film *The Necklace and the Bracelet/Al-tauq wal-aswira*, for instance, the camera pans slowly, closely, up the neck and cheek of a mother; later in the film, when the daughter has grown up, the camera will adoringly climb up the same neck, on to the same face (the same actress plays both roles). But the camera's caress cannot stop the story, each woman dies in horrible torture: of the head. This kind of irony appears also in Mohamed Khan's *The Wife of an Important Man*. An 'important' policeman who feels the world belongs to him gazes in erotic fixation at parts of his secluded wife: around and over one of her feet and later, almost studiously, at one of her earlobes. But when dismissed from his 'important' job, he staggers out of touch with all context, with all reality, and when he takes his starving wife out for what might be described as a 'Pyrrhic' feast, the camera now shoots, in ultra close-up, each bite of food; morbid and macabre, like carrion, lifeless bits of matter.

Egyptian realism old and new

What does one shot of one piece of food mean? 'The iconic enunciation,' writes the French critic François Jost, 'lacks a grammatical criteria which would permit it to signify the difference between transcription of reality and discourse on reality.'[14] If the camera is not used to pick and choose parts of the scene and put them into relationships of significance with each other or the context, what will? Since the first 'talkies', this role has been more or less taken over by the speaking person. If on the screen a single shot of a house seems meaningless, everything changes if a voice says, 'This is *my* house,' or 'This *was* my house.' Then that person is only one of a group who can all go on to talk, or even argue, about their houses.

This, it would seem, is the Egyptian version of realism – that is, if one judges from the films of the man known as 'the father of Egyptian realism', Salah Abou Seif. It is true that he has been judged guilty of the occasional slip into metaphor, but in general his films are so lively that no literary device would ever slow them down. It is people, not signs, that count. 'I might be the only director,' said Abou Seif in an interview with the Tunisian critic Khemais Khayati, 'who has known how to translate the "Egyptian personality" as it appears within reality, a personality which is not made up uniquely of costumes but of situations and sentiments.'[15] The point about costumes is particularly relevant as, no matter what the setting, his characters are never 'faces in a landscape'.

If anything, they are faces in society, faces engaged in constant games of give and take, in which the camera dips into the particular only to come bouncing back into the general. Because of this, some of his best films have already been mentioned in connection with the socially loaded genres of comedy (chapter 4) and melodrama (chapter 5). In fact, very often overtly demonstrating how economic conditions keep people glued to one level of society, some of his films can seem class-bound. Assistant in 1939 to Kamal Selim for *Determination/Al-azima*, which was known as Egypt's first realist film because of its inclusion of classes absent from the Arab screen until then, Abou Seif has continued to include these classes, particularly the lower middle class, sprinkling the screen with a multitude of their stories.

But, to be fair, Abou Seif's films are more complex than that. Where more mediocre directors would line up the good–poor characters against the bad–rich ones, Abou Seif stirs them all up. His 1975 film *The Liar/Al-kadhdhab*, though not one of his best films, is a good example of the tasty brew he makes. As a young reporter becomes fed up with the lying and posturing of the media world, that of the newspaper and of cinema too, he wanders off into a poor neighbourhood to live and experience a more authentic life among the people. The irony is that not only does he find liars and cheats there too, but also by disguising his own real identity, he is as guilty as everyone.

This is in fact an interesting aspect of some of Abou Seif's films: no one is really innocent. Often the hero himself has to descend into sin before he can rise above it. In *The Bully* the hero has to use hypocrisy and treachery, and in *A Woman's Youth* he has to descend into voluptuousness and sensuality. There are no glasshouses here; the corollary is that since all participate to some extent in vice, a catharsis must be a general one to be effective, and Abou Seif's films often end with whole neighbourhoods clamouring and crying out. In *The Liar* they advance on the camera, shouting 'We will talk!' Furthermore, given the date of this film (1975), the audience knows, by analogy, that the confession in question concerns not just the film's characters but all of Egypt, uncovering the hidden shame of the Nasser years.

And all of Egypt is usually the subject of Abou Seif's films. He likes to see all strata of its society interact, whether the film is set in a poor neighbourhood that the rich control and strut around in or is set, like his 1959 comedy *Between Heaven and Earth/Bain al-sama wal-ard*, in a stalled lift, with the rich in eloquent discomfort, wedged tightly up against the poor. This device, that of the social microcosm, which is familiar in Western cinema too, with its shared panic in crippled aeroplanes and sinking ships, is also used by Salah Abou Seif's son Mohamed Abou Seif in his 1988 *River of Fear/Nahr al-khawf*. Again all the national types are gathered up to interact in an enclosed space. Falsely accused of a vicious crime, a young man becomes hysterical and hijacks a Nile river bus. After lots of social interaction he finally proves not just his innocence but his real purity and humanity, and society takes him back into its arms.

Such an ending assumes, of course, a fairly cohesive society, for all its squabbles and class differences. It is a kind of Egyptian metonymy, with the individual fitting back into society if only to signify the coherence of that society, and Egypt's age-old integrity as a nation may explain why this kind of realism is largely absent from the cinema of younger Arab nations. It assumes a lot of elasticity, and there are those who say that Egyptian realism is now becoming even better because it is including on the screen the new classes from Sadat's laissez-faire (*infitah*) economy. Plumbers who have made good deals in the new building boom now enter previously sacrosanct territories, in society and on the screen.

Not only that, but any one of the new young actors, the 'generation of the star who lives next door',[16] could actually pass for a plumber. Gone are the glossy matinée idols limited to heroic roles. Roles are changing, new faces are grinning on celluloid and society/film is putting on weight. Or, is it becoming unrecognizable under its rolls of fat? How are film-makers to represent realistic behaviour, in totally new conditions?

Sometimes new conditions can be so disorienting one might as well be in a foreign country. For this reason, to step out of the belly of Egypt and get a little perspective, it might be helpful to mention two classic approaches to documentary, two different ways in to non-fiction reality, that of Flaherty and that of Grierson. Assuming there was a kind of primitive social integrity in farflung places, Flaherty would start with the centre, with the milieu, and then work out to the expected behaviour patterns. Grierson, on the other hand, filming some very evanescent moments in the British scene, would instead start with behaviour and work back in to the environment it logically created.

The distinction is schematic perhaps, but what would this mean in Egypt? Abou Seif, who knows the centre is there, has been doing it like Flaherty. The new Egyptian realists, who are perhaps not so sure, might be doing it like Grierson. Either the centre is not holding, or there is just no sense of it being there anymore. In Bechir al-Dik's 1986 *Journey's*

Road/Sikka safar, for instance, there is sliding in and out, not only from the Egyptian village away to work in the Gulf, but a slipping around of criteria, as people's motives are muddled by sudden and unexpected opportunities for wealth, for everybody. The village is breaking apart before anyone is even leaving it. In the same way, in Mohamed Khan's 1986 *Return of a Citizen/'Awda muwatin*, the wealth the older brother has brought back from the Gulf to his siblings in Cairo does not enrich the family circle and allow it to bloom in place. Instead, it tears it apart as each member of the family goes off on his own to realize dreams which in films of the 1950s or 1960s would have been prevented by lack of material means, as well as by a strong sense of moral propriety.

But if traditional relationships are decomposing, new relationships will emerge. The story of two housemaids in Mohamed Khan's 1988 *Dreams of Hind and Camilia/Ahlam Hind wa Camilia* would have been perfect melodrama material: each girl alone in the world and at the mercy of occasionally sordid masters or mistresses. But this film is not so; as the country girl and the city girl meet on their errands and chatter together, they weave a friendship which invents a whole new relationship, a whole family together, just the two of them, a sisterhood unusual in Arab cinema. Despite rough times in their environment and signs that they might be deluded, their own behaviour is so creative that when one of them has a child, a daughter by a fly-by-night lover, they call her Dreams (*Ahlam*).

Traditions die hard, though, as do old film conventions, and though the girls are basically honest, they do have to cut corners occasionally. But when the stronger, more steadfast of the two, Camilia, pockets one or two things that are not hers, she is rapped on the knuckles by at least one Arab critic, who finds it 'not consistent'.[17] But is that not the point about realism – the little aberrant detail proves the naturalness of the whole, making it look non-schematic? Also, part of the fun of realism is that the genre flirts with both slice of life (*sample*), and larger than life (*example*). However, there is in Egypt some disquiet about the new tinkering with traditional expectations and models, and one option is to point to Khan's foreign training (in the UK) and imply that he has smuggled strange forms back into Egypt. Certainly he sometimes does go a bit far, as in his 1982 *Half a Million/Nasf arnab*, in which his camera follows a timid bank clerk on the trail of a thief and into his world of crooks, both banal and odd. The whole exercise is voyeuristic, a kind of extended point of view, suspensefully held just a little out of reach of what it sees.

Camera

If there is one thing most people are sure about, it is that in the new Egyptian realism the camera itself has come back within reach, back into and on to the scene after many years of absence. This is not just a question of arid formalism, a bit more angling here, a bit more movement there. What seems to be happening is that the camera is an increasingly active participant in the current voyage beyond the secure and closed society of an older realism.

A particularly eloquent example is Atef al-Tayyeb's 1983 *The Bus Driver/Sawwaq al-autobis*. This film is a good example on all counts of Egyptian new realism, satisfying even that most basic of supposed criteria, being about the 'right' subject, and 'showing' the right people: the lower classes as well as some of the new social groups, the post-Sadat opportunists. But as the bus driver tries to get help from his better-off brothers and sisters to rescue their father's business and morale, the faces, places and stories begin to rise up and swirl around him in a nauseating circle of excuses and rationalizations which have as much to do with the splintering of the family as with the illusions of each of its individuals.

Foreshortening, parallax, all the canons of 'good' film-making are wilfully disregarded. This is not some expressionist game: the shabby flats and the crowds crawling all over the alleys are shot by a camera that is on the same journey as the hero and never lets go of his sleeve, a kinetic camera on a restless search.

Egypt is helped not only by some of its talented new cameramen (Sa'id Shimi, Tarek al-Telmassani, Mohsen Nasr) but, ironically, by the fact that the old studios are crumbling from neglect and no longer provide convincing décor. In Algeria there have never been real studios capable of building artificial sets. Everything is 'real' to start with and will simply be cut up according to cinema's mechanics. As Yusuf Sahraoui, one of Algeria's best cameramen said in 1982, 'The cameraman must become impregnated by a space which he will necessarily have to close, by framing.'[18] But like his Egyptian counterparts, when the Algerian director Merzak Allouache made *The Man who Watched Windows/Rajul wa nawafidh* in 1984 he went against the grain of 'correct' practice by circling around and around a dinner table, against the frame, to show what? an extended space? No, not at all, to show a restricted space. The family are finishing their meal, sitting in front of the television. They are not necessarily watching the television, or even watching or speaking to each other, or in any other way constituting a group, a family circle. Not at all: the camera goes around and around as if to pull them together, but all one sees is how apart they are. Moreover, the camera's persistent movement only increases the static, glaucous, still-life impression.

In Syria too, now, there is some play on 'the real' by the very mechanisms which supposedly ensure its perfect analogical image. In Ussama Mohamed's 1988 *Stars of the Day/Nujum al-nahar*, for instance, within the same frame a close-up on video of two children's faces very within the same frame a close-up on video of two childrens' faces very much at odds with the overall feeling of the wedding. This is metonymy with a punch! One image against another, or maybe 'reality' talking back to 'realism'.

Sample film: *Save What We Can*

Sa'id Marzuq's 1985 *Save What We Can/Inqadh ma yumkin inqadhuhu* is an Egyptian film which drags the naive one-to-one concept of cinematic analogy deep into the world of dialectic, as the camera and 'reality' perform a little tango. Broadly speaking, the story is about two young Egyptians who meet on an aeroplane returning to Cairo, and thereafter go in opposite directions: he into corruption, she into social commitment. His corruption is of the 'wine, women and song' variety and at his house towards the end of the film she has to be rescued, from 'a fate worse than death', by religious zealots who, like the US cavalry, arrive just in time. But 'the story of the film' is not the film, the real story is written in the film's cinematic figures.

If one could say that, visually, *The Bus Driver* plays the circumference off against the middle point, *Save What We Can* plays the foreground off against the background, a dynamic largely neglected since the Arab cinema of the 1960s. One facet of this is Marzuq's discursive use of depth of field. In several different scenes, as alliances are made and broken, the idea is conveyed visually by the forming and re-forming of triangles in space. As two people in the foreground converse, the odd man out marks the eyeline in the distance, but as opinions change and allegiance is shifted, one figure in the foreground moves back, out, and is replaced by the man who is now in. Not only is this unusual in a cinema whose space has been flattened out like that in a television studio or a US whizz-bang linear action tale, but also by seeing these couples forming and re-forming, emphasis is put on the one major couple, hero and heroine, which could have been formed, but never is.

There are barriers of all kinds here (social, economic, and so on) to the forming of this couple and so Marzuq literally uses barriers in much of his framing, shooting from behind a variety of obstacles: walls, columns, grillwork and, most significantly, people. The long tracking shot at the beginning of the film, when the heroine arrives at Cairo airport, follows her on a straight trajectory as she moves through the formalities, but she is seen only from behind the crowds who surge around her, between her and the camera. This is not simply a partial, fragmented, realist feeling; it contrasts with shots of the hero who lounges, full face to the camera, in the VIP lounge. He is a man with connections, and others clear away anything that might block his way.

It is as tedious for the heroine of modest means to get through time as it is to get through space. This is indicated by another technique, as Marzuq exploits montage rather more than is usual these days. As the hero and his friend speed away from the airport into various flashbacks, and then back into the present, guffawing over their various memories, it comes as a shock to see the heroine still in her taxi not far from the airport, blocked again, this time by traffic.

Marzuq does not always use the usual realist convention of continuity by contiguity, in other words, the idea that what one sees after a shot actually happens after that shot, with its usual corollary of cause and effect: that one sees afterwards what really happens because of what one saw before. Instead, Marzuq often organizes his scenes according to spatial principles, exploiting the *plan-séquence* more than is usual in Arab cinema. For instance, several sequences are shot in an L shape: the camera makes a short entrance into the depth of a room, followed by a long horizontal pan along it, creating an L, two of the four sides of a rectangle. The next scene is often related not chronologically or causally, but semantically and spatially. In other words, it is the same argument one had just heard, but argued in reverse, in the negative, and is shot as another L shot, only in mirror image, the other two sides of the rectangle. Thus, as both sides of the rectangle are explored in expanse and depth, both sides of the argument are also set out. It thus becomes clear that the sides are not only contradictory but also strangely complementary, adding to the complexity of what some had seen as a fairly partisan story.

But it becomes clear that Marzuq is using the camera to highlight the dialectics of reality when he exploits the circle, the 360 degree angle. An example is one of the scenes towards the beginning of the film, when all the viewer can see is . . . nothing. There are obstructions, sails are lowered, masking whatever is going on behind them. But muffled voices are heard and music, and it becomes clear that someone is starting to dance behind those sails. While the viewer becomes increasingly impatient to see, the camera begins to pan horizontally along the sails then, at last, reaches into the space behind. In deep angle shots, all the way around, 360 degrees, we see a girl dancing on a boat. It is not only a tantalizing dance, it is seen from every angle and every point of the compass. The tension induced by a desire to see had been so intense, and the revelation is now so total, that this must rank as one of the great dance scenes of Arab cinema.

Another aspect of the circle, its representation of a closed, self-referential system, is suggested in a couple of scenes involving the religious guardian of the hero's old family palace. At one point he trots around in a circle, parroting the axioms of English grammar, at another point he trots around again, this time mouthing axioms of religious piety. Here the circle confirms the axiomatic, and vice versa. As Giles Deleuze writes, the use of the camera-pen (*caméra-stylo*) exploits the 'necessity inherent in relationships of thought *within* the image' more than the older and more conventional 'contiguity of relationships *between* images (themselves)'[20] (my emphasis). So, if they were to read the message as it is written here by the medium, perhaps those who criticized this film as conservative, anti-West, pro-Islam, would realize that a film is not a thesis,[21] and realism is not 'show and tell' on screen.

Conclusion

So now, twenty-five years after Marzuq's noted critical demands for more realist films, are there any realist films in Arab cinema? If the 'real' means data, everything out there – in life, in its haphazard, unstructured state – yes, that does turn up, but either floating in some unsuccessful 'realist' film, or, more interestingly, in films trying to express relationships of the unconscious. If, however, 'realism' means a particular genre which integrates such data within life's experiences, within a story, yes, there are at least two versions of this in Egyptian cinema, the old and the new.

But does the new version of Egyptian realism simply mean modern accretions: new faces, new classes, new phenomena? Yes, but perhaps it means even more, and is similar to one of two dialectical forms in which Islamic history and Arab literature have expressed themselves. In the older versions of Egyptian realism characters (though often in changing and dynamic relationships) are mainly identifiable as parts of an integral society, much like the perennial Islamic vision of community (*umma*). In newer versions of Egyptian realism, though, that society is fragmenting and splintering, nearing the asocial nightmare of a particular moment in Islamic history, the time of civil strife (*fitna*). Furthermore, like the Arab literary traditions alluded to in chapter 3, these two versions of realism seem to look in different directions: the older, a centripetal vision, attracted to the centre; the newer, a centrifugal vision, drawn outwards to the periphery.

Many commentators have spoken of this schizophrenia as a reflection of Egypt's abrupt socioeconomic transformation. But as the French scholar, Michèle Lagny writes, 'History interrogates film as document, not on the realities of a society, but on the representation which it [that society] gives of itself.'[22] Realism, like any genre, is representation, a construction, whose codes are aimed at particular significations. Broadly, metonymy is used for denotation, metaphor for connotation, though the better the film-maker, the more he can blur this distinction. The positive aspect of the realist form is that, through metonymy, it can display exciting shifts in relationship between man and his environment. In its best examples it is existentialist, not essentialist, it does not allow the part to stay long enough anywhere, in the whole, to be catalogued and pigeon-holed.

In tired and hackneyed examples of the form, it is just the reverse, with the 'right' part always returning to the 'right' place. But if the metonymic phrase is thus limited, what of the theoretically unlimited associations of metaphor? Same problem, well-worn and limp symbols are just tossed in. These days to put some punch back into the old Egyptian realism two new methods have been tried. The first is that of accumulation: the piling up of new classes, new faces, new actors; it is a mechanism supposedly broadening the social scene and bringing it more up to date, making it look more 'real', or 'new'. The other method is acceleration: frantic action is invented and people are pushed and pulled around at a terrific pace, in order to make the film look, it has to be confessed, like the realist films imported from elsewhere.

The problem seems to be that this realism still is a genre championing monocular vision, with a nineteenth-century author still fitting all the pieces of the puzzle together to signify its 'natural' look. But by now so many Arab audiences know from experience where the pieces will go that the picture in the puzzle no longer looks natural. Does that of new realism look more so? This is almost beside the point. As the Russian formalist Tomachevski argued in 1925, 'realism' is simply the label all the latest, most contemporary artists claim for themselves. If 'realism' sprouts perennially, 'This phenomenon is always explained by the opposition of the new school to the old, in other words, by the substitution of old conventions, perceptible as such, by others which are not yet perceptible.'[23]

But whether a convention is perceptible or imperceptible has to do with a reading of the image and here it could be thought that Arab audiences would actually be ahead of some others. They are accustomed to scan the screen to see if all the 'real' items are in place, and what 'unreal' (metaphorical) ones stand in as substitutes, to be hurriedly transcribed. They thus 'read' well. But, if they are to catch up with some of the best new realist directors, transforming, if not actually subverting monocular vision, they will have to learn to read differently, paying attention not to the over familiar objects and faces *seen*, but to the unfamiliar ways and processes of *seeing* them. They will have to learn to read the writing of the camera.

7. Sound

'Every lover of musicals,' writes the American critic Leo Braudy, 'has heard the complaint that musicals are unrealistic and the viewer gets embarrassed when people start singing and dancing.'[1] When faced with an Arab musical, a Westerner unfamiliar with this particular genre might feel both embarrassed and frustrated. Subtitles, when they exist, do not extend to songs and, to most Western eyes, the sultry dance is apparently arbitrarily tacked on.

It is ironic that to the Egyptian bourgeoisie of the 1940s and 1950s these musicals seemed the very mark of modernity and of the American way of life.[2] The old-style musical has faded out, but in Arab films even today there is a song here, a dance there, and still plenty of talk. Why this perennial blooming of sound and movement?

Functions

In his analysis of American musicals, Braudy contends that the songs and dances of Fred Astaire and Gene Kelly were not just decorative but also functional. Can the same point be made in relation to Arab film? Songs and dances that seemingly materialize out of the blue hardly seem functional. Yet Salah Abou Seif, otherwise known as the 'father of Egyptian realism', slides song and dance in and out of his films as both conspicuous performance and functional act. If dance, for instance is often exploited as implicit seduction for the film viewer, in Abou Seif's 1955 *A Woman's Youth/Shabab imra* it acts also as explicit seduction within the story itself. Not only does the landlady, shot in angles from above and below, entice the young student by dancing for him, but this dance, filmed as a circular movement around him, suggests the spinning of a web.

This type of dancing, called belly-dancing in the West, can also occur in public celebration; in the context of a wedding Abou Seif fits it into his 1954 film *The Bully/Al-futuwwa*. Waiting for the bridegroom, the women dance in one room, the men sing in another. The groom, meanwhile, is struggling to get out of a locked cold store, and the scenes of dancing, singing and struggle – intercut in a crescendo of suspense and panic – feed off each other's frenzy.

In his 1954 film *The Monster/Al-wahsh*, Abou Seif pushes these narrative and performance inter-dependencies even further. As the police wait outside an inn to make an arrest, their accomplice dances inside. With the camera cutting back and forth between them, suddenly the pace is cut. The dancer stops for a kiss (very unusual in such scenes) and it is clear that breaking into the dance's rhythm is almost like suspending the whole story.

In Atef Salem's 1959 *Struggle on the Nile/Sira' fil-Nil* the story almost does stop. Because of the particularly erotic undulations of a dancing woman, the male crew of a Nile boat become so absorbed that the boat simply runs aground with a crash. On the other hand, in Yusuf Chahine's 1960 *Lovers' Call/Nida al-'ushshaq* it is as if the end of performance would mean death. The film's opening scene is a seductive dance which, when it ends, initiates a killing. This start–stop pattern then leads into film rhythms dominated by the dancer's restlessness, and space and perspectives setting off her legs.

In each of these films, dance is not just present as some incidental Orientalism but is intertwined with the film's chronology, playing itself out in relation to narrative developments, in diachronic terms. But what of the songs? Nothing seems less diachronic, less flowing, than these monologues that seemingly stop the story in its tracks. There are, of course, such metaphors as love songs sung in rose gardens, but in his 1954 *Love Taxi/Taxi al-gharam* Niazi Mustapha provides something more compelling, shooting lurching swings and roundabouts in deep angles from below and above as the hero sings of his vulnerability to the vicissitudes of fortune.

In general, however, the interplay between story and song is sufficiently cohesive that any dependence on visual props would be gratuitous. Often song and story have a parasitical relationship to each other. In Henri Barakat's 1952 *Song of Eternity/Lahn al-khulud*, two of the hero's main songs, lovely as they are, are ineffectual on their own: they cannot enter into the story until questions have been asked about their narrative reference. To which of two women are the love songs dedicated? that is the question. Or, which music are they fitting into? That is the greater question, since the film is not just about the singer finding the right girl but also about his finding a muse for truly Arab music. In this kind of film, song and story take turns opening up the narrative space.

But if song can work in close tandem with story, a word, or a few words, if declaimed insistently, can often contradict or reroute it. This is the effect of the heroine's 'No!' (*la!*) as she runs along with the city crowds in Chahine's 1973 *The Sparrow*. Ostensibly 'no' to Nasser's proffered resignation after the 1967 defeat, it is actually 'no' to everything swallowed by the Egyptians in the film (and in life) up to that point. So famous is that 'no' that in Sa'id Marzuq's 1985 *Save What We Can* the film's end is marked by the very same 'no', amplified by loudspeaker, uttered by a girl about to be raped, or, Egypt about to be defiled.

In both of these films, it is woman, as clear personification of Egypt itself, who cries out and redirects the narrative. But this role can also be played by a man if he is emerging from some sort of heedlessness. Thus in Hussein Kamal's 1971 *Chatter on the Nile/Tharthara fauq al-Nil*, an ageing bureaucrat rouses himself from a chronic hashish stupor to shout out, calling on Egypt to rise up; in Sa'id Marzuq's 1977 *The Guilty/Al-mudhnibun*, a tainted school principal does the same. Even the new Egyptian realist directors use that final cry: Bechir al-Dik's 1985 *The Flood/Al-tufan* ends as a young musician emerges from his isolation to call for an inquest into his mother's death.

The allusion, again, is to Egypt, in this case the death of Egypt: though many films are heavily larded with discussions of politics and other serious matters, it often seems as if only another register of speech will suffice to convey a caring, or patriotic message, only one which is sung, as it were. Of course, there are films in which a nationalist message is explicitly articulated in song, one of the foremost being Ahmed Badrakhan's 1966 *Sayyid Darwish*. Taking as its subject the life of a great Egyptian nationalist singer of the first part of the century, it is organized along lines familiar to viewers of comparable Western films. One sees the boy growing up and groping for the right music, hesitating between European classical music and Quranic intonations, but eventually finding the Egyptian folk and popular forms which he will reshape into rousing nationalist anthems.

The idea of an artist hunting for the right form is a theme which often turns up in the films featuring Farid al-Attrache, a Lebanese singer of Egyptian cinema fame. Is Farid, in Henri Barakat's 1956 *Shore of Love/Shati al-hubb* a serious actor or a dissolute entertainer? Answer: he will have to deal with his family before one knows for sure. Can Farid, in Mahmud Zulficar's 1965 *Out of Paradise/Khuruj min al-jenna* write music as seriously as his wife composes poetry? Answer: she will have to leave him so that out of despair, he will. Can Farid, in Henri Barakat's *Song of Eternity*, find the right music? Answer: the right girl will have to be found and (almost) die first. Even in Yusuf Chahine's 1956 *Goodbye to Your Love/Wada'tu hubbak*, admittedly one of his bread-and-butter films, the question is, can solitary, egotistical Farid sing about brotherhood? Answer: yes, but he will have to die on the last note.

Why all this kitsch romanticism: art or love, art or life? Here, the accusation that Arab musicals were borrowings from Hollywood musicals may well be true. The reason is that such dichotomies do not normally appear in Arab films, even in other musicals. Moreover, where there are dichotomies – the either/or choices so dear to melodrama – these are always stated in moral, not in teleological terms.

The role of the artist is much more interesting in two films starring Oum Kelthoum: Ahmed Badrakhan's 1940 *Dananir* and Togo Mizrahi's 1945 *Sallama*. In both of these the great Egyptian woman singer known as 'star of the East' (*kaukab al-sharq*) emerges from a simple Bedouin background as singing shepherdess to become an entertainer at court, articulating sophisticated ideas in eloquent Arabic, and in song. This is more than the 'little country girl making it in the big city' or the 'artist torn between extremes' of Western cinema. There are extremes here, but the point is that the artist bridges them. The dichotomies slide beautifully into each other: from desert to city, from ignorance to knowledge; this is the accepted genealogy of the Arab nation and of Islamic civilization. Through transformation in types of articulation, a clear sense of historical realization supports the narrative direction. Among the types of articulation are a Bedouin dialect[3] and a literary Arabic, indications of the peculiar situation of the Arabic language (see page 35).

Today, the term 'musical' is used almost exclusively of Egyptian films. But that does not mean that music is absent from other Arab countries' films, far from it. Even though intimidated for years, perhaps by the long chain of Egyptian films featuring one singer or another,[4] music stayed in the background of most other Arab films, and was used more or less as a token of regional differences. Nowadays, however, in North Africa such music is no longer simply folkloric: it has been shaped to please the young of Paris as much as those of Algiers or Casablanca. Like 'rap' songs, the music is often strident and subversive, thus when the Algerian director Sid Ali Fettar called his 1987 film *Rai* after the music of the same name, some of the music's punch might have been expected to enter the story. But it did not; short passages were simply inserted into empty background spaces.

Far more assertive and taking the opposite tack in his 1980 film *Trances/Ahwal*, the Moroccan director Ahmed al-Maanouni dug deeply into the eclectic origins and electric effect of the music of Nass al-Ghiwane, a highly popular Moroccan group. Though the film is a documentary, its kaleidoscopic form conveys how vibrantly Arab music is lived: from stadium performance to religious trance. This can be said of the music of any Arab country and Samir Zikra's 1986 Syrian film *Events of the Coming Year/Waqai' al-'am al-muqbil*, which makes the same point, will be dealt with in some detail at the end of this chapter.

If Egyptian music is foreign for Moroccans or Syrians, the irony is that even in Egyptian films there is often foreign domination of music. In older Egyptian films, especially, Western music slunk in through every open door, 'background music' being a very large door. Chahine even used Hollywood motifs in knowing and provocative counterpoint with Arab music. In more ordinary films, however, there was a pretty clear hierarchy: Western music for mood, Eastern for exposition, that is, Western melody at one point, Egyptian song at another. Even Barakat's *Song of Eternity*, whose subject matter is whether Farid will find the right Arab music, bundles in music by Tchaikovsky for the romantic mood moments!

Another classic example is Niazi Mustapha's 1956 *Quay Number Five/Rasif nimra khamsa*, in which the hero's fights take place as great waves of Western suspense music ebb and flow, though the narrative line is directed by a performer in a bar, who sings once to warn the customers of the arrival of the police, and later to cover up the noise of another fight. In this film the idea of divulging or withholding information through song is particularly mordant as the film's only witness to a murder is a mute woman.

Tensions

Silence and speech are not simply opposites in the Arab/Islamic cinema tradition, they are also like an amorous pair, constantly enacting the nuances of their relationship to each other. Gesture beckons to song and song to gesture, and film is full of the courting devices of delay or contradiction. A foreigner, bewildered by long garrulous scenes, or sudden patches of song, must not expect a purely linear narrative, with its interplay of action and reaction, chronology and causality. Arab films are often structured by means of tensions, not functions, by means of synchrony, not diachrony. The closest analogy in Western cinema would probably be the duos, trios and quartets, of declaration, contradiction and rebuttal so masterfully orchestrated in films such as Orson Welles' *Citizen Kane* which, in the 1940s, shocked and baffled a public accustomed to speech by one person at a time. Though in Arab films voices are rarely allowed to speak concurrently, none the less tensions lie in the harmonies and dissonances within different registers of language, different circumstances of performance, and different manners of articulation. It is not so much a matter of what is said but how it is said.

In some films there is even a battle between the written and the spoken word, which is not surprising perhaps in a culture very attached to books, and in particular the Book (the Quran). This battle often appears in melodramas, one example being Hassan al-Imam's 1962 *Sins/Al-*

khataya. Its hero, Abdel Halim Hafez, sings and laments throughout the film, wondering why he cannot remain in the bosom of the family in which he has grown up. The matter is not resolved until toward the end of the film, when his mother presents him with some documents, written revelations about the shady circumstances of his birth. Though singer and song were present and active, words already written and sealed, seemingly coming out of nowhere, are needed to identify the problem, to legitimize it, and so enable it to be dealt with.

The same point is made, but in reverse, in Hussein Kamal's 1971 *Chatter on the Nile*. Dipping his pen into the ink at the film's beginning, the ageing bureaucrat whose youthful political activism has been dulled by despair and hashish begins his report. The first lines are visible and legible, but as his voice-over drones on and as the pen scratches away, the page remains largely blank. The ink runs out, and so no words are visible, but his pen scribbles on regardless. Loss of lucidity means loss of licence to write.

But this film is no single-focus melodrama: the droning voice and blank paper are just one of its many forms of expression, others being the singsong ditties of the hashish addicts and their burlesque homilies on economics, history, and so on. Most of the other addicts are public personalities of screen, the press, the law, and so on, and thus the question of the legitimacy of their words hovers close to the film's surface. Furthermore, true to the film's initial dichotomy between the spoken and the written word, the film's pulsing spell of insouciance will at the end be broken only by words written, all too lucidly, by a sober young journalist.

With all its different versions of expression and performance, this film conveys a delight usually only found in comedies where scrambling of speech is just one of many 'mistakes', and is the law, not the exception. There is enormous expressive range in Arabic, so what can be scrambled is anything from a literary language (*fusha*) at one extreme to vernacular or colloquial languages (*'ammiyyat*) at the other. The result often brings to mind the sociologist Ibrahim Amr's description of Egypt's outdoor cinema: 'ritual disorder, mixing, like the Egyptian dialect, the most elaborate forms with one-off idioms, a structured sense sweating its effort and its history and a parasitical commentary'.[5]

A good example of the use of mixed idioms in comedy is Helmy Rafla's 1955 *Nights of Love/Layali al-hubb*. Though Abdel Halim Hafez again sings throughout the film, his eloquence is in competition with that of his sidekick, a master of jokey language as well as of ornate literary flourishes. Then there is the girlfriend's mother, who pulls bits of classical Arab poetry out of thin air, to the distress of her pedestrian husband. With the right sense of comic confusion and collision, these different articulations roll around like so many billiard balls.

To an Anglophone, these forms may seem somewhat like the regional or ethnic accents in the US, or those of class in the UK. But they reach further. According to Abdellah Bounfour, in search of a culture shunted aside during centuries of foreign domination, the Arabs of today often see two alternatives: a 'purist and ethnocentrist' tendency on one hand, and a 'digestive' more cosmopolitan tendency on the other.[6] Moreover, since some of Bounfour's most notable examples of the second, 'digestive' tendency are figures from the ninth century AD (al-Jahiz and Abu Nuwas) the terms 'purist' and 'digestive' should not be confused with those of 'traditional' and 'modern'.

An example of the digestive tendency is Fatin Abdel Wahhab's 1958 *Isma'il Yasin in the Navy/Isma'il Yasin fil-ustul*, in which the rough and tumble of comedy satirizes the rigidities of both modern and traditional verbiage. Isma'il is flanked by two buddies each possessing his own speech idiom. One speaks flippantly, off the cuff, with a new line for every new girl, the other soberly intones holy writ for every situation, though changing his reference book (religious precepts for navy manual) when necessary. Oblivious of these extremes, Isma'il muddles through a middle way, and into the arms of the desired girl. But she also is flanked by extremes, on the one hand, a docile, inarticulate father, and on the other a shrew of a mother who, when crossed, goes into trance-like fits. The film is not a musical, but plays on speech and rhythm are so much a part of its construction that verse and trance seem not far removed from song and dance.

Not only does the digestive option highlight extremes, it also undermines them by sliding words from one context to another. What does courtship mean in *Nights of Love*, for instance? It means that Abdel Halim Hafez sings to his love, the sweet young girl, about his love for her. But he also sings to an old gentleman, choosing exactly the right old songs that are sure to please him. This he does to escape jail, and because his tactic works, he receives from the old man what amounts to a royal pardon: courting . . . courtship . . . courtier.

Though implicit here, play on words is such a dominant principle in Arab film that it cannot help surfacing from time to time in the form of riddles. 'What can the eyes say to each other?' says the Bedouin to Sallama. 'The eyes . . . the eyes . . . the eyes . . .' she begins, 'when an eye sees her beloved, she talks to him lovingly. . . .' she replies. This riddle is of particular interest here because just before Sallama's reply she had been singing a dirge, beginning over and over with the words 'oh eye, oh eye' (*ya 'ein . . . ya 'ein*) in connection, of course, with crying.

In many cases words seem to levitate above signification, only momentarily fixed to shifting contexts. In *Chatter on the Nile*, when the young addicts want to display their delight at the bureaucrat's protracted draught of hashish, the expression they use is, 'oh eye, oh eye'. So here the words express pleasure, not pain. In fact, in Arabic there are not just plays on polysemy, on multiple meanings for one word, there is a phenomenon called *addad*. This is a word, or even a sound such as 'oh' which means both one thing *and* its complete opposite. So, when watching a film with a sung 'oh . . . oh . . .' going on and on, the thing to know is that this may mean either ecstasy or agony, and the fun for the audience is to drag out the suspense as long as possible.

This phenomenon mischievously clouds quality judgements, with the effect of maintaining Arabic's elasticity. For instance, the word for 'tune' (*lahn*) also traditionally meant 'improper Arabic' and one of its modern derivatives (*malhun*) means both 'incorrect' and 'poetry in colloquial Arabic'. And singing poetry in colloquial Arabic is what we last see the hero of the 1982 *Shame/Al-'ar* doing, as he dances an unsteady shimmy in a wobbly canoe. He is by now totally deranged, but his little ditty is not the last thing one hears. Another voice admonishes him. Echoing from above and beyond, we hear Quranic verses (Sura 91:7–10) being intoned to clarify the film's moral; that is, a transcendent register of language materializes to dot the *i*'s of an immanent one. Moreover, the words of the Book are not only used to confirm the film's message, but through rough rhythmic, syllabic and rhyme matchings the medium of one recalls that of the other.

This device of a heavenly voice heard at the film's end is used in three films of the 1980s scripted by Mahmud Abou Zaid and directed by Ali Abdel Khalek: *Shame*, *Hashish* and *The Run of the Beasts*. This device is new to Egypt's usually secular cinema, but despite the ideological reservations one might have, it is interesting because it seems to occur in a kind of counterpoint with two other types of articulation: a very tedious discursive base (law versus science, for example) and lots of episodic, singsong poetry, little 'singing in the shower' songs. Not only is this singsong language a kind of third option between literary and colloquial registers, but sung here by actors, not singers, it also pulls performance into life.

Performance

But are performance and life so very different one from the other? Is the persona so different from the person? In a culture which does not articulate this dialectic through figuration, through painting or masks, for instance, it often seems displaced into bodily or verbal expression. How, for instance, is the large javelin-like stick, carried by the peasants of Egypt, used in Atef Salem's 1959 *Struggle on the Nile*? Not only thrashed about in violent fights between men, but also held high and horizontal when the men dance, and even captured by a woman and flaunted provocatively. Below in the crowd, in the meantime, children dance too, but like adults, not like children. In fact, it can almost be said that in a good Egyptian film like *Struggle on the Nile* individual performance, collective celebration, imitation, seduction and even fighting dissolve into each other, into the same rhythms.

There are films in which, as in some of the old Hollywood films, a character's professional performance and spontaneous act are set up in contrast to each other. In Hassan al-Imam's 1972 *Watch out for Zou Zou/Khalli balak min Zou Zou* for example, Zou Zou and her university friends, full of vitality, break into song and dance irrespective of time or place. But when it appears that Zou Zou pays her university fees by performing professional belly dancing with the family troupe, she is deemed an inappropriate match for the rich, young theatre teacher. Hope and vitality sag until she makes the proper choice, giving up her profession for the teacher. Actually, however, this facile moral ending hardly holds, the film's dancing having swirled around in so many forms, surfacing as seductively in her own dreams as in men's fantasies, that both 'bad' and 'good' become equally volatile.

By and large, in Egyptian films it is more usual to have an avowed alternation, back and forth, between professional dancing and the spontaneous act, between persona and person. Though Atef Salem exaggerates more than a little in his 1973 *The Back Stairs/Al-sullam al-khalfi* by having no less than seventeen musical sequences, it is a good example of such films, representing all the singing and dancing (and starving and stumbling) going on in a large block of flats. Neither simply inserted performances nor psychic mirrors, these sequences often serve to link the various stories, and the whole is finally pulled together when the young singer in a jazz group serenades the girl on the balcony above. The performance may indeed be cliché, but it includes and sets off spontaneous responses from assorted servants and wives in the surrounding kitchens and bedrooms.

But is a serenade always a cliché? It does, as Braudy admits, often embarrass audiences of musicals. What if its actual performance is elided, as it is in Hussam Eddine Mustapha's 1987 *Bird in the Sky/Tair fil-sama*? In other words, what if the man sings to the girl about his love for her, but not staring into her face, breathing into her eyes? In this film Imam al-Bahr Darwish (son of the famous nationalist singer) runs around hills, gardens, pools, cavorting with his girlfriend while his voice-over sings the appropriate song to her. One is spared the eyeball-to-eyeball encounter, but also cheated of some very interesting performance dialectics.

An example of such dialectics is given by the seated, strumming, singing Mohamed Abdel Wahhab at the end of Mohamed Salem's 1963 *Ultimate Joy/Muntaha al-farah*. Of course, one can say that his song works and produces pleasure because it is the long-awaited song at the end of a sort of shaggy dog story: a film about getting a long-awaited song by . . . a man who was, and still is at 80, the epitome of the Egyptian composer/singer. Still, the performance might well seem redundant, as the song has nothing in particular to do with the non-story. But redundance, as described by Roman Jakobson[7] and echoed in the Arab/Islamic tradition, is the play of the pleonastic (*ziyadah*) against the concise (*ijaz*) and of the explicit (*zahir*) against the implicit (*batin*). Applied here, in Abdel Wahhab's performance, there is both exaggerated expression of desire and desire's containment, there and then, through that one expression only. Also, though the song's words are clear, the context is absent, so signification is held in suspense; by both giving and withholding at the same time, the film achieves a result that is electric.

Perhaps because most of the dialectics lie within performance, within the act itself, there is in Arab film a continuum in which speech, song and dance slide easily back and forth, in and among each other. This may be close to what Michel Fano (who was responsible for the sound for Robbe-Grillet's films) had in mind as desirable for speech, noise and music: 'some way of thinking them other than in isolation, in discrete terms'.[8]

But how, within such a continuum, does one pin down signification? Song and dance express what, on behalf of whom? Are feelings expressed in song because in life they cannot be expressed? How much does the other person really hear, anyway? Sometimes while being sung to, they look away in a vague manner and the song, which would seem the epitome of monologue, becomes dialogue, with the singer responding to his own pleas by the other's assumed rejection. There is also another possiblity: that the song, as monologue, is a refusal of necessarily banal or formulaic dialogue.

In Salah Abou Seif's *The Bully*, for instance, it is embarrassing situations that are papered over with formulaic repetitions. Not only when the penniless peasant greets his equally penniless city relatives does one hear, 'How are you, how is the family, how is your mother, how are you, how is the family . . .' over and over. Out on a picnic with his girlfriend, all the hero can find to say as endearment is 'How are you . . . how are you . . . ?'. As they walk along, trying to devise a plan to market produce fairly, real passion is heard below them, expressed by peasants singing poignantly about their land and its fruits. Finally, when they come up with a plan, it is by inadvertently listening to a *mawal*, a poem in colloquial language sung by an old café poet.

In this manner, by alternating circumstances, and playing formulas off against feelings, background against foreground, the collective against the individual, the modern against the traditional, Salah Abou

Seif assures both a continuum of sound and a density of signification to be found in the best Egyptian films.

What of films from other Arab countries? There is often plenty of music but it is projected differently. There is a notable absence not only of singing stars but even of on-screen individual performance. In Nouri Bouzid's 1986 Tunisian film *Man of Ashes/Rih al-sadd*, the one person who sings to camera is someone marginal, an old Jew who used to be a family friend before (political) 'events' broke up a once-cosmopolitan society. Actually, in North African films song is meant to cement recognized, already existing social relations. Song and dance occur at times of communal celebration: religious festivals, circumcisions and, above all, weddings. Weddings are particularly favoured perhaps because they are so clearly moments of transition, in which an individual moves from one state to another. The lengthy scenes of preparation in the bath house, and of make-up and dressing, seem to prolong the suspense, much as when an Egyptian singer lovingly prolongs the ambiguous words 'oh . . . oh . . .' before opting for a song of pleasure or pain.

Because what is transition if not a moment between extremes, or a moment even when extremes are mixed? Again, an Egyptian parallel might be the scene of masquerade in *Nights of Love* when, for a brief moment, the hero is neither pauper nor millionaire, neither inside nor outside society. But if for an individual this moment is ambiguous, it could also pass off as invisible were it not made visible by public show and declamation. So, it might be danced by all in a North African film, just as it is sung by a singer in an Egyptian film. In this sense, one sees vestiges of the Rabelaisian world described by the Russian critic Mikhail Bakhtin, in which:

> Everything that is in man is expressed by action and dialogue, in him there is nothing which would exist only for him and which cannot be 'published'. . . . On the contrary, everything which is in him only acquires its full sense by being expressed.[9]

So, in marriage ceremonies, what one sees on the screen in various North African films are group celebrations, with group singing and group dancing. Admittedly, these are single sex groups, with men in one room, and women in another, but if it is assumed that all experience this moment as equivocal, it is not surprising that the range of expression is so wide: from the staid, traditionally dressed matrons in Jilali Ferhati's *Reed Dolls* to the more frenzied, Western-dressed women in Abdellatif Ben Ammar's *Sejnane*.

But if communal expression dominates, is there no room for the private feelings of the individual? Usually not; the bride's face is painted and, like a doll, she does not speak. Emotions are expressed at another time, in another way. In *Reed Dolls*, for instance, the heroine's feelings and frustrations are articulated almost as a frame for the film, in melancholy songs at its beginning and at its end. These songs, however, are not seen to be sung by the heroine; they are sung off-screen, by a woman's voice intoning what can be assumed to be a general sense of unease, experienced by the women of Morocco.

This North African reticence about individual performance is noticeable in stories about men too. Using music by Nass al-Ghiwane, the group featured in *Trances*, the Moroccan Ahmed al-Maanouni also opened his earlier film, *Oh the Days, Oh the Days/Al-ayam, al-ayam*, with a doleful, off-screen lament. Presumably, again this was an expression not simply of individual distress but of general unease, since the film's young peasant recounts the ordeals of his generation in the Third World. He has difficulties making a living on the farm, but cannot get away to earn a better living elsewhere. That this story is narrated in the first person allows him to express some individual feelings, but this is largely because the film is basically a documentary. First person narration or even voice-over is a technique used only very selectively in Arab film.

Voice

Everything stops for a moment in blankness in Farouk Beloufa's 1978 Algerian film *Nahla* as Nahla starts her song with the word 'I' (*ana*) and cannot go on. Seemingly aping an Egyptian-style film revolving around a singing star, this film actually highlights three Lebanese women talking to, around and over a listening Algerian journalist. This kind of interplay between the consciousness of two different Arab nations is rare on film. Furthermore, as the film's background is a Lebanon falling apart, a song beginning with 'I' is clearly a little unseemly.

The narrative voice itself is treated with some reserve in Arab cinema. Often in Egyptian films a voice-over by the narrator is an indication of some sort of diminished mental condition. This is true for the droning voice of the hashish addict in *Chatter on the Nile*, and also for the voice of the young peasant in Atef al-Tayyeb's 1986 *The Innocent*, muttering and mumbling army slogans as glibly and naively as he does village pieties. And in Nabyl Lahlou's 1984 Moroccan film *The Soul's Braying/Nahir al-ruh*, the voice-over is simply that of a donkey, though a very shrewd and bitter donkey.

Full of songs beginning with 'I', it would seem that most Egyptian films largely steer clear of any other narrative voice, whilst other Arab countries use a personal narrative voice only when a personal crisis can be somehow associated with a collective crisis, like that of the disaffected peasant in *Oh the Days, Oh the Days*. In Borhan Alawiya's 1982 Lebanese film *Beirut, the Encounter/Beirut, al-liqa*, a young Christian girl and a Shi'ite boy, friends from college but now separated by the city's divisions, record their feelings and memories on to cassette for each other, as if monologues could be transposed into dialogues and the city be cajoled back together again. In Michel Khleifi's 1981 Palestinian film *Fertile Memories/Al-dhikrayat al-khasibah* it is two different types of Palestinian women who speak out. They not only reconstitute, in speech, their absent and invisible country but they also complement each other to the extent that as woman, the country seems as present in the kitchen of one as in the study of the other.

But Palestine as woman, is that not a problem for women? Despite Khleifi's sensitivity, the image of woman, as Laura Mulvey writes, is 'still tied to her place as bearer of meaning, not maker of meaning'.[10] This viewpoint is apparently shared by the two Arab women directors Lebanon's Heiny Srour and Algeria's Assia Djebar. Women should be seen on screen not just to be, or to speak, but to act, and to act meaningfully in history, as indeed they have in reality. In Srour's 1984 *Leila and the Wolves/Leila wal-dhiab*, mini-dramas are re-created to show the audience what women did and how they felt about it. Their feelings are then amplified by scenes of symbol and metaphor, supposedly originating in women's fantasy not in men's, and this is all extended back over time and throughout the Levantine space.

For Djebar, space, outside space, is one thing that Algerian women have not yet conquered.They are still enclosed creatures. Attempting to liberate them, in her 1978 *The Nouba of the Women of Mount Chenoua/Nouba nisa al-djebel Shnua* she has them tell stories, stories connected with their own activities against the French during the war for independence, and stories of their grandmothers in similar circumstances in the previous century.

The woman who listens is more liberated, a young woman from the city, and this allows Djebar to work out some musical counterpoint: the young heroine is backed by traditional Algerian flute music, but when the old peasants dance the soundtrack plays Bartok's 'Algerian Pieces'. This, Djebar points out, is because 'the more a woman is traditional, the less she needs to lean on folklore'.[11] Maybe, but in this film there is no counterpoint from men; the only male in the film, the young woman's husband, is mute.

Though it is normally dominant in Algerian films, the male's voice does not usually narrate. Narration is perhaps thought of as the natural role of the enclosed woman, at home. But looked at and talked about like an object, almost as a woman might be, Ali speaks out in Ahmed Rachedi's 1979 *Ali in Wonderland/Ali fi bilad al-sarab*. As a migrant worker in Paris, he seizes the narrative initiative and tells the viewer what he sees in France and what he thinks about it, unknowingly initiating an increasingly complex play between viewer and viewed.

An even more startling use of narration by a man occurs in another Algerian film, Merzak Allouache's 1976 *Omar Gatlato* (see chapter 3 for details). Though Omar can be said to speak for his generation, narrating the cause of the one as that of the many, it is a post-Revolution youth, lolling about without a cause, and the tone is not simply humorous, it is self-derisory. And self-derision goes beyond the dusty roads of denotation into the muddy bogs of self-doubt. This is precisely what Arab film, or even Arab culture, is in need of, says the Syrian director Samir Zikra: a little dose of Rousseau.[12] In fact, 'Confessions' is what he first thought of calling his 1986 film *Events of the Coming Year/Waqai' al-'am al-muqbil*, in which various people walk in and out of the hero's flat, trailing their tales of illusion or disillusion behind them (see the study at the end of this chapter).

But normally in Arab film, the idea of confession bears connotations of the insalubrious, of the criminal. (An example is Sa'id Marzuq's 1977 Egyptian film *The Guilty/Al-mudhnibun*, in which confessions of other, lesser, crimes are accidentally elicited by a police inspector investigating a murder.) So it is rare to have a whole film dominated by confession, but in Merzak Allouache's 1982 Algerian film *The Man Who Watched Windows/Rajul wa nawafidh* an ageing bureaucrat rambles on and on. Confessing what, to whom? That is kept open and never quite settled even by the film's end: voice and image at times accord, at times not. When confession comes into film, therefore, there is the risk that the voice is hiding as much as it is revealing: it is not the voice of denotation, of information, it is the voice of impressions and feelings, and in these exceptional Syrian and Algerian films it is a voice perhaps parallel to the 'I' so flaunted in Egyptian song.

One voice, certainly, is rarely heard in Arab film: the explicit authorial voice. But perhaps matching fantasy of approach to fantasy of subject, Merzak Allouache opens his 1978 *Adventures of a Hero/Mughamarat batal* with the words 'Once upon a time . . .', after which the hero, bent on salvation/revolution, charges through the myths of the world, and of cinema. Considering the great Arab storytelling tradition, it might seem strange that in other films the authorial voice is so resolutely shunned. This might be from a desire to make of cinema a very separate art, or from an idea that a performing hero and a storytelling voice is cinematic overkill, or it might be from so precise a concept of storytelling that it does not bleed out into anything else.

In some films, though, there is a commanding voice that does come from elsewhere, if not directing the narrative at least giving it its period political colouring of the 1950s and 1960s. This is the voice of Gamal Abdel Nasser, or of Egypt's famous radio station 'Voice of the Arabs', and its use is not limited to Egyptian films. It figures in Yusuf Chahine's 1958 Egyptian tribute to the Algerian revolution, *Jamila/Jamila al-jazairiyya*, in Borhan Alawiya's 1974 Syro-Lebanese *Kafr Kassem* and in Mohamed Malass's 1984 Syrian *Dreams of the City/Ahlam al-madina*. In all of these, the voice from Cairo sets out the parameters which will, in some way, affect those in the film who sit and listen to the radio.

The radio, as a speaking, interfering presence in the home, is nowhere so deftly used as in Mohamed Bouamari's 1972 Algerian film *The Charcoal Burner/Al-fahham*. It speaks to the husband about politics and it sings about love, and gives recipes, to the wife. It marks not only the space between husband and wife, but the silences between them also. Furthermore, using another dimension of sound, the piercing silence of the charcoal burner's primitive home in the woods is heard through the sounds of frogs, crickets, and creatures of all sorts.

This is unusual in Arab cinema: background noise, when used, usually stays in the background. Of course sound effects may soon become more prominent, as the new Egyptian realists are trying to tone down speech and song and bring out the environment in an effort to achieve a more naturalist effect.

In Arab films psychological effects are traditionally conveyed by pouring spooky music over suspenseful glances or over close-ups of evil deeds. That has been the usual Egyptian solution but in this too the North Africans are more innovative. Part of the power of Moumen Smihi's 1975 *El Chergui* lies in its evocative soundtrack. In a story of abandonment and solitude, the ticking of a clock resounds and reverberates while women's greetings are heard as meaningless, speeded-up gibberish. And in the 1981 collective Algerian work *Human Interest Stories/Ahdath mutanawwa'a* sound itself scratches and tears at raw nerves. In the first story of the quartet the nerves of a man back home after torture by the French have become so fragile that a dripping tap sends him into shock, and the incessant screaming of his child leads him to silence the infant for good, to smother it.

Sample film: *Events of the Coming Year*

What does sound have to do with a film introduced by the Sufi saying, 'Petrified knowledge is absolute ignorance'? This is the puzzle worked out in Samir Zikra's 1986 Syrian film, *Events of the Coming Year*: oral clues will eventually support his written statement.

With its constant hum of music, for instance, the film conveys a sense of music's omnipresence in the Arab world. Zikra shows, first of all, that sometimes that music is 'real', it is very obviously coming out of a radio, or many radios, and if it finally becomes important to hear someone talk, the radio can be switched off. Sometimes, on the other hand, the film's music is dramatic, the music is obviously in the head of someone, following him around from place to place.

Another reason that music is all over the place is that it is being performed by many different people. Not only are there the inevitable records of Mohamed Abdel Wahhab, Oum Kelthoum, and Feiruz (a famous Lebanese woman singer) on the radio, everywhere and all the time, but unknown people perform, here and there. In a cabaret, there is some vulgar and banal singing, in a restaurant some timid and folkloric tunes sung by a young Kurdish waiter and, in a bus, a perturbing medley by a shellshocked veteran that ends with the evocative and ambivalent plaint, 'oh night . . . oh night . . ' (*ya lail . . . ya lail . . .*)

Not only does music surround and pervade all the film's events, but it runs along in continuum with the film's dialogue. In fact, the dialogue is often 'performed', just like music. In other words, there are people whose speech is so familiar it sounds like an old record. This is particularly true of the hero's rival, a rather frenetic leftist whose sloganeering in a restaurant scene bleeds right into the mad patter of an insane doctor. There are also those who unconsciously speak in the formulaic constructs of their own countries: the voice-over, in a letter, of an American girl, going on and on about practical problems, followed by the voice-over, in another letter, of a Russian girl suffering from various anguishes of the soul.

How to get out of all this, all these petrified forms, how to think something new? On the level of speech, can one get near anything new with a little self-knowledge, a little confession? Maybe yes, maybe no. One woman, a frustrated old maid, comes to the hero's flat again and again, 'confessing' that she does not really care about men, she is too intellectual, but all the while with her eyes and appetite visibly fixed on his bedroom. Another, the girl he loves, also comes often, but only to say that because of a painful past she does not want to become involved, and she means it.

There is another suggestion in the film: what of inventing your own words? In the hero's *Thousand and One Nights* nightmare, the sultan asks his prisoner to tell him a joke, even if it is anti-regime; the man tells it in silence and then laughs uproariously to himself. None the less, he is beheaded. Why, what did he say? Is even silence dangerous because it is so articulate?

During the whole film, the soundtrack itself is really open, despite *and* because of all the music. Though the story is about a musician trained abroad who returns home to work, to compose, and it shows him searching through channels to be seen and heard, alert viewers will sense that he is also searching for the music that will end the film. The musical principles are on-screen. There is the idea of variations, for instance: one musical motif, the one he bases his dream symphony on, appears several times, in a jazz version as well as in a trumpet solo. Then, there is the idea of recurrence: a second motif from the same symphony is heard being practised by a young orchestra of the blind; this same motif is then heard in his head after a fight, and then again at the film's end, in strains of musicians tuning up.

There are also musical borrowings. At one point, constantly and distressingly broken off by blaring disco music, a piano plays a Chopin prelude. This surfaces later in particularly melancholy circumstances, played by a traditional instrument, the *bezo* (like an *'ud*), and shows, Zikra says, 'how expressive our somewhat primitive instruments can nonetheless be.'[13] Moreover, the ideal composition, the one which opens the film via the hero's daydream, is a Western-type symphony, but based on an Eastern key, the *nahawand* (*maqam al-nahawand*).[14] Finally, the piece he has to conduct, as a compromise, at the film's end is clearly what he had been putting together in his head throughout the film, and is basically a symphonic version of a dance melody from northern Syria.

So variations, recurrences, borrowings, synthesis; these are all musical means of escaping from a petrified knowledge. But the story of the film also shows that when the pompous declaration of theories is always given precedence over any concern with the means of their implementation, absolute ignorance cannot be far away.

Conclusion

The patterning of sound in Arab cinema is not always as complex as in Zikra's film, but the range is still wide. On the one hand, Egypt sings its story, on the other Algeria tells it, or at least so it seems from some of the examples here. Does this mean that Egypt concentrates on description and Algeria on narration? It is probably not that simple. As the French scholar Jacques Berque puts it, 'If the language [Arabic] had only been a collection of information, a tool of communication, it would never have been able, in this role, to resist world languages like French and English.'[15] Though Arabs complain of their own 'verbalism' (*lafziya*), he asks, 'Is this not a matter of compensation which rehumanizes the material aspect of the exterior world?'[16] In other words, both of these film extremes are different versions of rehumanizing, of covering the story's bare bones (*histoire*) with the flesh and blood of story-telling (*récit*). While an Egyptian film might add songs to different manners of speech, the Algerians might pile up narrative voices, public versions and private ones.

Whatever alternative is chosen, usually in the best films there is an underlying feel for the principles of music: of tone in the levels of language, of stress in the alternation of types of exposition, of frequency in the intervals of repetition. Why this should be so marked in Arab cinema can perhaps be partly explained by the holistic concept worked out by the Iraqi artist Issam al-Said.[17] First illustrating the bases of Arab/Islamic design, al-Said goes on to show how, mathematically and geometrically, the very same concepts of rhythm and balance occur in Arab poetry, and again in Arab music. They are not so obsure or unrealistic then, the slides and interchanges, the continuum between speech, song and dance in these films.

Still, seemingly intrusive and digressive, there remains the problem of the static scene: the story says 'go', the song says 'stop'. Ironically, though sound is the most linear of all film ingredients, in Arab film it can sometimes appear almost perversely anti-linear. Looking at Arab/Islamic art, however, again we see that this is how calligraphy is described: as an art that works on the interplay between the static and the dynamic,[18] between the 'stop' and the 'go'. Then also, calligraphy uses not only the three visual dimensions but also a fourth, that of movement.[19] So, enter dance. . . .

But what of repetition? Are there not lots of love songs, lots of protestations saying the same thing, over and over? Writing about the choice between invention or 'replay' in classical Arab literature, the Moroccan scholar Abdelfattah Kilito not only points out that 'repetition is the guarantee of the very life of speech',[20] he also evokes the vertigo induced by one of the main props of Arab culture and Islamic civilization: the relayer of tradition.[21] A good example of this occurs in Mizrahi's film *Sallama*, where the same words are repeated over and over – 'They say al-Qass loves Sallama' – by women talking, girls singing, men singing, children chanting, al-Qass himself; finally, Sallama sings about it. At this point, by evoking all the previous performances, and sung with the acknowledged mastery of Oum Kelthoum, the words have become a work of art: by repetition acquiring the patina of authenticity, but played off against multiple senses of *déjà vu*.

This replay in *Sallama* through speech, poetry and song has another aspect. Much has been made of Arab cinema's teething problems using the argument that the novel was a late development in Arabic literature, so that fiction could not be presented on the screen in those familiar terms. But the Russian critic Mikhail Bakhtin points out that at the base of the novel lies a willingness to pit direct discourse against indirect discourse,[22] what is said against commentary on it, even if such commentary is no more than parentheses, or a change in the tone of voice.

As pointed out in connection with synchronic tensions, these different tones are major operating principles in many Arab films, and are especially noticeable whenever music is concerned. This might go some way to explain why in general the voice-over and particularly the overt authorial voice are so largely eschewed: they might simply be subsumed in the film's already divergent discourses. This might also explain why songs appear so often not just in comedies but in melodramas too: a familiar story is made more exciting by an unfamiliar song. Or, to put it another way, the story's direct discourse might change significantly when supplemented, or even subverted, by an indirect discourse.

8. Sign

The sweet little heroine of *The Princess and the River/Al-amira wal-nahr*, Iraq's first full-length cartoon, directed in 1982 by Faisal al-Yassiri, is quiet but effective. Like the heroine of any fairy tale, she accomplishes the tasks set her and proves worthy of her kingdom. But what kingdom is this? The film's hesitant prince and valiant peasant appear to have more to do with contemporary wrangling over Arab policies and leadership than with ancient Mesopotamia. Do the film's huge edifices and their ominous shadows summon up memories of a bygone Babylon or models from Disneyland?

As for the quiet young hero of Qais al-Zubaydi's 1974 Iraqi film *Al-yazirli*, he has his own personal memories, or perhaps they are fantasies. Like any young boy about to enter a man's world, he watches the struggles of boss and workers around him, but he also remembers, or daydreams. Gritty black-and-white images of his work hauling barrels down to the sea alternate with overexposed, ethereal images of a mysterious woman in a carriage. Is she sexual figure or sister, fantasy or memory? The relationship of these images to the hero is as ambiguous as his own relationship to himself, neither child nor man.

As for the fantasies of the very young and completely silent hero of *Hardboiled Eggs/Al-baida al-masluqa*, one of three sketches in Brahim Tsaki's 1979 Algerian film *Children of the Wind/Awlad al-rih*, the child himself knows that they are founded on an illusion: on a film. While his old and alcoholic father is out peddling clockwork mice on street corners, the small boy goes around the local bars, selling the eggs he has cooked. One of the bar regulars, propped upright but lost in a fog of beer, is Boualem Benani, the star of Allouache's 1976 *Omar Gatlato* (see chapter 3). Despite the evidence of dissolution in front of his own eyes, the boy cannot resist dreaming about Benani as he was, as a movie star; he even fantasizes that Benani the star looks warmly down at him, a preferable father figure, a model, an illusion.

The boy's silence is perhaps not surprising: all the children in Tsaki's films are silent, and almost all his films' characters are children. In this film, in relation to the past, to memories, dreams or models, the silence is particularly significant. It is as if, in stilling conventional discourse, it would be possible to get back to something else, something with which children supposedly have not lost contact. But is this necessarily so? Does one have to assume some kind of pristine innocence in order to bypass the here and now? Cannot adults also bypass the politics of chapter 3, the society of chapter 4, the law of chapter 5, the reality of chapter 6, and the language of chapter 7, and dream a little . . . ?

Madness

Well, as fools or madmen they can, of course, and there are plenty of these in Arab films, though they are not all the same. A fool might be a fool in name only, as in Allouache's 1978 *Adventures of a Hero/Mughamarat batal*, a man who speaks about portents and miracles when it is convenient to seem possessed, but is otherwise quite capable of telling things as they are. Or he may be a lone and wily soul, like the fool in Tewfik Saleh's 1955 Egyptian film *Alley of Fools/Darb al-mahabil*, living off the community's piety by mumbling religious platitudes which happen to fit every circumstance. On the other hand, he may be a pure-spirited simpleton who sees no harm in saying the emperor has no clothes, or as is the case in Mohamed Chouikh's 1988 Algerian film *The Citadel/Al-qal'a*, in saying that he too wants to have the village prostitute, just like all the 'respectable', married, villagers.

Very often though, a fool or madman is neither bogus nor simple-minded, he is a normal man in some temporary diminished state brought about by past events. In *The Bully*, for instance, the mad beggar had been a strongman himself, before being crushed by his successor. In Mohamed Bouamari's 1974 Algerian film *The Inheritance/Al-irth*, the fool had been smart, the village teacher, before his village was blitzed by the French and he was tortured. As for Mahmoud Zemmouri's 1983 *Take 1,000 Quid and Shove Off/Prends dix mille balles et casses-toi*, he had been in France before humiliations drove him back to Algeria, down into madness.

When it is not a matter of events, of history bearing down in some way, when it is more a matter of the present or the future, there can be an extension across space which seems to imply the breadth of a 'mad' vision. In Souheil Ben Barka's 1972 Moroccan film *A Thousand and One Hands/Alf yad wa yad* the madman crosses the country, muttering and moaning, berating first the plains, then the mountains, and finally hurls his invective against the ocean. Momo, the eccentric in Mohamed Zinet's 1971 *Tahya Ya Didou*, is much more mellow, not moving from his crosslegged position on an Algiers pier, but his vision seems to extend over time; he sees all and knows all, at least about Algiers, and comments both on events just presented in the film and on those that will follow. Not only does this produce a kind of authorial prescience rare in Arab films but he constantly enlarges on the impact of his words by further commentary in poetry.

If a madman has any vision at all, it is usually enunciated in poetry, whether the religious doggerel of the alley beggar or Momo's ode to his city. This is particularly true when the words are portentous and hold the weight of the future. Playing a dishevelled and destitute madman, Mohamed Lakhdar-Hamina, the director of the 1975 Algerian film *Chronicle of the Years of Ashes/Waqai' sinin al-jamr*, has been made visibly distraught by the fact that no one hears him, or wants to hear him. Too bad, the words are thunderously ominous for Algerian man and for his history.

Such visions get dangerously close to the idea of real prophecy, though, and in Islamic films the rules about that are strict (first, Mohamed was the seal of the prophets; second, he can never be represented figuratively).[1] Thus most madmen characters may be raving but it is never implied that they are (divinely) inspired. Nor are they even major characters, except perhaps Algiers's Momo, or in this case one can also say Momo's Algiers, as the man *is* the city, which in turn *is* the poetry. Usually though, the madman is more marginal, a foil for the real world, a half-remembered melody in the head. The words belong to what: history, religion, archetype? At any rate, they are about something that is most definitely off-screen, at the most some figuration in the unconscious.

Like prophecy, the unconscious is quicksand territory in Arab film, and this becomes clear when dreams are concerned. They do not occur often and are not well handled. An exception, already mentioned, is the young boy's daydream in *Al-yazirli*, which is allowed to be both ambiguous and haunting. But when it comes to adults' dreams, such as that of the hunchback hero of Rabah Laradji's 1982 Algerian film *A Roof, a Family/Saqaf wa 'aila*, they are simply and unambiguously wish-fulfilments, and to make this clear, their inhabitants and places subsequently appear in real life. Most dreams in Arab films are actually nightmares. From the surreal spaces in *Brahim Yach* to the humiliations of *Zift* they have to do with real-life battles with faceless bureaucracy or multiform profiteers.

In other words, in most of these films there is a clear feeling that one's real conflicts with such and such a power reappear in nightmares, as is, though in somewhat more alarming colours. Though there is not quite the one-to-one Freudian symbolism of Hitchcock's *Spellbound*, there is the same feeling that anxiety is explainable in terms of real-life events. No unknown structure of the psyche emerges.

One Moroccan film, Ahmed Yashfin's 1984 *The Nightmare/Al-kabus*, does try, through dream, to tackle a particular identity problem: who is the modern Moroccan man? The husband of a determined feminist, the hero already looks out of place in his city house with its murals of Hawaiian beaches and panels of Grenadier Guards posters. Out on a business trip in the Moroccan countryside he gets lost and dreams that he is back in nineteenth-century Morocco, with its idyllic scenery, French occupier, and its arbitrary and oppressive local patriarchs, himself included. He is relieved to wake up after dreaming that his own injustice has brought about the death of his several wives. But the relief is only momentary: he finds the key to the dream house in the pocket of his city suit.

Myth

It is a simple enough allegory. But the effort to deal with what is inside people's heads as memories, fantasies or models, and then to transfer that to the screen is not easy, and not many directors have taken on this task. A notable exception is Algeria's Mohamed Bouamari, who takes on cinema stereotypes, his own included. His 1979 *First Step/Al-khutwat al-ula* for instance, begins as the actors step forward to have their roles explained and take their bows. The idea of roles is followed up as the film's husband and wife spar at home in scenes depicting what married relationships can be in Algeria, or what they often are in Algerian films, depending on a couple's socioeconomic conditions. The play on present cinema and gender roles in Algeria is augmented by reference to the country's past, and the roles determined by an avowedly patriarchal system. So, intercut with shots of the urban middle-class couple are those of stark and statuesque archetypes: the heroine and hero of epic tales.

Bouamari had already used these same figures from the past along with their schematic desert décor in his 1974 *The Inheritance*. In this film, the Algerians slowly begin to rebuild a country destroyed by the French. Rebuilding is slow because all could crumble again if relationships are not got right. To build on the rubble of beautiful sand walls, for instance, an entrepreneur offers bricks made mostly of straw, whilst the religious authority only mutters platitudes and the army officer speaks in the distant tones of a classical language and, more or less, looks the other way. Despairing of all these authority figures, the wife of the film's 'madman', the former village teacher, must bring him back to his senses. When he is finally pulled out of his autism, his first words point out and identify ruins of previous colonizers, the Romans.

Almost automatically pedagogical, the teacher's words have a broader significance. They have to do with signs, the 'traces in the sand' (*atlal*) motif of ancient Arab poetry. Though Bouamari's approach to stereotypes in history is still unusual, Arab cinema is now beginning to take some interest in archaeology, in its broadest sense. Under the sponsorship of UNESCO, there is now a bi-annual festival of film and archaeology in the Algerian town of Tipaza. It remains to be seen whether this will just be a scholastic adventure or whether the information to be exchanged between scholars and film-makers will elicit fresh imaginative approaches. So far, two projects of interest are emerging: the Tunisian Nacer Khemir's idea of filming the eleventh-century Andalusian classic, Ibn Hazm's *The Ring of the Dove/Tauq al-hamama*, and the Algerian Ahmed Rachedi's project of a film about Leo the African.

In terms of cinema itself, and its own archaeology, there are projects in Egypt to do remakes of two famous films of the 1950s: one of *Cairo: Central Station*, bringing it up to date, and one of *Quay Number Five*, transforming it into a comedy. But the comedy idea is not appreciated by the star of the original film, Farid Chauqi,[2] and in general, the past, whatever it is, is treated gingerly or with sobriety. Most Arab film-makers are content to be historians, getting the names and dates right. Some do not even bother with that. The Egyptian director Niazi Mustapha, for instance, who made no less than six films about the great pre-Islamic hero Antar, always made him look, act and talk like a perfect Muslim. But since the values Antar defended were the same as those later revealed by Islam, the director said, 'I filmed him the way I felt him.'[3]

Not much feeling can be discerned in Salah Abou Seif's 1980 *Al-Qadisiyya*, about the Arabs' ancient victory over the Persians. As a director of lively, modern Egyptian films, Abou Seif is not just on foreign territory, filming in and for Iraq; it is clear that the epic is not his genre. Full of all the sound and fury of *Lawrence of Arabia* and elevated by its enunciation in a classical Arabic that it is doubtful anyone ever spoke, it is as dry as the most banal nostalgia film: tourism in the past, clothes and décor. At least when, halfway through production, Yusuf Chahine took over as director of the 1963 Egyptian *Saladin/Salah al-din* (another story of Arab victory, this time over the Crusaders), he added a new level: theatre. It is a Shakespearian device, perhaps, but war as theatre within war breaks into the film's relentless alignment of events and sets up, on stage, two otherwise separate groups: the bickering coalition of Christians and the cohesive force of the Muslims, thus inducing, incidentally, desirable analogies with Nasser's pan-Arabism.

Aside from recorded events such as battles, very little material from the ancient past comes to the screen. But myths are told and stories are handed down, so how are film-makers to integrate them, or even just display them? In his 1972 film *Yusra*, the Tunisian Rachid Ferchiou tries to portray a mythical figure predating the Arabs' arrival in North Africa, along with a sensuality implied to have disappeared with the myth. But this Swedish coproduction, with its nude swimming and its French dialogue, resembles a European fantasy. The same could be said of another coproduction, the Tunisian–Czech *Ballad of Mamlouk/Sarab*. Directed in 1981 by Abdelhafidh Bouassida, this tale with its black, ideologically determined ending seems more like a cautionary tale from Eastern Europe than a Tunisian story of tasks set and rewards collected. And now it even seems that an Orientalist will have his turn in Tunisia, as the Tunisian director Tayyeb Louichi is to film the famous Arab love story of Qais and Layla not directly from the ancient poem, but from a prose version of it written by the French Arabist André Miquel.

The idea of a film solely guided by poetry does seem hazardous but an interesting example is the 1977 Algerian film *Hyzya* directed by Mohamed Hazourli. Though the Bedouin life depicted in this ballad of long ago looks too pretty to carry much conviction, that is probably beside the point as the full narrative load rests on the spoken word, the poetry of Ibn Guittoun. So effective are the scathing words of rejection the young heroine speaks to her suitor that he actually turns back and she gets her freedom. But what of cinema, as word *and* image? Though there is not space in this book to mention some of the very interesting Arab short films, the Tunisian Moncef Dhouib's medium-length 1982 film *Nest of Eagles/Nid d'aigles* is a neat parable on this subject. With the local storyteller's death his place is taken, in accordance with tradition, by his son. But his son is a mute. Never mind, the stories must go on, so the son makes giant marionettes and carries the stories around on parade, mustering the participation of others as he goes along.

In a not dissimilar way, the 1985 Lebanese film *Maarake*, directed by Roger Assaf, tells the story of the village of that name, storytelling here being combined with theatre, acting-out. In fact, the acting-out is double as Maarake's villagers re-perform both their recent martyrdom in struggles against the Israeli invader in their own streets, and the ritual Shi'ite passion plays about the seventh-century martyrdom of Hussein. These two traumatic experiences are simultaneously co-ordinated through the narration of a storyteller, so that the film is built on the concordance between now and then, between here and there, between experience and tradition. Such cohesion is unusual and it is powerful, but being based as much on religious as on artistic convictions, it is also provocative.

Using a famous story to make a polemical point can also be done with the reverse artistic means, via disengagement from the local scene instead of emergence from it. Taking his characters very definitely out of their own streets, or, as he says, out of locked rooms,[4] the Egyptian director Mohamed Abou Seif, son of the famous Salah Abou Seif, puts them on a desert island in his 1986 *The Apple and the Skull/Al-tufaha wal-gumguma*. It is a story about the birth of evil, complete with a woman and an appletree, and like his father's 1986 film *The Beginning/Al-bidaya* it is about how this necessarily concerns the control of scarce goods. Like his son's film, which is set on an island, the father's is set in a desert oasis, so the argument is neat: as scarcity is definitely a problem in both places. Though the two films' techniques differ, with the father's based on sketches and the son's a vortex of action and violence, the idea is the same: take people out of space and time and see if their behaviour is none the less predictable, like real life, only clearer in the desert/island sun. The interest is not in a never-never land, it is in reality.

Strangely enough, paring a décor down to a minimum in order that symbols will dominate and a message will come across is a technique rarely used in Arab cinema. Salah Abou Seif and some other directors may often lean on metaphor (see chapter 6) but overt symbolization, or parable, is usually avoided. Moreover, to lean on a universally known story like Eve's temptation with the apple is also rare. In fact, one of the few Arab directors to question never-never land itself is the Algerian Merzak Allouache, only his intention is not to support known stories but to subvert them. In his 1978 *Adventures of a Hero* Allouache propels his hero through time and space in order to personify most of the world's hero myths, and shoot them down. Just as he slays the sea monster (and gets the virgin) in one story, he bivouacs with freedom fighters/thugs in another. And when he was born, did not all the right messianic signs appear to announce him?

Memory

This is delicate, 'saviour', territory and Allouache's satirical approach has had little follow-up in Arab, let alone Algerian, cinema. What of these ready-made stories that spring into any man's mind as he tries to explain what he is doing and why? On the problems of Third World cinema Giles Deleuze, probably thinking of some of the films of the French ethnographer Jean Rouch, writes that the best approach might be to take a 'real man' and have him tell his tale (*légender*) to camera. Yes, but is a real–unreal discrepancy then clear, or is any headway made in trying to identify the tale itself? One Arab director is deeply involved in this problem. Since at least 1976 Egypt's Yusuf Chahine has taken on the problems of memory, dream and model. He seems to be working his way through the problem as stated by Roland Barthes: that there is never any real knowledge of the deep self, only different ways o speaking.[6]

What greater medley of ways of speaking is there than in cinema, even starting with performance *per se*, one of the best performances in a Chahine film being that of Chahine himself as the crippled hero of the 1958 *Cairo: Central Station*. And in some form or another, a performer hangs around the corridors of most of the films he has made since 1976, up to the 1987 *The Sixth Day/Al-yawm al-sadis*. In this, a young man cannot help singing and dancing, despite the smallpox epidemic raging around him. But as in the case of the hero of Chahine's 1978 *Alexandria Why?/Iskandariya leeh?*, this is not just any kind of singing and dancing, it is the Hollywood film variety, something in the air, irresistible, and also likely to make any ordinary man start thinking out his life in the plots of these Hollywood films. This is something Chahine knows a lot about, and something he convincingly shows.

But *Alexandria Why?* also projects performance into theatre: two theatres. There is the theatre of war, Egypt occupied by the British who are fighting off the Germans, and classroom drama, the students struggling to get through *Hamlet* and out into the world, or on to the world's stage. Actually, Hamlet's problem is not so far removed from that of some Arab cinema. According to the French scholar Jacques Berque, it is both 'what to do' and 'what to be' that makes the Algerian film-makers hesitate so much.[7] For this reason Chahine's 1976 *Return of the Prodigal Son/'Awdat al-ibn al-dall* is of particular interest as its hero, at least, has the 'what to be' problem solved: he is the 'prodigal son' returning. None the less, he still hesitates. Fitting into an ancient and well-known biblical story does not suffice. Like most Chahine films, story is layered on to story, one is written on top of another. In this case, there is a story about the nation state with its strong father figure, Nasser, and there is a story about a family, with its weak and reluctant patriarch. As the singing and dancing go on in the present, and flashbacks emerge from the past, the hero simply cannot fit himself into any of these stories, Biblical, national or social.

Here history is a series of events and story, as one way of speaking, seeks to order those events. Yet implicitly they are set up against each other, and in his 1982 *An Egyptian Story/Hadutha masriyya* Chahine adds another dimension by the fusion into his chronicle of that great detective story: the psychological analysis or, looked at in another way, the courtroom drama of the *mélo*. A film director, under anaesthetic for a heart operation, retraces his life to release the child in him who will tell the judge and jury where it all went wrong, and where his real identity is.

'He is still an orphan' is one of the conclusions of the film. Yet according to Morocco's Abdellah Bounfour, it is because of a 'refusal of the status of orphan' that there is in past and present Arab ideology an '"eternal return" to an authenticity motif (*asala*)'.[8] But the authenticity motif and problem of return are not just limited to the Arab world.

Writing about Caribbean cinema Stuart Hall observes:

> It is because the 'New World' is constituted for us as a place, a narrative of displacement, that it gives rise so profoundly to a certain imaginary plenitude. . . . And yet, this return to the beginning is like the imaginary of Lacan – it can neither be fulfilled nor requited, and hence it is the beginning of the symbolic, of representation, the infinitely renewable source of desire, memory, myth, search, discovery – in short, the reservoir of our cinematic narratives.[9]

In classical Arab poetry there is this same dialectic of place and displacement; it exists in the 'traces in the sand' (*atlal*) motif mentioned above. The poem would begin as the poet returns to traces, to an abandoned campsite, and tries to name who was there before him. Long misread as some kind of exercise in description, a search for a tribe, a person, and so on, such a poem is closer to what Hall describes, a manifestation of lack, of separation, of desire. As the classical poem develops, this feeling of incompleteness is assuaged as the poet leaves the desert and enters the state ruled by the perfect prince. All binary oppositions are then dissolved into the now perfect whole.[10]

Such a resolution, however, is no longer acceptable, especially to modern North African thinkers wary of a hegemonic discourse. The Moroccan Abdelkebir Khatibi writes: 'only the Outside rethought can tear up our nostalgia for the father figure.'[11] What he means by this 'Outside rethought' is a discourse which is 'decentred, subverted, rerouted from its dominant determinations': only that can 'distance us from "blind identity" and "brute difference." '[12]

How does decentring operate in Arab cinema? One approach is revealed in Chahine's style: a very lively, almost nervous montage that alternates with long complex scenes shot by a camera sliding in and out of the lights, in and out of the wings, a constant tracing and erasing, at the same time as various stories are being compacted one on top of the other. There is return, return again, traces left, traces over traces. . . .

Figures

As a strategy against the hegemonic discourse then, Chahine's method is one of excess. But another, more austere route is taken by some Arab directors. One cannot really call it lack, in opposition to excess, but there is certainly a lack of paraphernalia, all the little realist details. Not following movements into cars and out of cars, for instance, but refocusing, the camera follows the traces of abstract figures, follows relationships via space or via time. In his multimedia approach, Chahine often sets theatre up inside cinema, but what happens if, in film, theatre is merely the restricting space of the proscenium arch? This idea is explored by the New Tunisian Theatre Collective in their 1978 film *The Wedding/Al-'urs*. This work had already been produced successfully in the theatre, but in the film version the anxieties, and outright enmities, uncovered on a couple's first night together are increased by the pent-up atmosphere in this little box, in the enclosed stage. The enclosed space is then played off against a surrounding space, so that each time the camera exposes some new nook, some previously withheld cranny, this exposure acts like a discovery of some new character quirk. Space itself thus takes over, and eventually consumes the importance of the actors.

As for time, though in literature there may be an interest in origins, few Arab film directors like to delve back into the past, and few Egyptian directors, in particular, have dared to take on their Pharaonic legacy, let alone relate it in some way to the present. Shadi Abdel Salam dared to in his 1969 *The Night of the Counting of the Years/Al-mumia*. Though revealing about Egypt, the film is far from pedagogic; after all, according to this long-time director of Egypt's Experimental Film Centre, 'the term "documentary" has no sense, there are just short or long features'.[13] In *Al-mumia* people circle the past or its traces. There are European archaeologists, local tribesmen, one of them a young man with an uncanny resemblance to the young men of the ancient drawings and reliefs in the ruins. For this young tribesman it is memory, or rather lack of it, and a lack of names, which is disturbing. Not only is he ignorant of his tribe's graverobbing past, but he also does not know whose the graves were, where their names have gone, and why the European archaeologists know them and he does not. As his disquiet leads him to a break in solidarity with his tribe, his mother chillingly declares that henceforth he himself shall have no name.

To mark this place where traces are erased and names obliterated, Shadi Abdel Salam gives identities instead to figures of cinema, to time and to place. Each scene is shot as a sequence and has its own time. Because he considers transition shots to be 'just chatter',[14] there are none, and there is also a studied avoidance of any explanatory insert. As for place, each space is marked either by its own light or its own colour. As a result, the film has an awesome feeling of dimension, each unit of time becomes also its own unit of space, and as in the ancient Arab 'traces in the sand' (*atlal*) poetry, the question 'where is . . . ?' turns out to be the same question as 'when was . . . ?'.

But though to Shadi Abdel Salam transition shots may be 'just chatter', generally they are part of film's dominant discourse and those with less talent omit them at their peril. The end result can appear to be incoherent or, worse, folkloric. As the Moroccan Abdallah Laroui writes, 'Any cultural manifestation . . . which lays claim to the particular in face of the universal, which assumes naiveté, direct intuition, natural life in face of reflection and sophistication reserved for others, falls necessarily into folklore.'[15] In Mustapha al-Khayyat's 1984 *The Entanglement/Al-ouarta* and Mohamed Tazi's 1981 *The Great Voyage/Ibn al-sabil* it cannot be said that any 'reflection' is apparent; all action seems so 'natural' that it ends up as inconsequent. This is too bad, because both of these Moroccan films are about voyage and encounter and, traditionally, dense Middle East forms structure such random wanderings. One is the mystic (Sufi) idea of a voyage beyond self into God, another is the literary genre of the *maqamat*, in which one approaches recognition of the Other, and the last is the Karaguez shadow plays in which the hero of that name meets society in all its forms and triumphs over it.

All that seems to happen in these films, though, is that the eye wanders over the ethnographic variety of the faces seen along the way. So is it true of most Arab cinema, as the French scholar Louis Massignon wrote, that 'God pulls the strings as in a Punch and Judy show. And that is why there is no drama in Islam'?[16] Well, is there not some drama in watching the strings being pulled, or rather in focusing on the strings themselves?

In some Arab films strings or wheels or circles or mirrors very often submerge the viewer within their orbit and toy with him, as well as with whatever hapless Punch and Judy is on screen. Take the wheel, in Mustapha Derkaoui's 1985 Moroccan film *The Day of the Hawker/Le jour du forain*. It is a roustabout's wheel of fortune, used, misused, unused. The roustabout continually comes to a new town, sets up the wheel, people lose on it, lose interest in it, and he loses his reason to be there, so he goes on his way. Is he manipulating the wheel or is it manipulating him? His wandering from village to village is not aimless, it is structured in sequence, like the slots on the wheel. But will the right number come up, as the man himself fades behind the figure of the wheel, and the eventful fades into the habitual?

In Mahmoud Ben Mahmoud's 1982 Tunisian film *Crossings/'Ubur*, it is land, *terra firma* itself, which fades out in the film's very first shot. All light and all vision fade out too as the camera, inside the belly of a car ferry, films the door sliding down, producing total darkness. Two men without visas are on the boat and they will be doomed to shuttle back and forth between foreign shores, between borders, never to get off. One man is East European, the other an Arab, but it hardly matters which is which because the main figure is the circle in which they travel round and round. On every side the ephemeral ship's life of the other passengers goes on, but the action is not there. It is in the circles, as one man tries every door, every exit, every trick, to get out while the other slides inwards, into a personal vortex, into himself.

If the heroes of *Crossings* are lost in a circular space which is wiping out all time, time is stuck also in Jean Pierre Lledo's 1981 Algerian film *Empire of Dreams/Mamlakat al-ahlam,* in which the characters contemplate themselves in mirrors, in camera lenses, in books, even as dummies in shop windows. It is a film about making a film. But who are the heroes, who are the actors? Or, what kind of a film should it be, are there any precedents locally? Or if models from abroad have to be used are those not the roles the actors are living anyway, or think they are living? Where is the persona, where is the person? Or where is cinema, inside or outside the theatre?

Is it all made more clear if a film starts with a little piece of theatre, like Raafat al-Mihi's 1988 Egyptian film *Hurley Burley/Samak, laban tamar hindi?* As in Shakespeare's *A Midsummer-Night's Dream,* roles and intentions are explained, and to follow this up, the film ends with a procession of its characters, donkey's head included. But in between . . . all hell is let loose. In general, this film is about how the Third World is being lobotomized, the better to fit into a world order directed from elsewhere. As could be expected from the title, everything happens in the film, even the dead in the morgue are allowed their soliloquies, that is, when they are not being chased in and out of everywhere by various forms of Interpol. If the film seems a breathless series of surreal and bizarre gags, that is how the director wanted it, 'like shots fired from a gun', said Mihi.[17]

So, if Mihi's film is structured like *A Midsummer-Night's Dream,* that is, on the principle that 'this is crazy, and we told you it was theatre, but it is happening anyway', why not 'gunshot' scenes, scenes cross-cut with hyper rapidity but whose satire is aimed with deadly effect? And in Ahmed Bouanani's 1979 Moroccan film *The Mirage/Al-sarab,* why not theatre walls approaching and retreating from background to foreground, over and over? Like in *The Entanglement* mentioned above, another Moroccan film, a country man comes to the city and finds it disorienting. Unlike the situation in *The Entanglement,* though, the peasant's confusion arises from more than prosaic shock at high buildings and honking horns. On the contrary, in *The Mirage* the hero enters a city which is structured like a great German expressionist film set, with long walls which lean in on him, and a self-appointed storytelling guide who leads him on and off stages, sets and décors, or simply walls and buildings. As the hero tries to follow the exterior labyrinth of the city, his wife goes into her own labyrinth, inside, via the rhythms of dance and religious trance, accompanied by another self-appointed guide.

Tableaux

But is the usual guide, the linear narrative of history, any more reliable? The Moroccan Moumen Smihi seems to examine this question in his 1982 *Forty-four, or Bedtime Stories/Quarante-quatre, ou les récits de la nuit*. 'Forty-four' refers to the duration of the Franco-Spanish protectorate over Morocco and the film presents episodes in the lives over that time of two families, one more or less rich and Westernized, the other poorer and more traditional. Despite this historical structure, the narrative is episodic and what seems to give the film its bite are the three storytelling options which appear in different geographical locations. In the old city of Fez a professional storyteller flatters his audience and tells them traditional stories of Arab heroism, notably of the great pre-Islamic hero Antar. In the countryside, on the other hand, a wild and woolly-looking character, almost the stock madman, tries to fire the Berber people into political action with stories of Moha. Finally, coping in the city with all the cultivated sciences of classical Arabic and Islamic scholarship, a young student none the less acts in a mute version of *Othello*, while Verdi's music rings out.

So, panning not just across history but also across the traces of other narratives, the film seems like a fresco, a story fresco. As in some pre-Renaissance painting, each of the options operates in its own space, with no monologic perspective pulling them together. This refusal to make scenes cohere, whether through Renaissance perspective or narrative linearity, can be risky, and has analogies in serial music. Its enunciations are close to proverbs and maxims. In the prosody of these, according to the French scholar Jean François Lyotard, 'one recognizes little bursts of possible narratives ... this bizarre temporalization which clashes fully with the golden rule of our knowledge: not to forget'.[18] And in Najib Sefraoui's 1985 Moroccan film *Chams*, forgetting is one of the problems. The lovely young Chams appears and disappears, like some evanescent memory, in the mind of the old, tired politician. But who is his wife, who is his son? These other people seem to slip in and out of the narrative too. What are their relationships? Actually, there are at least two options in this kind of film and it seems the director tried both. Most of the film resembles traditional Arab poetry of description (*wasf*) in which it is possible, the scholar Andras Hamori writes, 'that successive emotions in the same person are not only fugitive but also fragmentary, and – being experienced as non-contiguous – unaccountable'.[19] That is one option, but toward the end of the film the director seems to accept another, the dominant discourse of cinema. There is, finally, melodrama's 'explanatory letter' and, with a sigh of relief, the film seems to slip into a more familiar, and more comfortable, slot.

In the 1985 Moroccan film *Hadda*, the director Mohamed Abou Wakar adheres to his principles right to the end: no explanations. At one point in the film, an old man in the corner, glowering out of some cursed existence, cries out, 'May it be damned, your "cause and effect"!' So all that is visible is that slight political waves undulate somewhere as a young son comes back to an almost abandoned estate deep in sand, two ethereal girls wave beautiful scarves about near a patch of grass and a mad/poet figure travails by carrying a great sphere on his shoulders. Tableau follows tableau, form succeeds form and, as for colour, the scarves are red, the grass is green and the sphere is white. Each thing stands out, as thing. If these people are outcasts, there is little sign of any society they are outcasts from. Maybe this is a pristine, pre-social space for the silent child, or an innocent, asocial space for the babbling madman. But perhaps another observation by Hamori, on another version of descriptive poetry (*wasf*), might also be appropriate here. 'The self has retreated; the speaker would keep the poet's give-and-take with the world but without hazarding an emotional investment in the temporal.'[20] From film with no 'emotional investment in the temporal' can an audience derive any memories, gather any dreams, or discern any models?

Sample film: *The Drifters*

Nacer Khemir's 1984 Tunisian film *The Drifters/Al-haimoun*, which ran for well over a year in Paris but was booed at its first showing in Cairo, is an example of the problem of 'traces' in Arab cinema. As one Arab critic, Jamil Hatmal, said, 'The film seems as if it is addressing the Western spectator, even in his own logic, i.e. presenting us to him as Eastern in a folkloric way, or as he wants the East to be.'[21]

'Eastern' meaning what? Mysterious? Or, as the Lebanese critic Walid Chmayt put it, more gently, 'the film unfortunately seems to have no first degree reading'.[22] No clear storyline, in other words. A young teacher goes into an almost deserted village in the south of Tunisia and finds mystery after mystery, absence after absence. Where are the men of the village? They seem to track back and forth across the desert but never return home. Who knows about this? Well, it is in a book, but the book is buried, or a treasure is buried or it is in Sindbad's boat which has reappeared and disappeared, or. . . . Even the government official, who comes in a jeep to clear things up by asserting his rank and making his scribe take down names and occupations, ends up circling round and round in the desert on a donkey. What is he looking for, anyway: Cordoba, the sea, the garden, the genie of the well, death at the gate, Sindbad's ship, buried treasure. . . . ? All of these are in the film, but as traces, in the heads of the schoolteacher, the children, the grandmother, the wise elder. . . .

This is exactly what upsets critics such as Hatmal: the film is all so confused, with the modern bus and the ancient boat side by side. Others have noted that the costumes owe more to Moghul miniatures than to Tunisia past or present. But Khemir says, 'our civilization is Islamic, not just Arab, it is Kurdish and Berber and Moghul, and so on'.[23] He adds, 'the desert is the zone of Arab Islamic civilization and the zone of the search for the gardens, which were Andalusia'.[24] Prodded to demonstrate what relevance all these old references could have for today, Khemir continues, 'For North Africa, Andalusia is *the* lost garden . . . like a parallel sign for all we have lost, Palestine, for example.'[25]

This idea of film's use as medium for a message – political, whatever – does not emerge solely in connection with realist films (see chapter 4). The term 'innovation' (*badi'*) was often used pejoratively in traditional Arabic literary criticism. This is because the purity of language of the innovators, the Moderns, was polluted by cosmopolitan accretions and thus unsuitable for exegetical studies, *ipso facto* useless.[26] Today, for those who innovate in Arab cinema, mostly North Africans, there is a similar tag, 'alternative' (*badil*) and clear implications, here also, that innovation is pointless, without value.

It is pointless, lacking value, as, in other words, displaying only the paraphernalia of a lost, 'Eastern', world: old costumes, old figures like Sindbad. But what is interesting in Khemir's film is that these 'traces' are not just there as décor, as things, as nouns. What gains in importance in the film are the verbs acting on the nouns. For instance, a garden is created in the film, in the desert, but how? Stealing and shattering all the mirrors in town, the children arrange them in neat patterns in the desert. There is water there too, somewhere, but it is sensed only by the sound of splashing which comes through the teacher's window. As for the song he hears, by the time he reaches the window, the singer has wandered off. In other words, all the driftwood of an Islamic civilization has assembled in this desert: fragmented, wandering, forgotten, disappearing, buried. Even as verifiable image the film plays games, a 360 degree angle shot, that great revealer of all context reveals . . . a mirage. As for the text, the words of the film, one story contradicts another, one person's vision of 'signs' and 'return' is immediately falsified by that of another. For this film, 'the story' is still waiting to be told.

Conclusion

'Narrativization of these quests for identity is almost never coded in the classical tradition of conflict, enigma, complication, resolution. Instead of the (Oedipal) drama, there is discontinuity, tableau, apparent randomness and fortuity in the sequence of events.'[27] Is this North African cinema, or is the following a description of the cinema of Chahine? 'The cinema, spectacle, the street, as places where the look is symbolically traded, become privileged spaces that actually structure identity outside the family.'[28] No, both of these are Thomas Elsaesser's descriptions of some modern German cinema, notably that of Fassbinder. But much of the cinema described in this chapter is as preoccupied as that of Germany with 'questions of identity, subjectivity, estrangement'.[29] [For greater detail on the classical option of arriving at resolution, and on the modern one of opening up to fortuity, one can consult Gilles Deleuze's *L'image-mouvement* and *L'image-temps* respectively.]

For Arab cinema, one can compare the cinematic patterns outlined in chapter 3 with those noted in this chapter. The heroes in the former are concerned with resolving their conflicts, here, now, on-screen. Those in this chapter are trying to find signs, traces, a memory, a dream, a model of . . . something . . . from then, from there, most likely off-screen. Is this something essentially Arab? Is there an Arab memory, an Arab dream, an Arab model? If we pursue this question, we encounter the Germans again: the Romantic idea of a *Volksgeist*, the spirit of the people. In Romanticism, the American critic Leo Braudy writes, 'The poet was inspired by what he saw and experienced and the intervention of any prior categories for the experience doomed the work to secondary value unless the forms that intervened were primitive forms – the folktale or the ballad. . . .'[30] In other words, if the films of chapter 8 are Romantic, it is first of all as negation, in opposition to the genres of chapters 4, 5 and 7, as well as to some conventions and 'prior categories' of chapters 3 and 6.

In a positive sense, what does this add up to? Take the idea of the individual poet/film-maker 'inspired by what he saw or experienced'. Take Chahine, who has exposed his sensitivity on the screen, dredging up scenes from his own memory for the general public. As is clear from this chapter, few other Arab directors seem to want to engage in this kind of individual catharsis in their films, even if such an exercise could be said to provide analogies with larger, political, problems. Psychology is resolutely kept at bay; unless it could be said that it is repressed psychologies which eventually surface in the 'madmen'.

On the other hand, what of that other source of Romantic inspiration: 'primitive forms, the folktale, the ballad'? Clearly, some of the films noted here try to work with this lore. But fewer than one might expect actually take the material and rework it. Apparently, one has to have strong convictions to take what has been quasi-sanctified by its antiquity and re-route it through cinema. Even then, the result might be the dubious one of reinforcing some partisan stand, political or even religious.

There is another way of looking at 'primitive forms' and that is as just that: forms. This is what the North Africans in particular seem interested in: structuring contemporary stories within older narrative patterns: episodic, serial, circular, or even refractory. And by refractory I mean works in which signs resist their integration into signification, in which, to direct you, the old man on the road will give you the words, but not the sentences they belong to. Or as the Tunisian author Abdelwahhab Meddab writes, 'I construct figures and I exile them from the events which they have brought about. And I put them on stage in the capacity of signs.'[31]

But how are these signs to be read? Reading signs is precisely the prerogative of religions, and it is interesting to note that in its early history Islam offered, theoretically at least, two ways in which man can arrive at knowledge of God: either through the Holy Book (kitab) and its revelations, or through the natural faculty of man (fitra) to discern God's signs in nature. The first is there for all to see and interpret, in the public domain, and even lends itself to symbolic readings. The second is a matter of personal experience, the book of one's life, a road that can be followed by one person, and only one step at a time. By analogy, one can actually switch the Romantic oppositions stated above. What was private: Chahine and a cinema based on his psychology; versus what was public: North Africa and a cinema based on its folk tales, now becomes: Chahine and a collective cinema, full of the history, stories and myths of a universal domain, versus North African cinema with its personal, private, labyrinths whose forms can only be distinguished from inside, as one inches one's way along, alone.

But these descriptions, based on a Romantic essentialism, keep lapsing into binary oppositions, the 'blind identity' or 'brute difference' Khatibi, Chahine, Hall, the North Africans, and others are all trying to avoid. So maybe it is better to go back and look at the 'traces' (atlal) themselves, not as things, as ruins, or columns, but as evanescent marks. In that case, there are again two kinds, but this time they are not mutually exclusive. The most obvious kind is that of the archaeological site, a place where each passing group has left some sediment. It might be Chahine's childhood memories, added to yours, added to that of your child. It might be Hollywood films, added to those made in Algeria, added to Algerian films made in France. Or it might be Shakespeare in an Egyptian film, theatre as a box in a film from Tunisia, or the city as theatre in a Moroccan film. These are all writings on top of other writings, a silting-up of the written, palimpsests, in other words.

Another kind of trace is that of something being formed, or rather, continously forming and reforming itself, a 'between two things', what the French critic Marc Vernet calls the *status nascendi*.[32] This is a story being told one way before it might just change and be told in another way, a sinuous line whose motion must be followed before its trace can be seen. This is a Moroccan man following the walls of a city at one moment and those of a stage set at another. Or, this is a Tunisian man travelling in a circle, outside in space, until the circle turns inwards, inside in time, into a personal vortex. This is theatrical scenes being fired into the audience in an Egyptian film.

To put this still another way, the first, archaeological kind of trace is of horizontal layerings, the second, serpentine, one of lateral extensions. Or, to rephrase again, the first is a paradigmatic axis, the second a syntagmatic one, and language, it is commonly accepted, arranges its signs with, and through, both these axes.

Part Three

African Film

Ousmane Sembene,
Taaw
(Senegal, 1970)

Ousmane Sembene,
Ceddo
(Senegal, 1977)

N' Gangura Mweze and Benoit Lamy,
Life is Beautiful / *La vie est belle*
(Zaire, 1987)

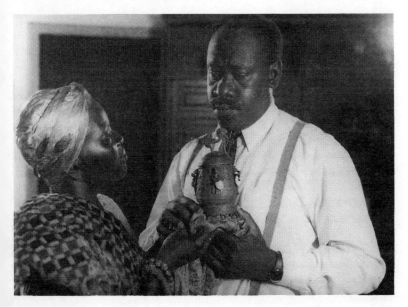

Kwah Ansah,
Heritage Africa
(Ghana, 1988)

Idrissa Ouedraogo,
The Choice / Yam daabo
(Burkina Faso, 1987)

Raymond Rajaonarivelo,
Tabataba
(Madagascar, 1988)

Ousmane Sembene,
Emitai
(Senegal, 1971)

Ousmane Sembene,
Xala
(Senegal, 1974)

Souleymane Cisse,
The Light / Yeelen
(Mali, 1987)

Idrissa Ouedraogo,
Yaaba
(Burkina Faso, 1988)

9. Voice

One starting point for a consideration of African cinema is the concept of voice, which is relevant at a number of levels. First, of course, there is the sense of a right to speak, which was denied under colonialism. Regardless of questions of artistic quality, the mid-1960s films made by black African film-makers have enormous significance in that with them, for the first time, the people of sub-Saharan Africa exercised their right to organize film images and sounds. Hitherto they had been merely the objects of the gaze of Europeans and their cameras,[1] their voices sought only as a contribution to the European codification of African 'traditions', their music recorded solely for the benefits of Western musical anthropology (or, later, Western commercial interests). It is significant that three film-makers chose as symbols of Africa young women who are either literally dumb (Ababacar Samb-Makharam's *Kodou*, 1970, and Souleymane Cisse's *The Girl/Den muso*, 1975) or denied all but an inner voice (Ousmane Sembene's *Black Girl/La Noire de . . .* , 1966). Acquiring a voice has an importance quite apart from what is actually said.

This first act of filmic utterance involved a Western technology, so that early film-makers wishing to make independent statements found themselves immediately and inextricably enmeshed with Europe, much as the first pre-independence novelists had been through their use of the language of the colonizer. The theme of the clash of cultures embodied in the lone individual – the 'been-to', the returnee – so common in literature[2] is found too in the cinema. Bassori Timite's *The Woman with the Knife/La Femme au couteau* (1969), Henri Duparc's *Abusan* (1972) and Pierre-Marie Dong's *Identity/Identité* (1972) are typical early examples. The theme has continued to prove of interest to film-makers into the 1980s, and was the subject of two films shown at the eleventh FESPACO festival in Ouagadougou in 1989. *The Healers/Les Guérisseurs* (1988), directed by the actor Sijiri Bakaba, traces the drift into crime of a young man whose two years in France have given him an overwhelming need for money. At a deeper level of investigation into the problems of identity, the Ghanaian director Kwah Ansah's *Heritage . . .*

Africa (1988) traces the progress of an African official, Kwesi Atta Bosomefi. As his career flourishes, he becomes a district commissioner and changes his name to Quincy Arthur Bosomfield, before a dream leads him to change course and seek out his African roots once more.

One of the more interesting examples of the early studies of readaptation is Oumarou Ganda's 45-minute autobiographical first film *Cabascabo* (1969). Along with Mustapha Alassane, another self-taught film-maker, Ganda was one of the pioneers of African film-making. Both directors were consistently hampered by lack of resources, and produced mainly short films and medium-length fictional works in their native Niger. *Cabascabo* reflects Ganda's early experience as a teenager fighting in the French army in Indo-China. In it, the director himself plays an ex-soldier who faces all kinds of difficulties in his attempts to reintegrate into African life. As soon as his money is exhausted he finds himself rejected by those he thought were his friends, but undeterred he gives up his acquired tastes for alcohol and tobacco and sets out to resume his life as a peasant. Like the rest of Ganda's early work – the medium-length cautionary tale of polygamy *Le Wazzou polygame* (1970) and the feature-length exposure of a manipulative marabout, *Saitane* (1973) – *Cabascabo* has an artless simplicity and derives its impact from its directness of expression.

A few other future film-makers were able, like Alassane and Ganda, to make their initial contact with film-making equipment in Africa – through collaboration with Jean Rouch,[3] for example, or work with Serge Moati at the French cultural centre in Niamey. But for most, film training involved study in Europe, with the result that many first short films are studies of European life as seen through African eyes: from Paulin Soumanou Vieyra's pioneering view of student life *Africa on Seine/Afrique sur Seine* (1955), through Désiré Ecare's *Concerto for an Exile/Concerto pour un exil* (1967) and Kwate Nee Owoo's London-made *You Hide Me* (1971) to the novelist Ngugi wa Thiong'o's first film exercises at his Swedish film school in the mid-1980s, which involved questioning Swedes about their image of Africa. The Senegalese film-maker Pape B. Seck, who studied at the IDHEC and made his first short, *Gare de Lyon* (1979), in Paris, subsequently worked in Germany on his first feature, *Africa on the Rhine* (1988). But despite the urging of some Europeans, such as Jean Rouch,[4] few of these African film-makers have returned to film in Europe: the only focus of African films is felt to be Africa itself.

Voices off

Obviously one key aspect of any form of utterance is the choice of language, but for film-makers in Africa this choice was not initially seen as being in any way problematic. The first feature films in Ghana and Nigeria were in English: Sam Aryeetey's *No Tears for Ananse* (Ghana, 1969), Ossie Davies's *Kongi's Harvest* (Nigeria, 1970), Ola Balogun's *Alpha* (Nigeria, 1972), etc. In Senegal, film-makers looked to France for at least partial funding of their work and could observe the use of French by those in authority all around them. The use of French therefore seemed natural, and Ousmane Sembene has recalled that it was only when he showed some of his early short films to peasant audiences that he saw the problem this caused:

> My attitude then was that there was nothing wrong with imposing the French language on the films, because the French language was a fact of life. But on the other hand the peasants were quick to point out to me that I was the one who was alienated because they would have preferred the film in their own language, without the French.[5]

This initial approach, combined with tiny budgets which precluded synchronous sound shooting, led to a situation in which the first African images of Africa produced in Senegal were set against French voice-over commentaries: Sembene's first works – *Borom Sarret* (1962), *Niaye* (1965) and *La Noire de . . .* Ababacar Samb-Makharam's short study of a returnee *And the Snow was No Longer There/Et la neige n'était plus* (1964), Mahama Johnson Traore's 55-minute first fiction *The Girl/ Diankha-bi* (1969) and Djibril Diop-Mambety's first personal and idiosyncratic studies of Dakar, *Contrast City* (1968) and *Badou Boy* (1970), the only films of this group to be made in colour. Such a combination of African images and an alien commentary is, of course, a commonplace of Western documentary. But the documentary form implies a degree of detachment not possessed in the mid-1960s by film-makers very much aware of being among the first black African film-makers to make films in Africa. Significantly, the first artistically successful feature-length documentaries were made only in the 1970s by directors living in exile, Med Hondo and Safi Faye.

Meanwhile the early Senegalese film-makers took the initial step in allowing Africans a voice – though an inner voice in a non-African language. Given the backgrounds of the film-makers involved – Sembene was already established as a major French-language novelist and Samb-Makharam and Diop-Mambety were both actors – the commentary often has a markedly literary tone. As a result, instead of resembling the various European-made adventure films set in Africa, superficially at least, these first tentative African voices followed the line of experimental French film-making inaugurated by Jean-Pierre Melville in *Le Silence de la mer* (1947) and brought to its point of culmination by Robert Bresson with *Journal d'un curé de campagne* (1950). The thematic material, however, was undoubtedly African and the soundtrack is characterized by a note of interiority: the inner monologues of characteristically proletarian and peasant characters from Sembene, the thoughts of a student returning from study in Paris from Samb-Makharam, three contrasting portraits of contemporary young women from Traore, and some irreverent comment on the contradictions of life and architecture in Dakar from Diop-Mambety.

For all the directors concerned, these were apprentice efforts,[6] but the three Sembene films show the difficulties involved in giving a voice to African thoughts and feelings in the neocolonial world of the mid-1960s. *Borom Sarret* is a simple 20-minute tale, a day in the life of a cart driver who plies his trade in Dakar and has his cart confiscated when he enters a forbidden part of the city (the Plateau, built for the colonizers but now inhabited by their successors, the members of the new African ruling elite). The voice-over is spoken in French by the cart driver himself, and the words uttered reflect his limited horizons. The voice does not organize the images, it merely reflects on what we see, defining, for example, the driver's relation to the various people who employ him. The driver begins his day with a prayer:

I beseech the divine protection of Allah and the merciful saints on me and my family. That they may protect me from laws and disbelievers.[7]

But God is notably absent from this world ruled by money and privilege. In keeping with the narrative stance adopted, the voice-over shows only limited insight into the structure of society (though the cart driver does note the connection between reading and knowing how to lie), and the key issues escape him. His final words as his wife goes off to procure the food he has failed to supply – 'Where's she going now? There's nothing to eat' – show a total lack of awareness that the only likely means at the woman's disposal is prostitution.[8]

The narrative of *La Noire de . . .* is also pared to a minimum, though this may be due in part to the distributor's requirements, which led to a reduction from Sembene's planned feature length to just under sixty minutes. This reduction was largely achieved, it would seem, through the omission of a colour sequence of the African woman Diouana's first reactions to France.[9] In its distributed form, *La Noire de . . .* traces with virtual documentary precision the alienation and suicide of an illiterate African woman brought to France by a couple returning from Dakar to Antibes and used unfeelingly as a housemaid. *La Noire de . . .* has a simple six-sequence (twenty-scene) structure, alternating sequences in France (mostly Antibes) and Dakar. The first scenes trace Diouana's first experiences in France and are followed by flashbacks showing how she was hired in Dakar, just as the subsequent build-up of tension is followed by a return to scenes of her in Dakar with her lover. The final quarrel, the suicide and its immediate aftermath in Antibes are followed by a concluding sequence in which the husband returns the maid's belongings to her mother in Dakar.

All but two of the eighteen scenes leading up to the suicide use a voice-over commentary by the maid (the exceptions are the drive to Antibes and a first quarrel, when Diouana stays in bed late). But whilst, in some of the French scenes, the commentary helps to communicate the maid's growing sense of isolation (which the images can only partly convey), much of the voice-over merely duplicates the images: listing the tasks she performs as we see her at work (scene three), describing the hiring in Dakar as we watch it unfold on the screen (scene seven), and so on. The postsynchronization forced upon Sembene by budget constraints means that the performance of the non-professional actress Thérèse M'Bissine Diop is accompanied by the eloquent voice of a trained actress. The stylistic possibilities which this doubling opens up – to create a complex portrait, setting external action and inner voice in juxtaposition – are largely ignored, however. Instead Sembene attempts to fuse image and sound into a seamless realism and this, combined with the film's basically simple moral stance, results not in the creation of a moving individual portrait, but in what is merely a convincing case study. It is hardly surprising therefore that most discussions of *La Noire de . . .* deal largely with its thematic content.[10]

Yet however much it reflects the concrete problems of production, the stylistic clash of African images and a linguistically alien inner voice does have real possibilities for the expression of the contradictions of African society, as Sembene's earlier *Niaye* shows. This film's strength lies in the lack of a purely literal connection between image and sound: Sembene's adaptation of his own story has rendered the narrative stance more complex. Whereas the original story has a straightforwardly linear third-person narration, the film's voice-over commentary shifts its location far more ambiguously, giving the film an unexpected richness. Running just thirty-five minutes, *Niaye* chronicles the decay of traditional authority in a remote rural village under French colonial rule. Though the French administrator makes only an annual visit (to collect taxes), his existence has destroyed the authority of the elders. These allow the village chief to go unpunished for sleeping with his daughter and making her pregnant, even after his wife has committed suicide to draw attention to the offence. Equally, the elders stand by powerless as the chief's younger brother seizes power by arranging the murder of the old chief – using as his instrument the chief's own son who has been driven mad by experiences endured while serving in the French army. The actions which the elders do take – punishing the son and exiling the young girl and her child – are not adequate acts of justice and represent little more than a covering up of events.[11]

Sembene's view of traditional authority as expressed in *Niaye* – like that of contemporary society in *Borom Sarret* – is bleak and unremitting and, as always, he puts the blame for Africa's misfortunes not on the largely absent colonizers but squarely on Africans themselves.[12] The film's power lies less in the simple black-and-white images than in the soundtrack, which largely comprises a complex set of variations on narrating style. The voice-over commentary introduces the characters to us but also addresses them directly, it records their words but also conveys their thoughts and feelings. The village *griot* – traditional poet and chronicler and the film's ostensible narrator – laments the decadence into which the village has fallen and is tempted to leave, though he is finally compelled by his conscience to resume his duties. Only at the end of the film do we see the girl who, with her child, represents the film's sole hope for the future. As Sembene notes in the introduction to the published story: 'Out of the defects of an old condemned world will be born the new world that has been so long awaited and for so long a part of our dreams.'[13] Sembene is not an experimental artist and the use of verbal language to convey complexity in this way (rather than to establish, say, class divisions in society) makes *Niaye* virtually unique in his output, its formal innovation unequalled until the equally audacious use of music in *Ceddo* some thirteen years later.[14]

While Sembene, with *The Money Order/Mandabi* (1968), led African film-making towards a more realistic approach (which will be examined in the next chapter), other film makers mixing documentary and drama followed the direction indicated by *Niaye* and by maintaining a more open and experimental stylistic approach were able to take full advantage of the potential of French-language voice-over commentary. Med Hondo's Paris-made *Soleil O* (1970) is a strikingly original work which provides a bridge between the somewhat tentative Senegalese mid-1960s approaches and the mature documentary styles of the 1970s. Hondo's background is in the theatre, and throughout the film he uses the same small group of performers, including one white-skinned Antillean, who take a variety of roles in a succession of dramatic scenes and sketches. These explicitly theatrical elements are set against songs, observational documentary footage, interviews and naturalistically played scenes to form a complex collage which continually challenges the spectator's easy assumptions. The range of issues raised is very wide: themes of disillusionment, housing, work and sexuality are treated, and both white rationalizations for racist attitudes and destructive differences among Africans themselves are probed. After a general opening in a theatrical style that depicts Africans being converted to Christianity and almost immediately turned into soldiers, the film is basically the story of a single African worker, newly arrived in Paris, who seeks both a job and an understanding of the situation confronting him. In a way characteristic of much early African cinema, *Soleil O* moves remorselessly towards personal alienation and an ending in which the hero screams with anguish as he witnesses a nightmare scene of destruction in a forest, as the images of Malcolm X, Che Guevara, Mehdi Ben Barka and Patrice Lumumba burn in the 'purifying fire of battle'.[15] But the body of the film contains many precisely expressed insights, and examination of the soundrack reveals a striking contrast with the interiority of the early Sembene films.

Soleil O's commentary begins with an unequivocal affirmation of African identity:

> We had our own civilization. We forged our own iron. We had our own songs and dances. We knew how to carve wood and work iron, how to spin cotton and wool, how to weave cloth and blankets. Our trade was not just barter, we struck gold and silver coins. We made pottery and knives. We made our own tools and cooking utensils, using bronze, brass, iron, quartz and granite. We had our own literature, our own religion, our own science, and our own methods of education.

This lesson in the African heritage addressed directly to the central group of characters could not be in greater contrast to the lesson in French which they later receive: a succession of tools held up and named, with a threefold emphasis on the roadsweeper's broom, the implement symbolizing the only work opportunity open to the immigrants.

Subsequently the authorial voice constantly shifts registers: arguing ('We've played our part in securing your economic and industrial capital. Don't we deserve our share of the interest?'), confiding the hero's delusions ('Sweet France. I've come to you. I've come home'), and savagely denouncing those, black or white, who are complicit in racial persecution ('You are a party to every crime committed on earth. You allow slavery, murder and genocide to go unhindered'). The dialogue is similarly flexible, probing, for example, the racism underlying sociological discussion of aptitude tests for immigrant workers, the rhetoric of African military rulers and the self-delusions of white racists ('I've nothing against "them" – I adore negro spirituals'). Equally effective is the use made of sound effects, as when farmyard noises are used to convey French reactions to a couple each of different race. *Soleil O* has all the qualities and defects of a well-directed piece of agitprop, some telling points, a few good jokes and the occasional passage of tedium, but what is crucial is that any trace of diffidence in putting forward an African voice – even though in French – has vanished.

Just a few years later, a relaxed self-assurance characterizes Safi Faye's two dramatized documentaries *Letter From My Village/Kaddu beykat* (1975) and *Fad jal* (1979), both set in the Serer village where she grew up. *Letter From My Village* is explicitly couched in letter form, beginning with the customary opening greeting: 'I write you this letter to ask how you are. As for me, I am well . . . Thanks be to God' – and the author invites us to spend a moment with her family. It ends equally personally, with a dedication to her grandfather, who figures in the film and died eleven days after filming ended. The film has a unique tone, at once personal and detached, since Faye's studies in Paris allow her to set her immediate response to these people in a wider context of awareness of the economic issues which shape their lives. But it is not only her voice (in French) that we hear. She also allows the people to speak for themselves, with their own words and in their own language:

> I give people a voice, they are enabled to speak about their own problems, to show their reality, and I take a position within that. I situate myself on one side or another, my voice criticises what is open to criticism or I provide some small explanation, but that's all. And I'm paving the way for the possibility of future self-expression because it is only they who can appropriately speak about their problems.[16]

Letter From My Village has a triple focus. Firstly, Faye's sharp black-and-white images give a vivid picture of everyday African village life, while her sparse commentary explores the different and complementary areas of responsibility of men and women, young and old. The director has explained that she sees this film, like *Fad jal*, as a document which is necessary for her children (and their contemporaries) 'so as not to deny them their African identity'.[17] The second element in the film is the daily ritual of assembly under the tree in the village, when the elders discuss the issues of the day. They lament the need to grow groundnuts for sale to the government, remembering the days when they grew millet and rice sufficient for their needs throughout the year. A reading (in French) of political speeches from a newspaper prompts them to offer somewhat disabused definitions of politics: 'having only one meal a day for six months of the year', 'having no dowry for their daughters', 'the need for their sons to go to look for work in the city'. The film's structure of voice-over commentary gives an added dimension to this aspect of village life. As a woman, Safi Faye would be excluded from these deliberations, yet within the film it is her voice on the soundtrack which has explanatory power and the ability to organize and make sense of the images. The theme of rural emigration forms the third (fictionalized) element of the film. Wishing to get married to Coumba, Ngor has to go to town in an attempt to earn the bride price. Like so many villagers before him, Ngor has little success and his father-in-law eventually has to settle for a goat. But Ngor does return able to give new thoughts to the elders seated under the tree. Safi Faye's awareness of the positive necessity to leave the village to acquire wider insight into the economic life of the countryside gives a very different tone to the theme of departure and return in *Letter From My Village* from that characteristic in the 1960s.

Narrative voices

Having acquired a voice, a number of African film-makers sought to use it to express stories drawn from – or inspired by – the wealth of African oral literature. As early as the 1920s (when the cinema was still silent), European students of African oral tales had expressed frustration at the limitations imposed by the writing down of oral tales:

> To reproduce such stories with any measure of success, a gramophone record together with a cinematograph picture would be necessary. The story suffers from being put into cold print.[18]

In the 1960s and 1970s several film-makers – Ababacar Samb-Makharam[19] and Inoussa Ousseini[20] among them – raised the question of a cinema rooted in Africa's oral literary traditions, but it took a decade or more before any films of this type materialized. Most African film-making has followed a pattern of socially realistic representation and has sought a novelistic richness of texture in its depiction of social interaction: the narrative structures which have resulted from such an approach are examined in a later chapter. But though only a handful of films – most made in the 1980s – can be said to bear the full imprint of Africa's oral tradition, these are undoubtedly among the most formally innovative works of African cinema and deserve a separate discussion here.

The first element of an oral tale is, of course, the narrator's voice and this normally has a didactic role; being used to reinforce the claims of society, the validity of the old ways. Typical is the attitude of the family *griot* in Fadika Kramo-Lancine's *Djeli* (1981) who criticizes the father for allowing his daughter to have an education ('if you spit into the wind, it will fall on your face'). By contrast, though many film-makers are happy to adopt a didactic stance, they tend to favour social change.[21] For this reason, their adaptations of oral forms tend to be subversions, giving greater weight to progress than to tradition, though Oumarou Ganda's *The Exile/L'Exilé* (1980) has an intriguing ambiguity in that it deals with an ambassador who has rejected his own government yet justifies his action with a tale of submission to the arbitrary claims of traditional society. It is the narrator's very different attitude to society, as much as the necessary distinction between an oral form and a modern recorded entertainment medium like film, which makes the application of traditional titles to film-makers so misleading, as when Ousmane Sembene is referred to as 'a Griot for Modern Times'.[22]

Some films inspired by traditional storytelling focus on a narrator who presents the story directly. Because of the way in which oral tales are collected, printed and analysed in the West we tend to think of them simply as verbal structures, but in fact the context is crucially important: 'Oral literature is by definition dependent on a performer who formulates it in words on a specific occasion – there is no other way in which it can be realised as a literary product.'[23] The performance depends on an intimate link between storyteller and audience in which the latter contributes to the telling, either through some ritualized pattern of statement and response, or simply through the interest (or lack of it) expressed as the story unfolds. Translating oral literature to the screen therefore involves more than merely filming a storyteller: filmic equivalents for the live performance elements also have to be devised and included in the text. Considering the oral tale as a performance gives some indications of how this may be achieved without losing too much of the original style:

> A particular atmosphere . . . can be conveyed not only by a verbal evocation of mood but also by the dress, accoutrements, or observed bearing of the performer. This visual aspect is sometimes taken even further than gesture and dramatic bodily movement and is expressed in the form of a dance, often joined by members of the audience (or chorus). In these cases the verbal content now represents only one element in a complete opera-like performance which combines words, music, and dance.[24]

Drawing their inspiration from this style of story presentation, many African film-makers have discarded a style involving a narrator's voice and illustrative images in favour of an approach in which the voice is internalized within the unfolding action, through the use of the various devices of staging, framing, editing, etc. which structure the filmic text.

If we consider oral tales as narrative structures, they have a number of characteristics which can be used by film-makers. First, they are set in a world away from everyday reality and often shot through with elements of magic, 'in a world in which existential barriers between humans and animals (and even non-animate things) are dispensed with so that all interact on the same plane'.[25] The characters tend to be stereotyped, so that 'it is very easy for the audience to discern and follow the drama in each tale and, at times, to guess the outcome as soon as the characters are announced'.[26] There is a concentration on individuals who embark on a quest of some kind, say, or undergo a rite of initiation. The task will involve a number of key actions (interdictions, transgressions, transformations, etc.) of a set kind. Vladimir Propp in his analysis of Russian folktales has shown how these actions, which he terms functions, recur in set patterns but in varied form throughout a number of tales. Often the recurrence leads to repetitions and sets of variations (a series of encounters or ordeals to be endured, for example). Protagonists are not defined in terms of an individual psychology (they are not well-rounded characters) but are viewed from without and embody just one or two clearly defined characteristics. The secondary characters are all best defined in terms of their relationship with the central protagonist (helper, enemy, etc.): Propp sees as the key aspect not the characters themselves but the set of roles, which may be occupied simultaneously or successively within the same tale by a number of characters.[27] Films based on narrative structures of this kind have a formal organization which sets them apart from the bulk of films exploring the social dynamics of contemporary African society or offering realistic appraisals of African resistance to colonization.

Haile Gerima's *Harvest 3,000 Years/Mirt sost shi amit* (1974), like Safi Faye's *Letter From My Village* a film made by an exile returning from study abroad, is a striking 1970s exploration of the value of the oral tradition even to a film-maker setting his work in the present. *Harvest 3,000 Years* was shot in Ethiopia in April 1974, on the eve of the downfall of the Emperor Haile Selassie and the takeover of power by a military government. Gerima used a crew and 16mm equipment from the University of California at Los Angeles (UCLA), where he was studying and where he edited the film. Like *Letter From My Village*, it has never been shown in its country of origin, but it is firmly rooted in Ethiopean culture and in Gerima's own personal background.

Filmed near the town where Gerima had once lived, *Harvest 3,000 Years* draws heavily for its rhythms on Ethiopian music and on songs and poems composed by the film-maker's father. It also reflects the moment of its shooting, ending with the intervention of soldiers who may or may not distribute the dead landlord's confiscated share of the harvest to the peasants whose labour has produced it. But aside from these touches of personal and contemporary interest, the basic structure of the film is that of an allegory of oppression, in which characters, gestures and objects take on a symbolic significance (the yoke with its connotations of 3,000 years of servitude, and the thundering lorries as indispensable emblems of a questionable progress). The timeless rhythms of peasant life are reflected in the slow unfolding of the film's two-and-a-half-hour narrative, but despite the use of Amharic dialogue, real peasant players and a mass of authentic realist detail, the film turns its back on the Western traditions of realist film narrative. The central figure of the holy fool, Kebebe, whose loss of his land and visits to Addis Ababa have opened his eyes to the realities of oppression, has his origin in the traditions of African oral literature. Similarly, the characters of the landlord and his servant, the peasant parents, the daughter Beletech and the son Berihun are not drawn in personalized, individual terms. They take on a wider significance, so that the jeers and abuse uttered by the landlord stand for a whole crumbling but centuries-old system of oppression, while the daughter's death and the eventual escape of the son are indications of the cost and potential of social change. We are drawn into a world of only partially articulated social conflict, but not in ways which allow easy empathy with the joys and sorrows of individual protagonists.

The world of externally observed reality is shot through with images and sounds representing the dreams, fears and memories of the characters, but the complex pattern of narrative, in which one character succeeds another like runners in a relay race (with the notion of freedom as the baton passed from hand to hand) denies us a purely personal involvement. The stylistic texture of the work, with its variety of visual tricks (freeze frames, slow motion, superimpositions, and abrupt and disconcerting transitions), also serves to maintain a distance between spectator and text, so that the broader issues of interplay between oppression and revolt are highlighted. Throughout *Harvest 3,000 Years* the images retain multiple levels of meaning: the closing freeze frame of the son clinging to the back of the lorry which will take him away from his home village is both a culmination of the struggles towards freedom of Kebebe and Beletech and also an emblematic image of Gerima himself: the Ethiopian film-maker clinging to his Arriflex and Nagra film equipment.

Two feature films dealing with storytellers that were made in West Africa at the beginning of the 1980s were to prove to be the last works of two pioneers of African cinema, Ababacar Samb-Makharam and Oumarou Ganda. Samb-Makharam's *Jom* (1981) uses the key figure of the *griot* – storyteller, celebrant of social values, historian of the people – to bring together a number of disparate tales. Though dealing primarily with a 1980 strike and its consequences, the film travels exuberantly through time to capture situations linked only by their common concern with the concepts of honour and dignity, the importance of keeping one's word and not being bought or corrupted. Throughout the film the need to relate present decisions to past events and outcomes and to draw strength from the history of the people, as recalled and embodied by the *griot*, is constantly emphasized. A similar moral stance is characteristic of Ganda's *L'Exilé*, but here the storyteller is an African ambassador (played by Ganda himself) who has resigned his post because of his disgust with the duplicity of politicians at home. In order to explain his decision to friends in Europe he tells a story, set long ago in his home country, about the importance of keeping one's word.

The bulk of *L'Exilé* comprises the tale told by the ambassador, filmed in a simple, direct visual style and featuring vividly costumed characters who have no psychological depth and who present, rather than embody, the actions of the plot. This has all the arbitrary happenings, unexpected twists, repetitions, ritual acts and oaths characteristic of an oral tale, but is held together by its single theme. The fable begins with a king overhearing two of his subjects agreeing that they would give their lives to be married for just one night to the king's daughters. Next morning the king summons them and grants their wishes, on condition that they agree to die in a year's time. The marriages are celebrated and time passes happily. A year later, having told his assembled court the tale of a king who gave his life to redeem his oath, the king summons the brothers and reminds them of the need to keep their word. The elder brother submits and dies, but the other, urged on and aided by his wife, makes his escape. Falling asleep under a sacred tree, he is saved only by the tribal healer's daughter, who demands marriage in exchange for her help. Travelling further, the group comes to a village where the young man must answer certain questions. Obtaining help from a young girl, who demands marriage as the price of her aid, he succeeds and becomes king. Ruling successfully, with three exemplary wives and three sons, the hero lives happily until his land is struck by famine. According to tradition, the land can be saved only by the self-sacrifice of the king: this time the hero submits willingly to his own death.

L'Exilé has a touching naivety and simplicity and shows how an 80-minute narrative can be built out of the fable's pattern of repetition and surprise. On the one hand there is the linearity of the hero's adventures (three dangers, three wives, three sons) which bring him back to the death he has sought to escape. On the other there is the reiteration of a single theme: an ambassador, revolted by politicians who do not keep their word, tells a story about how a king's two sons-in-law give their lives to keep their oath and in the course of this tale the king himself tells a story: about a king who gives his life to keep his oath. While a film like Sembene's *Mandabi*, with its contemporary setting, can show literacy and education used to dupe the poor and illiterate, *L'Exilé*, with its close links to Africa's storytelling past, can show in a vivid and narratively entertaining way the other side of the coin: the traditional importance of verbal contracts.

Two Angolan films of the mid-1980s, Orlando Fortunato's documentary *Memory of a Day/Memória de um dia* (1984) and Ruy Duarte de Carvalho's fictional *Nelisita* (1984), also show the oral tradition's great potential for shaping new mixed forms of documentary and fictional film-making. Both these films were shot in black-and-white, with the barest minimum of resources, but the imagination and inventiveness of their makers is always apparent. *Memory of a Day* begins with a well-chosen selection of photographic images of colonial rule set against a quietly lyrical, meditative text. It contains depictions of the customary range of aggressions by the colonizers – beatings, torture, forced labour – but these are presented through simple re-enactments performed by ordinary peasants from the region concerned. These scenes are illuminated by the direct testimony of witnesses who relate in personal, localized terms the history of the recent past (naming the colonial aggressors and their victims). To bind the film together, Orlando Fortunato uses the figure of an old peasant who moves ceaselessly through the landscape of oppression, eventually becoming the mute witness of the tragic aftermath of the 1960s massacre of Agostinho Neto's supporters which forms the film's principal focus.

A concern with a people's history and with using cinema to demonstrate truths about the past to a knowledgeable but unsophisticated audience is shown too in *Nelisita*. This film takes the form of a fable dealing with the last two families left alive in a time of drought. One man discovers a fantastic store of food in a warehouse guarded by mysterious 'ghosts' (easily recognizable by their dark glasses). Eventually he and his companion are captured and their families are turned into 'ghosts' as well, though the oppressors' greed causes them to leave alive one of the women who is pregnant – so that they may capture the child too. But the boy, Nelisita, grows instantly to manhood, survives all the tests and trials to which he is submitted, and turns the tables on the two families' tormentors. This simple fable – presented without the need for sophisticated props or acting – is commented on at intervals by figures representing the film's storytellers and audience, depicted as sitting among the players. This narrative device gives the story great immediacy and, though in itself quite simple, points to the subtle rethinking of the relation of film to audience which, on the evidence of these two films, underlies current Angolan film practice.

An equally simple film, on the surface at least, is Gaston Kabore's *God's Gift/Wend Kuuni* (1982), which is scripted in More, the language most widely used in Burkina Faso, and offers a look at Mossi culture before the arrival of the whites. The film tells of a young boy found in the bush who is brought up by a sympathetic family in a small village community and befriended by the daughter, Pongnere. The film builds its narrative out of a number of the story fragments typical of an oral tale: a missing husband, a rebellious woman, a foundling,[28] and its structure is made up of repetitions and variations. It was the death of his mother (driven out of their village when she refused to remarry after her husband did not return from a hunting trip) which – as we discover at the end of the film – rendered Wend Kuuni dumb. It is the shock of discovering a second corpse (an old man who has hanged himself after being publicly branded as impotent by the young woman forced to marry him) which gives him back the power of speech. The film strikingly subverts traditional values by its sympathetic treatment of female rebellion and youthful aspiration. There is no overt criticism in the film of Wend Kuuni's mother, though her village brands her a witch, or of the village woman who rejects an impotent husband, or of Pongnere for continually breaking away from her domestic role to join her brother in the fields. The key event in this virtually wordless film is Wend Kuuni's acquisition of a voice, which enables him to take over from the unseen narrator. But when he finally tells his story – explaining the film's otherwise enigmatic opening – it is not to those in authority (his new parents, the village elders) but to Pongnere out in the fields.

Souleymane Cisse's *The Light/Yeelen* (1987) is a perfect example of the linearity of the oral tale. The opening titles explain some of the elements of the underlying myth: the Komo, which represents divine knowledge; the wing of Kore, the sacred vulture, 'bird of space, hunting, war, wisdom and death'; and the Kolonkalanni, the magic pestle used to punish 'thieves, criminals, traitors and perjurers'. After two emblematic shots – a glorious sunset and a small naked boy who brings a white goat as an offering in the shrine of the Komo – the action gets under way with Soma continuing his ten-year pursuit of his wife and his now adult son, Nianankoro. The subsequent film constantly intercuts between pursuer and pursued, as Nianankoro follows a trajectory typical of the hero of a fable. His separation from his mother is followed by a prophesy uttered by a mysterious leopard-man: 'Your road will be good, your destination happy. Your future is grand, your life is radiant and your death luminous.' Captured as a thief, he gives a demonstration of his magical powers, whereupon he is given two successive tasks by the Peul king into whose territory he has ventured. The first task – defeat of the king's painted enemies – is successfully accomplished, but failure in the second task – curing the Peul king's barren young wife – leads to disgrace and banishment.

While Soma seeks the support of the initiates of the Komo, Nianankoro undergoes a ritual purification and is reunited with his uncle Djigui, who reveals the family history to him. Djigui, Soma's twin brother, was blinded and exiled after he had proposed that the Komo's secrets should be open to all. Instead the secrets were kept by Soma, whose misuse of his powers drove his wife to flee with her young son. Now, with the wing of the Kore (which Djigui had brought with him) reunited with its 'eye' (the jewel given to Nianankoro by his mother when they separated), the young man is able to confront his evil father, who at the moment of combat is deserted by the Komo because of his misuse of his powers and his contempt for humanity. In the final confrontation, good routs evil, though Nianankoro is himself detroyed. But his son by Attu, the Peul king's once barren wife, is seen in the film's final images as the hope of the future.

The success of these films comes not simply from their original adaptation of oral storytelling techniques, which gives them a tone unique in world cinema, but also from the aptness of their choice of thematic material. Together they deal with a variety of aspects of oral culture important for present-day communities containing a high proportion of illiterates: the articulation of revolt (*Harvest 3,000 Years*), the lessons to be drawn from stories of past struggles (*Jom*), the importance of verbal contracts (*L'Exile*), the power of eyewitness testimony (*Memory of a Day*), ways of talking of oppression (*Nelisita*), the importance of acquiring a voice (*Wend Kuuni*), the diffusion of knowledge (*Yeelen*). But there is nothing reactionary about their treatment of oral culture: the traditional status quo is called into question, and rebels are celebrated, not punished or brought firmly back into line. And, as is customary in most of the best African film-making, women who seek to alter their situation are offered respect, not branded as scolds, whores or witches.

10. Space

Along with the need for African film-makers to claim a voice, there is a generally felt need to show African reality as seen through African eyes. As André Gardies concludes:

> Of the two major functions attributed to fictional film making – showing and telling – the black African film undoubtedly favours the former. True, it stages events and sets out actions and characters, but it does so to further an exploration of referential space, as if the first urgent undertaking was a gesture of symbolic reappropriation. Reversing the normal process of classical narrative cinema, it tells in order to show, in order to allow the spectators to see what other cinemas do not show them: images of themselves.[1]

For a generation of film-makers trained in European film schools one obvious exemplar was Italian neorealism. Some critics have claimed to detect a direct influence. Inoussa Ousseini, for example, is struck by the contrast between film-makers whom he regards as 'conditioned' by the neorealists and the mass of spectators 'conditioned by American action films'.[2]

Certainly there are affinities between the neorealists and the African film-makers of the 1960s and 1970s. Both groups wished to intervene in the mainstream of commercial distribution with films of realist intent made with limited means, and both had to attempt to reach an audience whose tastes had been shaped by escapist entertainment movies. On another level, both groups were to some extent cut off from the mass of the people, the Italian neorealists by their generally middle-class origins and the African film-makers by their Westernized education and study abroad. Just as the Italians aimed to offer a truer image of Italy after decades of Fascist rhetoric and the upheavals of war, so too the Africans wished to uncover the world concealed beneath the lies and distortions of the colonial era, of which they could not fail to be aware after the largely successful conclusion of Africa's struggles for national independence. But rather than chronicle (or construct) yet another instance of supposed Western influence, this chapter looks at the specific ways in which spatial reality was organized in this project of giving an image of Africa as seen through African eyes.

The organizing eye

Indications of the distinctive African approach to the filmic depiction of spatial reality are to be found in some of the earliest films of the 1960s. On the surface, Sembene's *Borom Sarret* is no more than a day in the life of a Dakar cart driver, seemingly filled with a fairly random variety of encounters. But in fact, as Maxime Scheinfeigel notes, 'This film is a fiction and, as such, it reinvents reality, as the narrative is organized according to codes which are appropriate to it, chosen codes. One of Sembene's choices, the key choice perhaps, is that of symmetry.'[3] This symmetry exists on several levels: in terms of plot (in the balance of beginning and end), within the protagonist (his noble descent but present poverty), in terms of his customers (the pregnant woman and the dead baby), and so on. But central to the film is the geographical split which divides the city itself, setting in contrast the Plateau – built as the colonizer's residential quarter and from which horse-drawn carts are still excluded – and the poor quarter around the Sangara market where Borom Sarret lives. This split triggers the key reversal of the plot, in which Borom Sarret's cart is confiscated because he has ignored the prohibition and crossed into the Plateau.

Borom Sarret contains a mass of concrete detail of life in Dakar, but the principal locations are not given their specific names. Just as the cart driver, despite his interior monologue, is less an individualized character than a representation of *any* poor African struggling for a living, so too the geographical locations have a generalized meaning: this is *any* African city with its residential quarter for the wealthy and its popular market. This approach comes to be a feature of most subsequent filmic depictions of contemporary African life. For example, Dakar is never named in *Mandabi* and the labelling, in French, of certain key locations – the town hall, police station, bank – is a mark of their use within the narrative not as individualized sites but as institutions indicative of the financial and bureaucratic transformation of African society. Likewise, the emphasis placed on the nameplate 'Mbaye Sarr, Agent d'Affaires, Diplomé de l'Ecole de (sic) Hautes Etudes' is primarily a mark of Mbaye's status as representative of the new, rapacious and deceitful French-speaking petty bourgeoisie. The same approach can be seen in the work of other film-makers. Bamako is clearly recognizable as the setting of Souleymane Cisse's *The Wind/Finye* (1982)[4] and the film's plot was clearly inspired by the 1980s student riots in the Malian capital.[5] But again the locations are not given their specific names, and the mechanics of the plot even imply that the military governor is in charge of a provincial town away from the centre of power.[6]

There are a number of possible reasons for the adoption of such an approach. First, it may be an expression of the conscious pan-Africanism which led to the foundation of the film-makers' association FEPACI, and results in virtually all African film-makers talking about the problems of the whole continent when they discuss their work. At the same time, it is clearly a useful tactic to be able to say, when confronted by local censors, that one is not attacking one's own government, just making a statement about conditions common throughout Africa. Whatever the reason, the effect is to reinforce the difficulty of seeing African films in terms of 'national cinemas'. The films produced in any one country are, in any case, very few in number – three or four dozen at most. Often two or more different languages will be used within a single 'national' output, so that generalization is only one of the factors inhibiting the emergence of a strongly defined and distinctive national identity. But the combined effect is clear: just as films based on oral traditions and using African languages such as Amharic, More or Bambara can be readily approached as expressions of a storytelling tradition common throughout the continent, so too the studies of contemporary life and history are best understood less as specific accounts of the situation in, say, Senegal or Mali than as statements about *Africa*'s current problems and potentials.

In terms of spatial organization, the effect of this abstraction and generalization is to allow specific geographical divisions (as, in Sembene's *Borom Sarret*, between the Plateau and the Sangara market in Dakar) to repesent the social and economic divisions of Africa as a whole. In *Borom Sarret* the camera emphasizes the physical distinctions to an extent not called for by the plot itself, panning up the towering white apartment blocks of the Plateau and tracking through the squat and scattered buildings of the Sangara district. We are here far from the situation in classic Western film narrative, where the setting is no more than a location for the action and every element of the decor is ideally 'used up' as the action unfolds.[7]

The presentation of place in *Borom Sarret* lays such emphasis on specific contrasting characteristics that we cannot fail to understand it as the representation of a society now divided as rigidly between rich and poor as it once was between colonizer and colonized. Subjects which allow this kind of binary logic that can be expressed in spatial terms – Plateau/Sangara, Europe/Africa, modernity/tradition, corruption/virtue, etc. – are a feature of African film-making. Jean-Michel Tchissoukou's *The Chapel/La Chapelle* (1980) from Congo, for example, is built around the clash of an imposed Christianity and the traditional ways. And the rich visual contrast between a traditional healing ritual and treatment in a modern hospital, for example, is used in both Ababacar Samb-Makharam's *Kodou* (1971) and Moustapha Diop's *The Doctor From Gafiré/Le Médecin de Gafiré* (1983). Similarly, Borom Sarret's words when he finally reaches home ('This is my district, my village') anticipate one of the key organizing concepts of all African filmic space and narrative: the contrast of town and village which recurs regularly from Tidiane Aw's *The Bronze Bracelet/Le Bracelet de bronze* (1974) through Daniel Kamwa's *Our Daughter/Notre fille* (1980) and Kollo Sanou's *The Emigrant/Pawéogo* (1983) to Gaston Kabore's *Zam Boko* (1988).

Sembene's first full-length feature, *Mandabi*, is a beautifully worked-out comic variant on this contrast. Though Ibrahima Dieng lives on the outskirts of Dakar, he in fact inhabits a traditional world whose values are inherited from the village community. Here, though without a job, Ibrahima can feel himself to be a man of substance, as a true believer with two wives and seven children. Sembene does not idealize this world. The shopkeeper Mbarka ruthlessly exploits his customers and the imam prowls constantly trying to sniff out money. Even Ibrahima is aware that danger lurks on the roadway outside the family compound (warning his wives not to talk about money on the street). Yet the values of the local community are positive: if people flock to share Ibrahima's good fortune when they think he has money, they also rally round with gifts when they think he has been robbed and beaten.

Ibrahima becomes a richly comic character when his world is upset by what might have been a stroke of unexpected good fortune, a money order for 25,000 CFA francs (500 French francs) from his nephew Abdou who works as a roadsweeper in Paris. As Françoise Pfaff notes, the images of Paris which accompany a reading of Abdou's letter indicate not only Abdou's social alienation but also 'the alien aspect of the money order which comes from a society dramatically different from Ibrahima's'.[8] The money order must be cashed, and in attempting to do this Ibrahima enters a new world, marked by values inherited from colonialism, expressed in alien documents such as money orders, cheques, birth certificates and identity cards, and administered by a bureaucracy with no sympathy for an illiterate who speaks no French and is visibly out of his depth in modern Dakar. Sembene offers a savage portrait of those at home in that world, who prey on those needing a cheque cashed or a photograph taken.

But his greatest venom is reserved for the bilingual elite, since, with the sole exception of Ibrahima's helpful nephew Amath, everyone with a mastery of French scorns, abuses or cheats him. Language, which had initially been seen as neutral by film-makers of Sembene's generation, has in *Mandabi* become a key feature of the binary logic: spaces are differentiated linguistically as well as in terms of décor and furnishing. Another film to emphasize this point is Mahama Johnson Traore's *N'Diangane* (1975) in which the six-year-old protagonist moves from the happiness of his family circle to two successive alien spaces, the Quranic school in a nearby village and the streets of Dakar, where he is forced to beg. But after he has been killed by a car, the film introduces a fourth space – the world of the French-speaking bureaucracy – as the driver of the car and a police officer discuss the affair in a relaxed manner in French: no problems, no case to answer, just one of those beggars, no one's claimed the body, we can use it in the medical school. . . .

A dozen years after *Mandabi*, we find the same key geographical distinction in Kramo-Lancine Fadika's *Djeli* (1981), this time expressed as the contrast between the Plateau of Abidjan and a nearby rural community. As students at the university, Fanta and Karamoko have fallen in love, which is perfectly acceptable in their shared world of Abidjan, characterized by modern apartments, cars, records and the French language. But when they return to their village home, the traditional barriers of caste reassert themselves: Karamoko, as a member of the inferior *griot* caste, is unacceptable to Fanta's father. *Djeli* adds complications to this simple binary logic by embedding within the opening Abidjan sequence a brief sepia flashback dealing with the mythical origins of the caste system, and by showing inside the rural community a modern concrete villa being built by Fanta's father. Fanta herself is half traditional: she needs the village community as well as Abidjan, she wants to choose her own husband for love but also keeps to her traditional role in family councils. Her father is half modern: he is building his modern villa and has allowed his daughter to have a college education. She can even choose her own husband, so long as this does not mean crossing caste boundaries. The father's elder brother, the family headman who dresses in traditional robes, is also conciliatory, advising the father to accept a world where caste barriers no longer count. But the basic opposition between the values of Abidjan and those of the village, between modernity and tradition, remains, and Fanta is driven to attempt suicide.

At the climax of the film, her father and Karamoko meet by her hospital bed (a final symbol of modernity), but the film ends with a freeze frame a moment before a decision is made. In a sense it is the symbolic language of geography, in which the clash of values has been visualized, which stands in the way of resolution: the skyscrapers of Abidjan and the traditional dwellings of the village belong to irreconcilable worlds, however much goodwill may be present between the characters.

Another way of formulating the basic binary scheme is to set physical and mental space in opposition, and once again Ousmane Sembene's early work points the way. *La noire de* . . . is built around a series of external oppositions – black/white, employee/employer, Dakar/Antibes, past/present – which give the film its air of being a case study. But the essential drama is internal, and the forces which drive Diouana to suicide are conveyed partly (as we have seen in chapter 9) through the device of an interior monologue, but also partly through the spatial organization of the film. Diouana's memories of Dakar are full of vitality: finding a job, meeting her new lover, working with the children, enjoying her dream of France. The space is open and animated, a mixture of interior and exterior scenes, and the setting for a richly enjoyed life. By contrast, in the 70 per cent of the film set in France, the forces pressing in on Diouana are represented by interior shots only, the blank walls of the flat, the location of her eternal round of cooking and cleaning, the monotony of which is relieved only by images of the African mask which she gave to her employers when she first took up her job. Antibes itself is virtually absent, conveyed only by two street signs ('ANTIBES' and 'CHEMIN DE L'ERMITAGE') and a reiterated static long shot from Diouana's window. Interestingly a similar approach was adopted a dozen or so years later by Mory Traore from the Ivory Coast, whose *The Man From Elsewhere/L'Homme d'ailleurs* (1979) traces the loss of identity and eventual suicide of an African teacher of French in a Japan which we barely glimpse. The interaction of protagonist and social environment is a subject dealt with more fully in chapter 11, but in passing it is worth noting that what might, in another system of film narration, be seen as a problem of time (the lack of a future) is conveyed in these two films in spatial terms, with the lack of a viable social context (in Antibes or Tokyo) being deemed explanation enough for suicide.

In the work of some of the less talented film-makers, particularly those who favour a didactic or moralistic approach, this type of spatial organization based on binary oppositions can result in a mechanically predictable style of narrative. But its full artistic potential is dazzlingly apparent in Djibril Diop-Mambety's *Touki-Bouki* (1973). The basic anecdote is a simple story of two students, Mory and Anta, who meet, make love and decide to go off to France. They steal the necessary clothes and the money for the tickets and manage to evade the police. But though Anta boards the boat, Mory finds himself unable to tear himself away from home.

This story is set in a contemporary Dakar full of recognizable landmarks (the market, the footbridge, the harbour, etc.), but this realistic space is both fragmented and questioned. The spatial realism of Dakar is fragmented by the editing, which juggles with both time and the imaginary. The film is full of tiny echoes of events which have already happened and more substantial anticipations of what is to come (as when Anta is twice shown running down to the beach to make love).

Reality and imagination are also constantly intertwined, as when the stealing of the clothes leads directly to Mory imagining his triumphal return from France (a presidential-style drive through Dakar and a praise ceremony organized by Aunt Oumi, now transformed from his chief enemy to his most fervent supporter).

More significantly still, the realistic space is called into question by being held between two conceptual spaces: a memory of rural Africa and a dream of France. The opening and closing images of the film depict a small boy riding across the savannah leading a herd of oxen, and this boy is visually linked to Mory, who has an ox's skull fixed to the handlebars of his motorbike. Images of oxen recur through the film, and when Mory's dream ends, he finds the skull broken. This imagery from the traditional past – memories of Mory's childhood? – spreads forward through the film and eventually makes Mory unable to leave. At the same time, in an opposite motion, the soundtrack draws the couple towards a future imagined space, Paris (through the constant reiteration of two songs, Josephine Baker's 'J'ai deux amours, mon pays et Paris' and Mado Robin's 'Paris, Paris, Paris'). At the end of the film this space in turn is concretized in the images of the gleaming white liner, the *Ancerville*, which takes Anta away from Africa.

A further and more original way in which spatial organization is handled in *Touki-Bouki* is in the treatment of secondary characters. Both Anta and Mory are marginalized individuals. Anta's dress at the beginning of the film denies her femininity (indeed her gender is in some doubt until she strips off her shirt before making love to Mory) and Mory himself is ambiguously located (as Anta's mother sarcastically asks, 'Does he think he's riding an ox or a motorbike?'). Clearly it would be possible for them to pass anonymously through Dakar without any but a functional link to its inhabitants. But this is not allowed to happen. Diop-Mambety has devised a structure that fills out the spaces through which the protagonists pass with secondary characters, perhaps because traditional African approaches demand a link between hero and community, or perhaps, on the contrary, out of a purely modernist impulse to allow the narrative to generate itself. Certainly the narrative of *Touki-Bouki* is a perfect example of that type of modern fiction which Alain Robbe-Grillet describes as being characterized by a present tense

> which is continually inventing itself, as if it were at the mercy of the writing, which repeats itself, bisects itself, contradicts itself, without ever accumulating enough bulk to constitute a past – and thus a 'story', in the traditional sense of the words.[8]

In *Touki-Bouki* it is as if the mere passage of the protagonists through the space generates the characters whom the film stays to observe. The little boy's ride at the beginning of the film leads not just to the slaughterhouse, but to an extended fourteen-shot sequence of bloody killing; Mory drives under the footbridge and from the second shot of this emerges the fat postman who plods his way through the film; Anta passes the women drawing water and the camera stays to observe a fight between two of them; Anta and Mory drive off after their robbery and we see a long shot (lasting more than two minutes) of the fat homosexual Charlie on the telephone reporting the theft and chatting up the police sergeant, and so on. None of these little sequences is necessary in terms of narrative economy, but together they give a vivid portrait of Dakar and its environs. But the most audacious instance of the creation of a new space (in this case imaginary) is when the cawing of some crows startles Anta and 'creates' the figure of a savage in a tree, who scares Anta out of her wits and becomes a sort of *alter ego* for Mory, riding (and eventually crashing) his motorbike.

Thus, by the beginning of the 1970s, in a number of films of which *Mandabi* and *Touki-Bouki* are simply contrasting (if both excellently realized) examples, African space had found its authentic place on the screen. Its use in European-made action movies as a mere background for the loves and exploits of European explorers, soldiers and missionaries had been superseded. Now we were offered a space seen through African eyes, foregrounded and organized so as to reveal the order and economics of African society, as well as the imaginary life (memories, dreams, aspirations) of its inhabitants. Subsequent film-makers have built on this foundation to explore ways of expressing African politics and history in a similar way through the spatial organization of image and narrative.

The politics of space

It is widely recognized that one of the limitations of photographic naturalism is the fact that appearance and reality are not one: a photograph of a bank or a factory gives in itself little indication of the underlying reality of the organization of financial or productive forces. But such forces can be more clearly revealed if photographs are brought together, put into a context, used to form part of a collage. The African system of using binary sets of oppositions as a way of organizing spatial representation can be seen as in many ways akin to collage. So far we have largely considered film sets as static units, but within African film narratives they are often actively antagonistic and oppositional. Ibrahima's community and the bureaucratic institutions of Dakar in *Mandabi* are not simply contrasting, contiguous worlds, they are also in active conflict. As the film clearly shows, the tentacles of the monetary economy are extending outwards, transforming Dakar itself (as Ibrahima remarks, 'even begging has become a profession now') and extending to the adjacent community (symbolized by Mbaye's efforts to get possession of Ibrahima's house). The film's ending – Ibrahima's proclamation that he is going to become 'a wolf among wolves, a thief, a beggar, a liar' – may not be altogether convincing, but it is indicative of Sembene's conviction of the need for ordinary people to fight back.

The difficulties of fighting are clear in Jean-Michel Tchissoukou's *The Chapel*, in which the Catholic priest is on one level a comic character (cycling incongruously through the grasslands and riding like a potentate on a litter carried by four bearers), but imposes his will ruthlessly, setting an alien space (a Catholic church) in the midst of a traditional community. At the beginning of the film the conflict between Christianity and tradition seems equally balanced, with the priest's baptism of the chief intercut with a healing ceremony performed by Ta Ganga, who is traditionally clad with a painted face and a headpiece of feathers and cowrie shells. Ta Ganga wins his argument at the catechism classes by his assertion of traditional wisdom, and his powers of healing are shown to be real, whilst the building of the chapel demanded by the priest causes nothing but troubles. But at the end, when the priest returns with armed soldiers, Ta Ganga is overcome by sheer force. Wrongly accused of burning down the chapel, he finds his attempt to defend himself in his own language only reinforces the presumption of guilt in the eyes of the priest who – in French of course – orders his arrest and the burning of his hut. The presence of soldiers will ensure the rebuilding of the chapel.

The logic of antagonistic interaction between opposed spaces need not, of course, be as negative as in *Mandabi* or *The Chapel*. Gaston Kabore's optimistic and life-affirming first feature, *Wend Kuuni*, similarly sets two spaces in opposition. The first is the intolerant village of Wend Kuuni's early childhood, the village from which his mother was expelled. The second is the supportive community into which he is adopted after being found in the bush. The weight of the first space hangs over much of the film, since Wend Kuuni's experiences have quite literally deprived him of his voice. But the second space – that of the loving family (exemplified by Pongnere) which takes him in and regards him as God's gift (the literal meaning of the title) – has the power to contain these negative forces from the past, as the film's climax shows. On the surface level of plot, Wend Kuuni's recovery of speech is triggered by a negative incident: the discovery of a suicide's body. But its impact is wholly positive. By telling the past – his mother's expulsion as a witch and her subsequent death in the bush – Wend Kuuni shows that his place in his adopted family is secure enough for the past not to be a personal threat. The film's narrative reflects this by illustrating Wend

Kuuni's account with images that are clearly marked as flashback illustrations and in no way threaten the stability established by the narrative.

A more ambiguous interaction of contrasting spaces lies at the heart of Souleymane Cisse's ambitious second feature film, *Work/Baara* (1978). This is a film which many critics have found confusing because it lacks a clear single plot line, but it is better understood in terms of the interplay of three distinct urban spaces. The first part of the film depicts the life of a market porter named Balla in a large African town: a traditional outdoor space of lively personal interaction. One of his jobs takes him to the house of a middle-class engineer who on learning that they share the same name, befriends him. When Balla is arrested because his papers are not in order, the engineer secures his release from jail and finds him a job in the factory where he works. From this point onwards the film shifts its attention to two further spaces, both key elements of the emerging modern economy: the production line of the factory where the workers operate in appalling conditions, and the work and domestic spaces of the factory owner, characterized by deceit, profiteering and, eventually, murder. It is the inevitable clash of these two opposing spaces, rather than the simple logic of plot development, which leads to the film's climax: the murder of the engineer and the arrest of the factory owner.

The precise working out of oppositional conflict is seen more clearly in Sembene's *Xala* (1974) where all the various aspects of social and domestic politics are worked out in spatial terms. The film's opening allegory of the rise of the black petty bourgeoisie is an excellent example of this. The first moment of independence is represented by a crowd celebrating and dancing as a small group of Africans mount the steps of the Chamber of Commerce. There they eject, first, the objects in the committee room (including a bust of Marianne and, incongruously, a pair of army boots) and then the whites themselves, who clumsily gather up their belongings in full view of the crowd. The African group, still in traditional dress, then emerges at the top of the steps to acknowledge the cheers of the crowd. The second act begins with the appearance of African soldiers, led and controlled by a white man, who push back the crowd, separating it from the subsequent action, which goes on behind closed doors. In the Chamber of Commerce the African businessmen, now resplendent in gleaming evening dress (whereas the whites wear sober business suits), arrange themselves around the table where each receives from the whites (who assume an ostensibly advisory function) a briefcase crammed with banknotes. When, at the end of the session, the red carpet is rolled out over the steps and each businessman in turn is ushered (by a white) into one of the Mercedes limousines lined up before the Chamber, their separation from the people could not be more apparent. The two scenes are linked by the opening address, in French of course, by the new president of the Chamber, which moves from a simple chronicling of events ('Never before has an African been President of our Chamber') to ironic counterpoint, the scene of bribery being heralded by the words, 'We have chosen socialism, the only true socialism, the African path to socialism, socialism with a human dimension.'

Other conflicts in *Xala* are also worked out to a considerable extent in spatial terms. El Hadji Abdoukader Beye's opposition to the beggars (whose leader imposes the *xala*, a curse rendering him impotent on his wedding night with his third bride) is expressed by getting the police to remove them from in front of his shop and to transport them out into the countryside. Their response is to invade his domestic space (the home of his first wife) for the ritual in which he must submit to being spat upon in order to be released from the *xala*. On a domestic level, the tension between his two existing wives is also expressed spatially. Adja asserts her sense of status as first wife by refusing to enter the home of Oumi, the second wife. The latter asserts her claims by refusing to sit alongside the chauffeur while Adja sits next to El Hadji, so that all three have to ride to the wedding ceremony crammed into the back of the Mercedes. Even El Hadji's inner contradictions are in part expressed spatially. He is keen to define himself as a member of the modern business class, refusing to participate in the traditional ceremony designed to ensure a successful deflowering of the bride. But his future mother-in-law is not taken in: 'You're not a white man. You're neither fish nor fowl.' Her observation is borne out during the two trips out of town in which El Hadji visits village marabouts in attempts to have the *xala* removed. On the first visit he appears incongruous in a rural setting in his Western suit and with his inevitable briefcase; on the second he pays with a cheque (which unfortunately bounces, resulting in the reimposition of the *xala*).

Linguistic space is also a site of opposition in *Xala*. The businessmen use French in all their dealings, but a new spirit is shown by a young man selling *Kaddu* (a real magazine – the first in Wolof – founded by Sembene himself in 1972). El Hadji wants all the traditional patriarchal authority of a Moslem polygamist, yet quarrels violently with his elder daughter Rama who replies in Wolof when he addresses her in French at home. Later the tables are turned when, threatened with expulsion from the Chamber of Commerce, El Hadji asks to address the meeting in Wolof. The response is unanimous: French is the sole language of business and in wanting to use Wolof he is showing himself to be 'racist, sectarian, reactionary'.

Souleymane Cisse also uses attitudes to France to differentiate the views of father and daughter in one of the opening scenes of *The Wind/Finye* (1982). When Colonel Sangaré tells his eighteen-year-old daughter Batrou that he is sending her to France to continue her studies, her response is to accuse him of having France as his 'second homeland' and to explain that she wants to study at home, since she would feel abandoned in France. The confrontations which mark the widening gulf between Sangaré and all those around him are carefully located in spatial terms. Initially domestic and political spaces are separate as Sangaré is secure in his position as head of the household and state governor. But this separation gradually breaks down. Political events invade his domestic space (as when he confronts Batrou about the student pamphlet) and the domestic forces itself into the political (his daughter Batrou becomes a rebel and his third wife, Agna, confronts him in his office: 'Power is making you blind. Restrain yourself'). The climactic confrontation with Kansaye, representative of the traditional authority he has usurped, takes place at the country property he has acquired illegally, and his response is to have Kansaye's compound ransacked by troops. Throughout the film, most of the space falls within Sangaré's authority, but at the end, thanks to the intervention of the minister, his grip is broken, so that Kansaye and the protestors can march off knowing their demonstration will not be impeded. Part of the richness of *Finye* comes too from the inclusion within its social picture of spaces which are neither domestic nor political. Among these are the images of the dream which features the union of Batrou with her student boyfriend Bah (aspects of which are included in the film's opening and provide its final images) and the sacred grove where Kansaye summons the now powerless gods: 'The sky is changing colour, it is getting darker. The divine forces have deserted us. Act now according to your strength and what you know.'

The workings of antagonistic spatial logic in African cinema are seen with particular clarity in the various historical studies of aspects of colonization, since here control of the physical space is sought by the colonizer and resistance takes the form of defending one's land. What is initially remarkable about films otherwise as diverse as Ousmane Sembene's *Ceddo* (1982), Med Hondo's *West Indies* (1979) and *Sarraounia* (1986) is their comparative lack of concern with time. *Ceddo* is set in a very vaguely defined seventeenth century, and aspects of colonization which occurred separately in time (the intrusions of white slave traders, Catholic and Islamic missionaries) have been telescoped together to form elements of a filmic conflict that is worked out spatially.[10] Similarly, *West Indies* deals with some four centuries of colonial impact and a variety of forms of slavery in the Antilles, but it does not offer an alternative history as such (in terms of the names and dates of the oppressed). Rather the film gives us visual, spatial enactments of revolt and the celebratory anticipation of the dawn of liberation through the whirling colours and shapes of popular dance.

Both film-makers favour anachronism. Sembene includes a modern sunshade in *Ceddo*,[11] and allows the missionary a vision of a modern Catholic ceremony in Dakar. Hondo uses a similar device in *Sarraounia*: 'At the end of the film, there are people dressed in modern clothes. Sarraounia goes out of frame with history, and we are left with people just walking about, as in any street in Africa or Europe.'[12]

These historical studies may also move into the timeless world of the fable or oral folktale: the opening sequence of *Sarraounia*, for example, can be viewed as the ritualized education of a legendary heroine, while Dior Yacine's killing of the imam provides *Ceddo* with an ending as satisfying as that of any fable.

With the exception of a small amount of documentary footage of plantation economies in the pre-credit sequence, *West Indies* locates all the action within a single stylized studio set of a slave ship, built in its entirety at a disused railway station. The social stratification of the Antilles is conveyed spatially through the levels of the slave ship. Over the centuries, the slaves and the common people act out their scenes in the hold, the middle classes and the *assimilés* (the bilingual administrative elite) frequent the lower decks, while the upper deck is occupied by those in power – the colonizers and their principal allies.[13] Again the stratification is reflected linguistically: French is spoken increasingly as one ascends towards the upper deck and those in command. Social conflicts and the rise and fall of characters are conveyed spatially by means of progress through the holds, passages and stairways of the slave ship, which also serves as the location for the key dream sequence, the newly elected deputy's vision of becoming emperor. Through the use of this setting to locate its interwoven mixture of music, sound effects, dance, declamation and song, *West Indies* is able to encompass the continuing story of exploitation in the Antilles, from the transport of slaves and their sale in the West Indies to the twentieth-century emigration of workers seeking their fortunes in the metropolis.

In a very different way, Sembene's *Ceddo* makes equally effective use of the spatial divisions it creates as the basis of its narrative. The imam's takeover of all power and authority in the *ceddo* (pagans living in accordance with African traditional beliefs) community is slow and inexorable and hence, viewed as a single phenomenon, lacks real dramatic power. But by beginning at the moment when the pressure exerted by the imam has created a split between the king and one of his subjects (who has kidnapped the king's daughter as a way of stopping the forced Islamization of the *ceddo* community), Sembene is able to articulate two spaces, the village with its precisely demarcated ceremonial area, and the much more loosely defined space – 'somewhere outside the village' – where the *ceddo* holds Dior Yacine captive. Though this latter space is little more than a corner of scrubland, the *ceddo* gives it identity and dignity through the way in which he treats the initially arrogant princess. He addresses her through his *griot* – just as the debates in the village will be conducted through the spokesman Janaaf – and when she refuses to be tied up, he uses a single length of rope stretched out on the ground to define the boundary of her prison. It is therefore wholly appropriate that the king should respond with equal formality, sending two successive champions, her brother and one of her suitors, each of whom confronts the *ceddo* in a duel which the latter wins by superior guile. In this way we come to understand the ceremonial formality of the operation of traditional *ceddo* society in the resolution of internal disputes.

Ceddo lacks the dance which Hondo uses so effectively in *West Indies*, and makes a very different use of music, here employed largely to counterpoint the action (as when the operations of the white slaver are accompanied by an American gospel song, 'I'll make it home some day'). But it shares with *West Indies* a basically declamatory style and frequently theatrical manner of presentation, in which the spatial positioning of the characters is paramount, as when the *ceddo* kidnapper confronts the princess or when the followers of the king, Demba War, speak at the council. The dialogue makes full use of Wolof proverbs and sayings, such as, 'Trying to provoke a coward is like drawing blood from a turnip', 'If a lizard makes fun of a turkey, it's because there's a tree nearby', or 'The wind which knocks down a baobab tree only bends a millet stalk'.

The imam's form of authority has no need for ceremonial. He (and through him, Islam) is the sole source of power, and his white-clad followers are reduced to clicking their fingers and chanting in unison, 'Allah protect us' or 'Allah be praised'. The imam moves from symbolic appropriation (taking possession of the king's ceremonial umbrella) through verbal imposition of his authority (insisting on the sole use of Islamic law and the exclusion of non-believers from the royal council) to the actual seizure of power through bloodshed and the murder of the king. He then proceeds to the forcible conversion of all the *ceddo* of the village. The imam's response to the *ceddo* kidnapper displays the ruthless logic which exemplifies Sembene's view of Islam: he dispenses with all ceremony and sends two servants who gun down the *ceddo* from beyond the range of his arrows. With the death of both the king, Demba War, and the *ceddo* kidnapper, the split in society is removed. All territory is now under the imam's control, and Dior Yacine can be brought back to the village. The imam feels his position is now unassailable, but the princess avenges her father by slaying the imam in front of the assembled people, to give the film its dramatically satisfying ending.

Most films dealing with the politics of space do so by detailing an interplay of two or more spatial areas within the wider African rural or urban landscape. Yet the problematic of the possession of their own land, which underlies the African film-makers' foregrounding of space, is nowhere more apparent than in a film limited largely to a single location. The film in question is the account by Ousmane Sembene and Thierno Faty Sow of an authentic wartime massacre, *Camp Thiaroye/Camp de Thiaroye* (1988). The spatial constraint here is the result of the demands of what is, in essence, a prison camp story; the dramatic tension stems from the fact that what is at stake is not simply the lives of the protagonists but their very existence in history. A group of *tirailleurs* is repatriated to Dakar in 1944 after long years of military service in Europe. But instead of being sent back to their local communities, they are placed in a transit camp, and for one of their number, Pays, the effect is devastating. Having been imprisoned in Buchenwald, he cannot believe that on his release he will find a similar prison in Senegal. For Sembene, 'Pays is Africa':

> He has been abused and traumatised. He can't talk. He is alive, he can look and see, he can touch, and he can see the future. He is the beholder of the drama of the past, of the concentration camps, of colonisation, very disciplined, very alone. Very solitary, but he can't explain it.[14]

The other characters are equally representative figures, bearing names or nicknames linking them directly to the administrative divisions of France's African empire and forced to communicate among themselves in pidgin French (*petit nègre*). But if the camp itself is in this way a kind of metaphor for colonial Africa, it is an Africa in which a new sense of independence has come into existence. The soldiers' experiences in Europe have destroyed the myth of white superiority and their new attitude is reflected in the US army uniforms they wear when they disembark in Dakar. Many of them weep when made to revert to the shorts and bare feet of the conventional French *tirailleur*. None can take on again the subservient role forced upon them by a racist French colonial administration, and the dislocation is greatest for Sergeant-Major Diatta, an intellectual cut off from his family by his Westernized education (and French wife), from the men by his interests (the music of Albinoni and Charlie Parker, the novels of Vercors and Roger Vailland), and from the French officers by his colour but also by his superior linguistic abilities (he can speak English as well as perfect French and so can communicate with the US troops stationed in Dakar).

In one sense, the tragedy of those quartered in the Camp de Thiaroye is their lack of synchronization with the development of the societies from which they stem. Their service in the French army has given them attitudes which may become acceptable with independence in the 1960s but which are anathema to the French colonial military authorities in 1944. But the film develops their story not in these temporal terms, but through spatial interactions: the development of a society within the confines of the empty camp, the sorties outside and the increasingly tight encirclement. These *tirailleurs* are allowed to be in Africa only on the terms dictated by the colonizer, and when they talk of their rights and kidnap a French general to make their views understood, retribution is swift. Despite the French general's word of honour 'as a French officer', the camp is razed and all its occupants are massacred at 3 a.m. on 1 December 1944. The physical elimination of space entailed in the destruction of the camp allows it subsequently to be elided from French colonial history.

11. Story

A third concern of African film-makers – having acquired a voice and in the course of revealing African space – is to tell stories about contemporary African society and African history in which Africans can play leading roles. African approaches to narrative have generally been severely criticized by European critics. An extreme example of French impatience is Daniel Serceau who, in the course of a spirited attack on the 'failure' of *Emitai* and Ousmane Sembene's 'mistakes', offers this generalization:

> The fact is that in general African film-makers experience great difficulties in constructing their stories correctly. Mastery of so many of the elements that go to make up filmic narrative – the sense of concision and ellipsis, the question of repetitions, the arrangement of dramatic effects – more or less escapes them.[1]

It is clear that Serceau is taking as his implicit model against which to measure supposed African deficiencies what we may for convenience call the Hollywood movie (the form of film storytelling prevalent in Europe as well as North America for fifty years or more). But no explanation is offered as to why this should be regarded as a more appropriate yardstick for evaluation than, say, the Hindu melodrama, the European art film, or the Brazilian *chanchada*. Serceau simply assumes – without arguing the point – that classic Western narrative structures are 'correct' and that all deviations from them must constitute 'errors'.

In the course of analysing African filmic narrative structures in the pages that follow, I too shall be making reference to the Hollywood movie, as a form of storytelling with which the reader may be assumed to be familiar. But I must make it clear from the outset that it is in no way my aim to argue for some mythical Western 'superiority'. Rather, my concern is to define the particularity of African film narratives. There are a number of reasons why the African approach to film storytelling should be different from a European or North American approach. Two of these have already been touched upon. The first is the heritage of the oral storytelling tradition, which lays stress on linearity and repetition, and on sets of equally weighted variations, instead of favouring a division into plot and subplot. The second is the very different approach to – and use of – space in African cinema, which has important implications for story structure. The third, and perhaps crucial, factor shaping the development of a distinctive African film narrative is the very non-European view of the relationship between individual and group. But before turning to this, we need to look at questions of overall structure.

Structural principles

In an analysis of the films of Ousmane Sembene and Haile Gerima which has wider implications for African cinema in general, Mbye Baboucar Cham points out some of the major aspects of the structural organization of their films. Among these is a plot

> characterized to a large degree by a linearity of movement from conflict to conclusion. This movement, focusing usually on one central idea, is a characteristic of most African oral narratives. The overriding preoccupation with one central idea, and the urgency and clarity with which this issue needs to be conveyed to the African audience eliminate any tendency to dabble in intricate, convoluted subplots.[2]

This is clearly true of the films adapted directly from the oral tradition, such as *L'Exilé*, *Wend Kuuni* or *Yeelen*. Beyond this, a plot need be little more than a movement from one social space or community to another. The Ghanaian director King Ampaw in *Kukurantumi* (1983) uses the device of a lorry trip across the country. Elsewhere we find a journey out of the poor quarter to the Plateau (*Borom Sarret*), into the city from the outskirts (*Mandabi*), from village to city (*Letter From My Village*), from Dakar to Antibes (*La Noire de . . .*). Alternatively, all that is needed is the arrival of someone who disturbs the community: a man returning from military service (Oumarou Ganda's *Cabascabo*), a stranger mistaken for the government's inspector general (Mahama Johnson Traore's *Lambaye*), a young man who stirs the social awareness of the young (Jean-Michel Tchissoukou's *The Chapel*), a political activist advocating independence (Raymond Rajaonarivelo's *Tabataba*). The simple displacement of a character creates in itself sufficient material for a film story, reinforcing the tendency to dispense with subplots. The thinking behind this attitude is very clear in Ousmane

Sembene's response to a question as to why he had failed to show the contradictions of polygamy in *Mandabi*:

> I am against polygamy, but my purpose was not to deal with this subject in this film. Its unity of action would have suffered.[3]

In Sembene's work, potential subplots are invariably left undeveloped. The rise of the pickpocket which parallels the decline of El Hadji in *Xala* is merely sketched in, and the two never come face to face, though he is El Hadji's replacement in the Chamber of Commerce. Similarly Mbaye's scheme to get possession of his uncle Ibrahima's house in *Mandabi* is underdeveloped, since Ibrahima never learns of Mbaye's involvement. Even more striking is the way in which the white slave-trader and the Catholic missionary who appear in the first two shots of *Ceddo* (before the imam) remain marginal figures in the ensuing narrative. Despite the historical importance of European intrusion, Sembene's film maintains its unity of action and concentrates unrelentingly on Islamic conversion.

But as well as unity of focus, linearity also implies a view of time as succession, as simple chronological development: this happens, then this, then this, and so on. In a structure of this kind, troubles and disasters may pile up for a character as the narrative progresses, but no suspense is generated. To take a tiny example, at one point in *Mandabi*, Ibrahima raises a loan of 2,000 CFA francs on a gold bracelet belonging to his second wife, for which he had paid 15,000 francs. He has three days to repay this loan and 500 francs interest, or the bracelet will be forfeited. Clearly a situation of this kind could be used (in, for example, a Hollywood-style narrative) to build suspense, intensify the drama and reinforce our identification with Ibrahima: what will he do to cash the money order in time to recover the bracelet? But in Sembene's film (as in the original short story) Ibrahima goes to Dakar, is beaten up by the photographer's assistant and takes to his bed for three days. We see him again only after the bracelet has been lost, and this particular reversal becomes merely one of the series of disasters which befall him.

In a narrative system of this kind, new events and discoveries are totally unexpected and come as a surprise to audience and protagonist alike. Nothing in *Xala* leads us to anticipate El Hadji's impotence or to guess that the perpetrator of the *xala* is the beggar; no suspense is generated by Diouana's suicide in *La Noire de . . .* (she carries through her resolution without hesitation) or by Mory's decision not to leave Dakar in Diop-Mambety's *Touki-Bouki* (he turns away from the liner abruptly and totally unexpectedly). Even a film as different in style and theme from these as Cisse's *Finye* follows its various interwoven plot threads in a similar, purely chronological fashion, with no attempt to motivate Anga's affection for her step-daughter Batrou (though she is trying simultaneously to seduce Batrou's boyfriend, Bah) or to create suspense through the punishment of the students at the end (Seydou, Bah's friend and one of the key student activists, simply collapses in long shot, whereupon we are told that he had been ill before being imprisoned).

While this stress on successivity and comparative neglect of causality may have its roots in oral storytelling, it is by no means retrogressive. Indeed, it can be closely related to contemporary developments in European art cinema, where film-makers in the 1960s were struggling to dispense with the rigidities of Hollywood formulas, in much the way that Africans were attempting to free themselves from the grip of cultural neocolonialism. For example, Harold Pinter's account of his own approach in *Accident*, directed by Joseph Losey in 1967, could stand as Sembene's credo in *Mandabi* and *Xala*:

> I do so hate the becauses of drama. Who are we to say that this happens because that happened, that one thing is the consequence of another? How do we know? What reason have we to suppose that life is so neat and tidy? The most we know for sure is that the things which have happened have happened in a certain order: any connections we think we see, or choose to make, are pure guesswork. Life is much more mysterious than plays make it out to be.[4]

Beyond successivity, one of the simplest methods of story construction is repetition, and this can again be linked to oral storytelling: the series of pranks played on villagers by the local trickster or the succession of tests and ordeals undergone by the hero. In an oral storytelling presentation the repetitions and doublings may vary according to local circumstances or audience response. Occasionally, chance occurrences can also influence the structure of a film, as in *Yeelen*, where the doubling of Soma and Bafing (both of whom seek Nianankoro with a magic pestle) is the result of the death of the actor Ismail Sarr (Bafing) in the course of the shooting. The sequence featuring him is included as a homage to one of Souleymane Cisse's favourite actors. Systematic repetition is the organizing principle of most films based on oral material, and it comes as little surprise that the hero of *L'Exilé* acquires three wives (each of whom gives him a son), or that both a successful use of his magic and a failed attempt precede Nianankoro's final confrontation with his evil father in *Yeelen*.

But a pattern of repetition is also at the base of certain contemporary and historical films. In Mahama Johnson Traore's *N'Diangane*, the action falls into two distinct halves, the second of which is a virtual repetition of the first. A 6-year-old boy, Mame, from a traditional

family is sent away to a Quranic school in a nearby village, where he is
appallingly treated, eventually being tied up, brutally beaten and left
out in the sun. He manages to escape and is welcomed home by his
mother. But his sufferings begin all over again, since his father takes him
back to the school and even beats him in front of the marabout. This
time Mame is taken by the marabout's son to the city, where his
sufferings continue as he is forced to work and beg on the streets, until
he is run over by a car.

Equally based on repetition is Sembene's study of colonial
oppression, *Emitai*. The 17-minute pre-credit sequence shows the
methods used by the French to recruit Africans into the *tirailleurs*: a
mixture of brutality (pressganging lone passers-by) and psychological
pressure (an old man is left tied up in the village square until his son
surrenders himself for army service). The methods are successful and
the new recruits are marched off to a chant of 'Maréchal nous voilà.'
After a title – 'One Year Later' – and the credits, the film's final
seventy-five minutes constitute an extended repetition of the themes
and methods of the pre-credit sequence. This time the French are
seeking the bulk of the year's harvest of rice, and to obtain it they arrest
the women of the village and hold them captive in the square, until the
men deliver the rice. They also impede the proper burial of the dead
chief. As in the previous year, the pressure brings results: after endless
deliberations, the men hand over the rice, only to be promptly shot
down by the colonial forces.

Even when pure repetition is absent, we often find a structure in
which the parts are not tightly linked but are merely successive in time.
Thus in *Finye* the first fifty-four minutes (twenty-one scenes) work
through a conflict of generations in purely social terms (Bah's failure in
the examinations, his drug-taking and violence, his reconciliation with
Batrou). Then the scene in which Colonel Sangaré shows his daughter
Batrou the student pamphlet ('We want an honest leader, not a greedy
profiteer') introduces a political dimension for the first time, and in the
final fifty minutes (twenty scenes) the conflict becomes a struggle
between students and military authorities. The view of time and
causality which underlies the extensive use of linearity, successivity and
repetition in African cinema precludes the intricate manipulation of
time which for the past sixty years or more has characterized the
Hollywood movie. This manipulation finds its key organizational
expression in the three-act structure which characterizes films as
seemingly diverse as *Casablanca* and *Kiss of the Spider Woman*, *North by
Northwest* and *Kramer vs. Kramer*.[5] The audience response is controlled
through a patterning which hardly varies from film to film. The
triggering incident (setting the action in motion) will normally occur in
the first ten minutes and the act one climax (often followed by a change

of direction or location) will come within thirty minutes. The second act, which runs for an hour or more, is the longest and most complexly plotted, and leads to a climax which reverses the act one climax and to a personal crisis for the protagonist. A succession of short scenes in the swiftly moving, 15–20-minute third act takes the film to a final climax which resolves the crisis and is followed by a very brief (2- or 3-minute) coda.

One of the few African features to display a clear three-act structure is Diop-Mambety's *Touki-Bouki* and this film, significantly, has been accused by African critics of being over-Westernized.[6] Here the 24-minute, eleven-scene first act unrolls under the impact of the slaughterhouse imagery of the opening sequence (echoed in the reiterated images of Aunt Oumi's ritual killing of a goat). The act culminates in the lovemaking of Mory and Anta and their decision to go to France. The longer second act (thirty-seven minutes, seventeen scenes) traces the couple's attempts to acquire the necessary money, opening with Aunt Oumi's curses and ending with her sung praises of Mory (which he imagines). The third act is set in motion when Charlie phones the police about the robbery at his villa; it is interspersed with shots of police cars presumably in pursuit of the couple. It is notable, however, that each act is given its unity less by a tight narrative organization than by its distinctive thematic identity: the mixture of images of love and death in act one, the fantastic plotting and wild imaginings of act two, and the threat of arrest and reality of separation in act three.

In place of a multiple act structure, African films tend to adopt a form of structural organization which Mbye Baboucar Cham aptly characterizes as a division into primary and secondary sets of complementary polarities. This organization corresponds, on a narrative level, to the division into binary oppositions which, as we have seen, characterizes African cinema's handling of space. In Cham's analysis, which refers specifically to Sembene's *Emitai*, *Xala* and *Ceddo* and to Gerima's *Harvest 3,000 Years*, the purpose of the primary set is to analyse and expose 'the real nature and dynamics of oppressive and exploitative systems which are capitalism, neo-colonialism, feudalism or a combination of these'. As such, primary sets are 'less concerned with individuals than with individual representatives of a system or a certain view of human beings and relationships'. In contrast, secondary sets focus not on systems but on 'the inner details and implications (human and otherwise) of these oppressive and exploitative systems'.[7]

If we apply Cham's categories to *Emitai*, their usefulness as an analytic tool is immediately apparent. The primary set in each of the two parts of the film is the opposition between the French colonial forces and the Diola villagers whom they are seeking to exploit. The method of exploitation is in each case to split the unified Diola community and, by applying pressure, to bring about the desired outcome. In the pre-credit sequence, the French exploit the traditional loyalties and obligations of the villagers by binding and humiliating one of the elders. They can rely on the upholders of tradition (the man's two daughters) to accomplish their purpose for them by persuading their brother to give up his individualistic rebellion and exchange his liberty for that of his father. The French tactics in the main body of the film are similar, but more subtle. They isolate the women (who as growers of the rice are its traditional guardians) in the village square as a way of bringing pressure on the men (so that a secondary set, Diola men/Diola women, is formed). The women remain firm in their resistance, holding their unity in face of provocation and breaking out as a group when a small boy is shot dead. But the men, dismayed by the failure of their gods to help them against the French and disoriented by the task given them (the rice is traditionally the women's concern) split to form a further secondary set (warriors/appeasers). With the defeat of the warriors, and with the French still preventing a proper burial for the dead chief, the men capitulate and fetch the rice. Only at this point is the split between men and women dynamically bridged by the women's chant as they celebrate their defiance by performing the burial rites of the chief and the little boy. But the consequent revolt of the men is futile, as they have already handed over the rice. Their refusal to act as porters merely results in their execution. Looked at in these terms, *Emitai* is far from being the failure which Serreau claims to expose. It emerges instead as an exemplary demonstration of the workings of oppression, totally free from the personalization of issues which customarily vitiates Hollywood-style studies of war.

Sembene develops a similar structure, but in more complex ways, in his second historical film, *Ceddo*. At the beginning of the film three potential primary sets are introduced (the intrusion of white slave-traders and both Catholic and Islamic missionaries), but only one of these is fully developed. The Catholic missionary has only a single follower and is killed when the imam takes power, whilst the slave-trader disappears from the narrative at the same point (about half an hour from the end of the film), leaving the imposition of Islam as the sole primary set. Initially the kidnapping of the king's daughter, Dior Yacine, by one of the *ceddo* sets a united front of king, nobles, imam and converts against a helpless if protesting community and, of course, arouses the antagonism of the princess. The opposition between king and *ceddo* kidnapper is expressed through battles with the two champions sent to kill the latter (Biram/*ceddo*, Saxewar/*ceddo*). But the *ceddo*'s valour transforms the opposition *ceddo*/Dior into a new grouping (*ceddo* + Dior/imam), leading to the reversal at the very ending when Dior becomes the *ceddo*'s 'champion' and vanquishes the imam. But before he dies, the imam's tactics have split the royal group (the new heir, Biram, from the previous heir, Madior, and then nobles from king). This prepares the way to his seemingly unassailable authority, achieved through a night of bloodshed which sees the elimination of both his rivals (the Catholic missionary and the king). All these shifting conflicts and alliances are less a matter of personal involvement than of social position, and through them both the strength and cultural richness of traditional society and the ruthlessness of the Islamic intruder are exposed.

Med Hondo's *Sarraounia* is in many ways a complementary work to *Emitai* and *Ceddo*, since it chronicles the exemplary resistance of the pagan queen of the Aznas to a powerful and well-armed French force led by Captain Voulet. Sarraounia unites all her people and acquires new allies in the struggle (her estranged lover, the warrior Baka, and Dan Zarki, son of the ruler of the neighbouring Moslem community of Matankari), but the French force steadily disintegrates as Voulet's mad ambition and grandiose vision of empire cause a rift between himself and the French high command, dissension among the white officers who follow him and, eventually, conflict between the whites and the black *tirailleurs*. The escalating series of clashes which form the secondary sets grows in intensity as the ferocity with which Voulet had treated those he vanquished is turned against his own followers and fellow French officers. By the time Voulet dies, shot down by his own soldiers, he has already renounced his allegiance to his superiors and killed the white colonel sent to recall him to his duty.

The concept of the primary set as the key element in the organization of the narrative as a whole allows us to answer a question posed by James Leahy: 'What are the Tuareg doing in a story of Sarraounia and the Aznas against Voulet and the French?'[8] Despite its title and the 15-minute opening sequence devoted to the upbringing of the queen, *Sarraounia* is not the story of an individual princess and her prowess. Its primary set is the white intrusion into Africa at the end of the nineteenth century, and it therefore adds a number of elements to the novel by Abdoulaye Mamani on which it is based. Voulet's efforts are placed in the wider context of the European invasion of Africa through the inclusion of such new elements as the figure of Colonel Klobb, who brings Voulet his orders from the French high command, and the brief scene featuring two British soldiers guarding the entrance to Sokoto. But Hondo is also keen to show the whole range of African responses to the invasion, so he includes not only the responses found in the novel – those who aid Sarraounia (Dan Zarki), those who actively intrigue against her (the Emir of Sokoto) and those who do nothing (Serkin Gobir) – but also those whose lives are only peripherally touched but who fear the new order imposed by the Europeans (namely the Tuareg slave-traders, who play no part in Mamani's novel).

The same division into primary and secondary sets can be used to analyse films set in contemporary Africa. In *Finye* the primary set is clearly the struggle for freedom against a brutal military power which acknowledges no restraint ('Children without a state, sons of the devil, how dare you oppose us? Neither you nor your fathers helped us to take power. Our guns made it possible'). This finds secondary set expression in two political struggles (students versus military and traditional authority versus military dictatorship) and is paralleled by two main domestic conflicts (Sangaré/Batrou and Sangaré/Agna). While Sangaré remains inflexible throughout, refusing even to acknowledge his daughter when she opposes him ('No favouritism. Kill her if you want to'), the film is given dramatic power by the shifts undergone by the governor's adversaries (Bah and the students moving from drug-taking to political activity, Kansaye giving up his traditional ways and throwing in his lot with the young protesters, Batrou and Agna both articulating protests against patriarchal authority), as the wind of change sweeps through the community.

While primary sets – the major conceptual polarities – are given from the start (being inherent in African history and society), it is clear from this analysis that the secondary sets – the human implications as worked out in action and reaction – are created as the narrative proceeds. Such a structure allows a sharp interplay of oppositions in terms of narrative as well as space, and the film need by no means be static. Cutting between sets can give the film-maker control over rhythm and pace as the story unfolds in time. But the lack of subplotting means that no additional story material is brought into the narrative, and the resultant turning in on itself of the story can on occasion lead to stasis and an inability to find a satisfying resolution. Such an effect is reinforced by the particular focus of African cinema – the foregrounding in primary sets of major social divisions or historical forces which by definition move slowly (if at all) and are here expressed, as we have seen, to a very considerable extent through a spatial rather than a temporal logic. Nothing in this kind of overall narrative patterning generates the kind of relentless drive towards a resolution which characterizes Hollywood-style storytelling methods. But this drive is itself inseparable from the particular Hollywood definition of the individual protagonist and, as we shall see, special factors concerning the relation of individual and social group come into play in African culture.

The individual and the group

The distinctive African relationship between individual and group has been well formulated by Tahar Cheriaa, who asserts that in true African cinema

> the individual is always pushed into the background, and the hero – African films are rich in characters in the classic sense – never occupies the foreground. The principal character in African films is always the group, the collectivity, and that is the essential thing.[9]

It is not my purpose here to trace the origins of this relationship in African history or to test its general validity in African culture. My concern is merely to examine whether it offers potential insight into the formulation of a distinctive African approach to film narrative. Looked at in this light, Cheriaa's assertion offers us the third key element in African film narrative structure, since it defines the implications in social terms of the system we have already seen producing a foregrounding of spatial organization and a granting of primacy to sets defining major socioeconomic forces. A concentration on geographical spaces (such as town and country) and a use of these to create conceptual spaces (modernity and tradition) inevitably leads to emphasis on the group, since it is groups (the petty bourgeoisie and the peasantry) which physically occupy such geographical spaces and embody the opposing concepts they represent. Similarly, an emphasis on a broad issue (such as the anti-colonial struggle) as the primary set of a narrative also shifts focus away from the individual (who would be helpless in such a struggle) to the collectivity (which alone has the potential to embody power or to offer viable resistance).

The stress on the three wholly compatible elements of space, set and group creates an African film narrative system which is totally coherent. But this system is bound to arouse the incomprehension of those who take Hollywood procedures to be the sole method of film storytelling, since it is diametrically opposed to the underlying assumptions of those procedures. Whereas African film narrative begins and ends with collective entities (social spaces, socioeconomic forces, human groups), the Hollywood procedures focus almost exclusively on the individual protagonist. In the Hollywood ideology, a human being is a free individual, able to make personal choices as the basis for action. Whatever the dangers, these choices are free, and a human being is seen as comprising essentially the sum of his or her freely determined acts. Certainly it is through their decisions transmuted into actions that we judge and empathize with Hollywood characters. Both systems can be defined as an interlocking of three levels, but whereas the space, set and group structure of African film narrative operates at a collective level, in Hollywood the inner, the personal and the social are all internalized within the individual protagonist.

Sembene's *Emitai* is a significant film because it stands in much the same relationship to subsequent film explorations of African history as *Borom Sarret* does to investigations of African society. We can see in clear outline the basic structures which later films will develop. In *Emitai* the traditional division of labour (the women growing the rice, the men acting as warriors) is translated into spatial terms (the women hiding the rice in the forest and being held captive in the village square, the men locked in debate at the shrine with the gods who seem to have deserted them). The primary opposition between colonizer and colonized is acted out in the public space of the village (the trussing-up of the elder in the pre-credit sequence, then the imprisonment of the women) and gives rise to a number of secondary oppositions. Since subplots are of little concern to Sembene, some potentially interesting secondary oppositions are ignored (such as that between white officers and black soldiers). Those oppositions which are developed involve major groups of villagers (men/women, then warriors/appeasers). Personal issues are never allowed to cloud the clarity of the primary divisions into space, set and group, with the result that characters who, in Hollywood terms, would be seen as the most dramatically interesting – since they internalize the essential conflict – are ignored. Thus, after the young man in the pre-credit sequence has abandoned his individualistic revolt, we never see him again. He is not picked out as the group of recruits are marched off, and his reactions to the subsequent speech by the white officer ('France is doing you a great honour') go unrecorded. Even more significant is the refusal to develop the character of Sergeant Badji in the main section of the film, since Badji is a man of (presumably) split loyalties: regarded by the French as their best non-commissioned officer, but also a native of the village.

Souleymane Cisse's *Finye* develops its two central figures, the governor's daughter Batrou and her lover Bah in more personal terms. Bah's conversion to militancy is presumably influenced by the death of his close friend Seydou (though this is never explicitly stated) and Batrou articulates her revolt in family terms ('Now I see more clearly, I know we have different needs. I even wonder if we are the same blood'), and her last words in the film to her father make clear a very personal impulse ('You won't let me stay with the man I love'). Such motivations can obviously be related to those in Hollywood-style movies, but any examination of the overall structure of *Finye* shows the inadequacy of an explanation of the film in such purely personal terms. The lives of all the main characters are left in suspense. The governor's third wife, Agna, simply vanishes some thirty minutes from the end, and Batrou disappears ten minutes later. The final confrontation is between the governor, Colonel Sangaré, and Bah's grandfather, Kansaye, but we last see Kansaye marching off with a group of young people whose sole slogan is 'Kansaye, Kansaye', whilst the outcome of Sangaré's meeting with the president is left open. Bah is released from prison, but then simply disappears from the frame as the camera stays focused on the prison bars and walls. Even the final shot of the film – an echo of Bah's dream of union with Batrou – shows the small boy who had offered them water from a calabash, but omits the lovers. Clearly *Finye* is fully understandable only in so far as these characters are seen not as personalities carrying the whole weight of the narrative but as representative of the various groups engaged in the power struggle.

Given this focus on the group, the African film protagonist lacks the totally individual autonomy customary in the Hollywood movie. In virtually all the film studies of African society and history there is no possibility of a separation between values and the group. The protagonist is necessarily defined by his or her relationship to the community, which may form part of a polarized set (of the tradition/modernity type) but within which alone values are located. A character who rejects or is cut off from the values of the community without having the opportunity to join an oppositional group is doomed. Diouana in *La Noire de . . .* , the hero of *The Man from Elsewhere*, the mothers in *Wend Kuuni* and (presumably) *Yeelen* all die isolated, Fanta in *Djeli* is driven to attempt suicide. Coumba in *Letter From My Village* and the eponymous heroine of *Kodou* both suffer breakdowns when their links with the community are disrupted. A particularly interesting character in this respect is the king's nephew, Madior Fatim Fall, in *Ceddo*. When he learns that under Moslem law he is no longer heir, he disputes vigorously with the new heir, Biram, insults the king and flamboyantly renounces his adopted faith. But though he reverts to *ceddo* garb, he is now excluded from any role in the community: he can only be an observer of the fate of the king's champions and his words at the king's council go unheeded. Though he embodies so many key aspects of the film's conflicts, when the imam takes over he simply vanishes from the last forty-five minutes of a narrative in which, as a mere individual, he now has no part to play.

A corollary of the failure of the individual cut off from the community is the stress on the group as the only source of renewal. In Africa, as in most parts of the world, the message of a film dealing with contemporary society is likely to be positive if the state production company has had a major role in the funding of it. What is noticeable in the state-funded films produced in Africa in the 1980s, however, is that the source of regeneration is never a lone individual. In Arthur Sibita's *The Co-operators/Les Coopérants* (1983) it is a group of well-off students who volunteer to assist in a programme of rural development in Cameroon. In Paul Zoumbara's *Days of Torment/Jours de tourmente* (1983) the young people in a Burkina Faso village get together to confront the lethargy of their elders and dig a much-needed well. In Idrissa Ouedraogo's *The Choice/Yam daabo* (1987) it is a family which sets off as a unit to build a new life for itself instead of simply waiting for food relief, whilst in Flora Gomes's *Mortu Nega* (1988), the first feature film to be made in Guinea-Bissau, it is a whole community rebuilding itself after the costly, if successful, struggle against the Portuguese colonizers.

In any clash of social groups, an attempt to take up the role of the mediator is generally ineffective, whether in the case of the two small boys who help the women imprisoned by the French in *Emitai*, the uncle who tries to resolve the family conflicts in *Djeli*, the *ceddo* who kidnaps Dior Yacine in an attempt to force a change of mind on the king, those *tirailleurs* who seek to negotiate with the kidnapped general in *Camp de Thiaroye*, or the engineer who attempts to mediate between workers and management in *Baara*. But though the task of mediation is difficult, this is no cause for despair, as Idrissa Ouedraogo's charming study of growing up in a rural community, *Yaaba* (1989), shows. The film is largely concerned with the playful interaction and childish rivalry of Bila and his young cousin Nopoko. One of Bila's schemes is the reintegration into the village of the old woman Sana, who lives on the outskirts and is generally regarded as a witch. Getting over his initial fear, Bila 'adopts' the old woman, stealing a chicken for her, calling her *yaaba* (grandmother) and promising to rebuild her hut when it is burned down. After Sana has responded by procuring help for Nopoko when the little girl is taken ill, Bila even wins over his mother, who sends him to the old woman with food. But when he reaches her hut, he finds her dead. Only then is the truth about Sana's 'crime' revealed to Bila (and to the audience): her mother had died in childbirth and her father soon afterwards so that, as an orphan, she was unable to find a place in a community based on kinship relations.

Though there is little or no sign of oral narrative influence on the story pattern of *Yaaba*, it does share much with films like *Yeelen* and, especially, *Wend Kuuni*: a focus on attractive young protagonists, a timeless village setting and a moral climate where women who stray morally are not automatically blamed (here sympathy is shown towards the wife of the village drunk who takes a lover when her husband fails to meet her needs). Still, despite the wealth of sentiment to be found in the film, Sana cannot be brought back into the community.

Occasionally, however, there is the possibility of reintegration for an individual who is isolated: In *Letter From My Village*, Ngor is able to rejoin the village community after the fruitless spell in Dakar, and at the end of *The Chapel* the outsider Adouki looks forward to a future with Atsono, tilling the land rather than working for the European priest. Similarly, Sarraounia's allies, Dan Zarki and Baka, find a congenial community in the ranks of her army. But, in general, individual forays into the city or abroad can lead only to disaster, whether the cause is work (*Borom Sarret*), army service (*Cabascabo*) or university study (*Djeli*). The heroine of Sembene's early short *Niaye* is virtually the sole protagonist for whom a positive future is predicted after she has been driven without resources from the community (but this is a film, it must be noted, which adopts unchanged the storyline of a tale already published in French).

As a result of the general powerlessness of the individual, characters in African film narratives are generally the static representatives of the values of a particular social group. What becomes of them is less the expression of a personal destiny than a reflection of the viability of the group's values in a divided society, a society split by colonialism or still bearing the marks of alien influence even after independence. As Europeanized members of the bureaucracy, the client who lures Borom Sarret into the Plateau, the car driver who kills Mame in *N'Diangane* and the treacherous Mbaye in *Mandabi* are all secure. By contrast, Djimako the warrior chief of *Emitai*, Kinsaye the grandfather in *Finye*, and Nianankoro's evil father Soma in *Yeelen* find that the gods (and hence the values) by which they have lived are outmoded. El Hadji's fate in *Xala* and the calling to order of Colonel Sangaré in *Finye* point to the fragility of the position of both an aspiring urban petty bourgeoisie operating without independent capital and of military personnel in a situation where all power belongs ultimately to the president. But in each case these film narratives must be read as the expression of a view of society as a whole, rather than of a concern with the fate of an individual, if their structure is to be seen as clear and coherent.

The stereotyping of African film protagonists which stems from their representative role is clearly reflected in the use made of costume. A character's social position is instantly pinned down by the choice of dress: Ibrahima's flowing traditional robes in *Mandabi*, the dark glasses worn by the 'ghosts' in *Nelisita*, the paint and feathers of Ta Ganga in *The Chapel*, the contrast in *Xala* between the traditional eldest wife, Adja, in her African robes, the sophisticated second wife, Oumi, in her Western dresses and the committed, modern-minded daughter, Rama, in her jeans, and so on. Seldom, if ever, is there any ambiguity here, and a change in dress comes not as the reflection of a slow and carefully plotted individual development (such as that chronicling, say, the rise of a gangster in a Hollywood crime film[10]), but as a total social reversal of some kind. We see the pickpocket in *Xala* just three times: when he steals money, when he buys a Western-style suit and when he is invited to join the Chamber of Commerce. Similarly, when they steal clothes from Charlie's house, Mory and Anta in *Touki-Bouki* are immediately transformed into the sophisticates of their dreams. The entrepreneurs in *Xala* are definitively separated from the community the moment they shed their African garb, and the burning of Kansaye's traditional robes in *Finye* is an instant but irrevocable step.

The concentration on the group has important implications for narrative structure in terms of both pace and values. As far as pace is concerned, it inevitably results in a slow and more measured rhythm, since groups change only slowly over time. *Emitai* shows this vividly. The colonizers do not change at all: in both halves of the film they have clear-cut objectives and a worked-out plan of action from which they do not deviate. The Diola women are equally unmovable: they unflinchingly endure all the humiliations inflicted upon them before making their one final act of revolt. More dynamic change occurs among the men, but it is still distinctly limited: some take up arms and some hesitate, but after defeat all capitulate, only to make a final futile act of defiance. *Finye* is explicitly a film about change ('The wind awakens the thoughts of man'), but because of the focus on representative figures rather than notionally free individuals, the actual changes are minimal. Colonel Sangaré does not deviate at all (though the minister compels him to act differently), the students instigate a revolt that ends in personal defeat and capitulation (though with perhaps an ultimate victory beyond the confines of the narrative), and only Kansaye undergoes a fundamental change, accepting the inefficacy of the old gods and throwing in his lot with the more politically minded young people.

Concentration on the group also limits the extent to which the revelation and discovery of values can play a key role in the narrative, since groups embody values explicitly. In *Emitai*, the colonizers colonize, the resisters resist, and the waverers hesitate and are lost. In *Finye*, the young revolt against the authoritarian values of the old, and the latter either resist blindly (Colonel Sangaré) or join forces with the new spirit (Kansaye). In *Ceddo* the imam imposes his will without a hint of self-doubt and, since the king and nobles have already been converted, the *ceddo* are left confused and fatalistic. With the exception of the kidnapper (who is killed) and one family which chooses exile, they submit to conversion, and it is difficult to see how Dior Yacine's slaying of the imam will have a long-term impact.[11] The developments within the secondary sets which could potentially have brought something new have confirmed values known from the start and already expressed in both the oppositions of the primary set and the binary polarity of the spatial logic. Since characters are not individuals notionally free to make personal choices, but representatives embodying the values of specific groups, there can be no echo in the African system of film narrative of the essence of the Hollywood movie: the construction of the individual protagonist over time in relation to the espousal of values which are uncovered as the narrative unfolds.

The emergence of African narrative cinema has not been the occasion for manifestos or collective statements demanding adherence to any particular style or approach to reality. The film-makers at their various conferences in Ouagadougou, Niamey and elsewhere have been largely concerned with the practical issues of finance and distribution, relations with their own governments and with foreign funding sources. Similarly most writing about African cinema has been concerned with themes and content, with what the films are *about*. But as the preceding chapters show, the film-makers' shared backgrounds and the pressure of the context in which they are compelled to work have led them to a common way of seeing African reality and telling African stories. In adopting methods of documentary production developed in the West, they have devised ways of giving a direct voice to the African people. Their adaptations of stories taken from oral traditions have not fallen into the trap of viewing pre-colonial Africa as some kind of mythical golden age. Instead the films have been both formally innovative and consciously structured stylistically so as to allow the need for social change to be always apparent. The film-makers may have studied abroad, but in telling stories about their own societies they do not ape the methods of, say, Italian neorealism. The depiction of spatial reality in African films shows a distinctive and original response to the problems of portraying societies which are both divided within themselves and in a process of transition towards a still uncertain future. Though African screens are dominated by imported films showing epic heroes performing incredible feats with total disregard for social constraints, African film-makers have shown a striking common refusal to treat the individual protagonist as the driving force of the narrative. Individuals can be no more than representatives of groups or communities whose values they espouse. In societies still struggling for economic and cultural autonomy, the primary shaping force of any narrative study of history or society must be those broader socioeconomic forces which render the lone individual helpless.

APPENDIX:
Dictionary of Film-makers

This list covers the major Arab and African film-makers dealt with in the text. The major focus is on film-makers active in the 1980s but – as in the case of Abdel Salam and Diop-Mambety – some particularly important directors of an earlier period are included. For comprehensive documentation on those who careers did not extend into the 1980s or whose work falls outside the scope of this volume, see the valuable listings on Arab cinema contained in Thoraval (1975), Cluny (1978), Berrah et al. (1981) and (1987) and Nouri (1986) and those on African cinema in Binet et al. (1983) and Boughedir (1987).

ABDEL KHALEK, Ali (b. 1944, Cairo, Egypt)
A 1966 graduate of Cairo's Higher Cinema Institute, Abdel Khalek's first film, the 1973 *Song on the Road/Ughniya 'alal-mamarr*, was hailed for being one of the few Egyptian films concerned with Palestine. Since then all that can be said is that, in his prolific output, he manages to keep up with all passing fads. 1980s features:

The Torment of Love/'Adhab al-hubb – 1980
The Devils/Al-abalisa – 1980
Not by Love Alone/Al-hubb wahduhu la yakfi – 1981
Roadless Voyager/Musaffar bila tariq – 1981
My Love was Lost There/Wada 'a hubbi hunak – 1982
Shame/Al-'ar – 1982
The Bribed/Al-sadat al-murtashun – 1984
Daughters of Satan/Banat iblis – 1984
Execution of a Dead Man/I 'dam mayyit – 1985
Hashish/Al-kayf – 1985
Fish Warehouse/Shadir al-samak – 1986
Al-Hanakish – 1986
Furnished Tombs for Rent/Madafin mafrusha lil-ijar – 1987
Mud/Al-wahl – 1987
The Well of Treachery/Bir al-khayana – 1987
Four on an Official Mission/Arba'a fi muhimma rasmiyya – 1987

The Way of the Beasts/Jary al-wuhush – 1988
To Us!/Ilhaquna – 1989
Rape/Ightisab – 1989
The Charlatan/Al-baida wal-hajar – 1990

ABDEL SALAM, Shadi (b. 1930, Alexandria, Egypt)
Abdel Salam studied at Oxford, the Institute of Fine Arts in Cairo, and graduated in architecture. Assistant and artistic adviser to many foreign directors, from 1968 until his death in 1986 Abdel Salam directed Cairo's Experimental Film Centre. Though only one of his films is feature length, it is deservedly famous abroad.

The Night of the Counting of the Years/Al-mumia – 1968

ABDEL SAYED, Daoud (b. 1946, Cairo, Egypt)
A graduate of the Higher Cinema Institute, Abdel Sayed came into feature films via the National Centre for Documentary Films in Cairo and is part of the group known as the New Egyptian Realists.

The Bums/Al-sa'alik – 1985
Searching for Mr Marzuq/Al-bahths 'an al-sayyid Marzuq – 1990

ABOU SEIF, Mohamed (Egypt)
Son of the famous Egyptian director Salah Abou Seif and a graduate of the Cairo Higher Cinema Institute, Mohamed Abou Seif has to his credit so far one fairly schematic film and one fairly realistic film.

The Apple and the Skull/Al-tufaha wal-gumguma – 1986
The River of Fear/Nahr al-khawf – 1988

ABOU SEIF, Salah (b. 1915, Cairo, Egypt)
Called 'the father of Egyptian realism', Salah Abou Seif graduated in commercial studies. Known for his direction of many lively films, he also once taught at the Higher Cinema Institute, directed the nationalized cinema organization and founded a scriptwriting school.

Always in My Heart/Daiman fi qalbi – 1946
The Avenger/Al-muntaqim – 1947
The Adventures of Antar and Abla/Mughamarat Antar wa Abla – 1948
Street of the Acrobat/Shari' al-bahlawan – 1949
The Falcon/Al-saqr – 1950
Love is Scandalous/Al-hubb bahdala – 1951
Your Day Will Come/Lak yawm ya Zalim – 1952
Foreman Hassan/Al-usta Hassan – 1953

Raya and Sakina/Raya wa Sakina – 1953
The Monster/Al-wahsh – 1954
A Woman's Youth/Shabab imra – 1955
The Bully/Al-futuwwa – 1954
The Empty Pillow/Al-wisada al-khaliya – 1957
Night Without Sleep/La anam – 1957
A Thief on Vacation/Mujrim fi ajaza – 1958
The Alley/Al-tariq al-masdud – 1958
That Is What Love Is/Hadha huwwa al-hubb – 1958
I Am Free/Ana hurra – 1959
Between Heaven and Earth/Bayn al-sama wal-ard – 1959
The Anguish of Love/Law'at al-hubb – 1960
Dead Among the Living/Bidaya wa nihaya – 1960 (also known as *The
    Beginning and the End*, a title closer to the original)
Don't Put Out the Sun/La tutfi' al-shams – 1961
Letter from an Unknown Woman/Risala min imra majhula – 1962
No Time for Love/La waqt lil-hubb – 1963
Cairo '30/Al-qahira thalathin – 1966
The Second Wife/Al-zaujat al-thaniya – 1967
Case 68/Al-Qadiya 68 – 1968
Three Women/Thalath nisa – 1969 (sketch with Barakat and Zulfikar)
A Certain Pain/Shayun min al-'adhab – 1969
The Dawn of Islam/Fajr al-islam – 1970
The Baths of Malatili/Hammam al-Malatili – 1973
The Liar/Al-kadhdhab – 1975
The First Year of Love/Sana ula hubb – 1976 (sketch with others)
In an Ocean of Honey/Wa saqatat fi bahr min al-'asal – 1976
The Water Carrier is Dead/Al-saqqa mat – 1977
The Assassin/Al-mujrim – 1978
Al-Qadisiyya – 1980
The Beginning/Al-bidaya – 1986

ALASSANE, Mustapha (b. 1942, Niger)
Pioneer of Niger cinema. Introduced to cinema by Jean Rouch in
Niamey, he spent a brief period studying animation with Norman
MacLaren in Canada. He has made eight completed fictional,
documentary or animated short films, beginning with *Aouré* (1962).
After a 50-minute parody of the Western, *The Adventurer's Return/Le
retour de l'aventurier*, he has made three 16mm features:

Wife, Villa, Car, Money/FVVA (Femme, Villa, Voiture, Argent – 1972
Toula, or the Water Spirit/Toula, ou le génie des eaux – 1974 (co-director
    Anna Soehring)
Kankamba – 1982

ALAWIYA, Borhan (b. 1941, Beirut, Lebanon)
A graduate of the Belgian film school, INSAS, Alawiya has made memorable feature films on a Palestinian massacre and the plight of Lebanon.

Kafr Kassem – 1974
Beirut, the Encounter/Beirut al-liqa – 1982

ALLOUACHE, Merzak (b. 1944, Algiers, Algeria)
One of the few graduates of the short-lived Algerian film school, Allouache is particularly notable for the variety of his narrative approaches and an unusual, ever-present, wry humour.

Omar Gatlato – 1976
The Adventures of a Hero/Mughamarat batal – 1978
The Man Who Watched Windows/Rajul wa nawafidh – 1982
A Paris Love/Un amour à Paris – 1986

AMPAW, King (b. 1940, Ghana)
Studied film-making at various schools in Potsdam, Vienna and Munich and subsequently worked in German television. His first feature was shot in the German Federal Republic and both his subsequent features had German production links. On his return to Ghana in 1976 he worked with the Ghana Broadcasting Corporation. Features:

They Call It Love – 1972 (in Germany)
Kukurantumi – 1983
Juju – 1986 (co-director Ingrid Metner)

ANSAH, Kwah (b. 1941, Agona Swedra, Ghana)
Studied theatre design at the Regent Street Polytechnic and worked briefly in a minor capacity for RKO in the USA. His first play, *The Adoption*, was staged off Broadway and his second, *A Mother's Tears*, after his return to Ghana. His two 35mm features both explore questions of identity and the continuing force of values acquired under colonialism.

Love Brewed in the African Pot – 1981
Heritage . . . Africa – 1988

ARAFA, Sharif (Egypt)
A graduate of the Cairo Higher Cinema Institute, Arafa is notable so far for the unusually stylized whimsy with which he treated two marginal territories: the world of dwarfs and that of sports fans.

The Dwarfs are Coming/Al-aqzam qadimun – 1987
The Third Class/Al-darajat al-thalitha – 1988
Listen and Shut Up/Sama' huss – 1990

ASSAF, Roger (Lebanon)
After studying theatre in Strasbourg, Assaf returned to Lebanon to innovate on stage, founded his own storytelling theatre troupe and taught drama. His first feature film reflects a similar willingness to invent his own forms.

Battle/Maarake – 1985

BADRAKHAN, Ali (b. 1946, Cairo, Egypt)
Son of the famous Egyptian director Ahmed Badrakhan and a graduate of Cairo's Higher Cinema Institute, Badrakhan made a name for himself with his first film, *The Love that Was/Al-hubb aladhi kan* (1971). A second feature, *Al-Karnak*, followed in 1975. 1980s features:

High Society/Ahl al-qimma – 1981
Hunger/Al-ju' – 1986

BALOGUN, Ola (b. 1945, Aba, Nigeria)
Balogun studied at the IDHEC in Paris, worked as a writer and as press attaché at the Nigerian Embassy in Paris. He is the most prolific of black African film-makers, with ten short films and ten features between 1969 and 1984. Though he has worked in Brazil and Ghana, he has been most influential in introducing the Yoruba folk-opera directors to cinema. Features:

Alpha – 1972
Amadi – 1975
Ajani Ogun – 1976
Musik-Man – 1977
Black Goddess/A deusa negra – 1978
Fight for Freedom/Ija Ominira – 1979
Aiye – 1980
Cry Freedom – 1981
Orun Mooru – 1982
Money Power – 1982–4 (two feature-length parts)

BEN AMMAR, Abdellatif (b. 1943, Tunisia)
A 1964 graduate of the Paris IDHEC film school, Ben Ammar moved over from direction into production after two very well-received feature films.

Sejnane – 1973
Aziza – 1980

BEN MAHMOUD, Mahmoud (b. 1949, Tunisia)
A graduate of Belgium's INSAS film school, Ben Mahmoud also studied archaeology, journalism, and wrote scenarios. Though he has directed only one film so far, its disturbing treatment of exile has been widely appreciated.

Crossings/'Ubur – 1982

BESHARA, Khairy (b. 1947, Tanta, Egypt)
Beshara graduated in 1967 from the Egyptian Higher Cinema Institute and came to feature films via documentaries. One of the New Egyptian Realist directors, he pops up as an actor in cameo roles in the films of his friends.

Bloody Destinies/Al-aqdar al-damiya – 1982
Houseboat 70/Al-'awwama 70 – 1982
The Necklace and the Bracelet/Al-tauq wal-aswira – 1986
Bitter Day, Sweet Day/Yawm murr, yawm hulw – 1989

BOUAMARI, Mohamed (b. 1941, Guedjal, Algeria)
Self-taught, Bouamari has brought a refreshing boldness to Algerian cinema, willing to tackle both women's experience and men's roles, even risking one weak film (his latest) along the way.

The Charcoal Burner/Al-fahham – 1972
The Inheritance/Al-irth – 1974
First Step/Al-khutwat al-ula – 1979
The Refusal/Al-rafd – 1982

BOUZID, Nouri (b. 1945, Sfax, Tunisia)
A 1972 graduate of the Audiovisual Institute in Brussels. Bouzid's first film stunned audiences by its sensitive handling of a taboo subject.

Man of Ashes/Rih al-sadd – 1986
Golden Horseshoes/Safaih min dhahab – 1989

CHAHINE, Yusuf (b. 1926, Alexandria, Egypt)
One of Egypt's leading directors, Chahine studied at the Pasadena Playhouse in California and is often more appreciated abroad than at home. From 1973 on, most of his films are unique in Arab cinema in their thematic density and formal complexity.

Papa Amin/Baba Amin – 1950
Son of the Nile/Ibn al-Nil – 1951
The Big Buffoon/Al-muharrij al-kabir – 1952
The Woman on the Train/Sayyidat al-qitar – 1952
Women Without Men/Nisa bil rijal – 1953
Struggle in the Valley/Sira' fil-wadi – 1954
The Demon of the Desert/Shaytan al-sahra – 1954
Struggle in the Port/Sira' fil-mina – 1956
You are My Love/Inta habibi – 1957
Goodbye to Your Love/Wadda'tu hubbak – 1957
Cairo: Central Station/Bab al-hadid – 1958
Jamila/Jamila al-jazairiyya – 1958
Yours Forever/Hubb lil-abad – 1959
In Your Hands/Bayna aydik – 1960
Call of the Lovers/Nida al-'ushshaq – 1961
A Man in My Life/Rajul fi hayati – 1961
Saladin/Al-nasir Salah al-Din – 1963
Dawn of a New Day/Fajr yawm jadid – 1964
The Seller of Rings/Bayya' al-khawatim – 1965
Golden Sands/Rimal min dhahab – 1966
People and the Nile/Al-nas wal-Nil – 1968
The Earth/Al-ard – 1969
The Choice/Al-ikhtiyar – 1970
The Sparrow/Al-'usfur – 1973
Return of the Prodigal Son/'Awdat al-ibn al-dall – 1976
Alexandria Why?/Iskandariya leeh? – 1978
An Egyptian Story/Hadutha masriyya – 1982
Farewell Bonaparte/Al-wida'a Bonaparte – 1985
The Sixth Day/Al-yawm al-sadis – 1987
Alexandria, again and again/Iskandariya, kaman wa kaman – 1990

CHOUIKH, Mohamed (b. 1943, Mostaganem, Algeria)
Initially a well-known Algerian actor, Chouikh is now having his own say on Algerian myth and reality as director.

Rupture/Al-inqita' – 1982
The Citadel/Al-qal'a – 1988

CISSE, Souleymane (b. 1940, Bamako, Mali)
Studied for eight years in Moscow, first as a photographer and projectionist, then as a film-maker at the VGIK under Mark Donskoi. Cisse made three short student films in Moscow, then on his return to

Mali a number of newsreels and documentaries for the Mali State Information Services and a 40-minute documentary, *Five Days in a Life/Cinq jours d'une vie* (1972). His four subsequent features have made him the leading figure in the second generation of African film-makers:

The Girl/Den muso – 1975
Work/Baara – 1978
The Wind/Finye – 1982
The Light/Yeelen – 1987

DERKAOUI, Mustapha Abdelkrim (b. 1941, Oujda, Morocco)
After studying theatre in Casablanca, and cinema in Poland and at the IDHEC in Paris, Derkaoui returned to Morocco and worked first collectively with Mohamed Reggab and then set off on his own to pursue alinear narrative experiments.

The Cinders of the Yard/Les cendres du clos – 1979 (with Reggab)
The Beautiful Days of Sheherazade/Ayyam Sherezad al-jamila – 1982
The Day of the Hawker/Le jour du forain – 1985

DHOUIB, Moncef (b. 1952, Sfax, Tunisia)
Dhouib has so far made only short or medium-length films, but these have been noted for their imagination and their insight (remarkable in a man) into spaces reserved for women only.

Eagles' Nest/Nid d'aigles – 1982 (medium-length)
Hammam D'hab – 1986 (short)

al-DIK, Beshir (b. Damiet, Egypt)
After graduating with a degree in commerce from Cairo University, al-Dik made his reputation as a scriptwriter. Several New Egyptian Realist films owe their scenarios to him and he has directed a couple of his own.

The Flood/Al-tufan – 1985
The Journey's Road/Sikka safar – 1986

DIOP-MAMBETY, Djibril (b. 1945, Dakar, Senegal)
After three years as actor with the national theatre, the Théâtre Daniel Sorano in Dakar, and two idiosyncratic short films, *Contrast-City* (1968) and *Badou Boy* (1970), Diop-Mambety made his sole feature film, one of the most brilliant and unclassifiable works of African cinema, in 1973. He returned to film making with the short, *Parlons grandmère*, in 1989. Fictional feature:

Touki-Bouki – 1973

DUARTE DE CARVALHO, Ruy (b. 1941, Portugal)
A writer and film-maker who originally studied social science, Duarte was raised in southern Angola, which forms the subject of his poems and stories: *A decisão da idade* (1976) and *Como se o mondo não tivesse leste* (1977). A naturalized Angolan citizen since 1975, he has been very active as a documentary film-maker: five shorts contributed to the series *Sou angolano, trabalho com força* (1975), and there have also been a number of medium-length films, *Generaçao 50* (1975), *Uma festa para viver* (1976) and *Faz la coragem, camarada* (1977), the series *Presente Angolano, tempo Mumuila* (1980), etc. Fictional feature:

Nelisita – 1982

DUPARC, Henri (b. 1941, Guinea)
Duparc studied cinema in Belgrade and at the IDHEC in Paris before settling in the Ivory Coast. His first film was a medium-length fictional film, *Mouna, or An Artist's Dream/Mouna ou le rêve d'un artiste* (1969). Subsequently he made a number of commissioned shorts and a series of feature films:

The Family/Abusan– 1972
Wild Grass/L'herbe sauvage – 1977
I've Chosen to Live/J'ai choisi de vivre – 1987
Bal poussière – 1988

ECARE, Désiré (b. 1939, Abidjan, Ivory Coast)
Ecare studied first drama and then cinema (at the IDHEC) in Paris and his first films, the medium-length *Concerto for an Exile/Concerto pour un exil* (1968) and his first feature were shot in France. Fifteen years later his first African-made feature was a great commercial success. Features:

It's Up to Us, France/A nous deux, France – 1970
Women's Faces/Visages de femmes – 1985

FADIKA, Kramo Lancine (b. 1948, Ivory Coast)
Fadika studied at the University of Abidjan and the Ecole Nationale Louis Lumière, rue de Vaugirard in Paris. On his return to the Ivory Coast he made a number of short films on rural development and a single feature film which was highly successful with critics and African audiences wherever it was shown:

Djeli – 1981

FANARI, Mohamed Mounir (b. 1949, Syria)
A student at the IDHEC in Paris, Fanari worked in Iraqi television before making his first feature.

The Lover/Al-'ashiq – 1986

FAYE, Safi (b. 1943, Dakar, Senegal)
The first black African woman to direct a feature-length film, Safi Faye was a schoolteacher when she was chosen by Jean Rouch for a role in his film *Petit à petit* (1971). Subsequently she studied both ethnography and film-making in Paris, making her first short, *The Passer-by/La passante* (1972) as part of her studies. After her two feature-length studies of rural Senegal, she made short and medium-length films for foreign television companies and international organizations: *Goob Na Nu* (1979), *Man Sa Yay* (1979), *Souls in the Sun* (1981) and *Selbe And So Many Others* (1982). Feature films:

Letter From My Village/Kaddu beykat – 1975
Fad Jal – 1979

FERHATI, Jilali (Morocco)
After studying cinema in Paris and making a first film with his brother, Ferhati made a second notable for its sensitivity to milieu and character.

A Breach in the Wall/Une brèche dans le mur – 1978
Reed Dolls/'Arais min qasab – 1981

GANDA, Oumarou (b. 1935, Niamey, Niger; d. 1981)
A pioneer, with Mustapha Alassane, of Niger cinema, Ganda's experience of fighting with the French troops in Indo-China is reflected in his role in *Moi un noir* (1957), directed by Jean Rouch, whose assistant he became in Niamey, and in his own first medium-length film, *Cabascabo* (1969). His other films include other medium-length and short films – *Le wazzou polygame* (1971), *Galio de l'air* (1973), *Cock, cock, cock* (1973) and *Le Niger à Carthage* (1978) – and two features:

Saitane – 1973
The Exile/L'Exilé – 1980

GERIMA, Haile (b. 1946, Gonda, Ethiopia)
Gerima went to the USA in 1967 to study first at the Goodman School of Drama in Chicago and then at UCLA, where his first shorts, *Hour Glass* (1971) and *Child of Resistance* (1972), were made. Now resident in the USA and teaching at Howard University in Washington, he has become

a leading figure in black American cinema with several US-made features to his credit: *Bush Mama* (1975), *Wilmington 10, USA 10,000* (1979) and *Ashes and Embers* (1982). His sole film shot in his native Ethiopia is a work of masterly complexity:

Harvest 3,000 Years/Mirt sost shi amit – 1976

GUERRA, Ruy (b. 1931, Lourenço Marques, now Maputo, Mozambique)
Guerra studied at the IDHEC in Paris and most of his features have been Brazilian or internationally financed films: *The Hustlers/Os cafajestes* (1962), *The Guns/Os fuzis* (1964), *Sweet Hunters* (1969), *The Gods and the Dead/Os deuses e os mortos* (1970), *The Fall* (1977), *Erendira* (1982), *Opera do Malandro* (1986). His sole African feature is a remarkable study of colonial violence remembered:

Mueda, Memory and Massacre/Mueda, memória e massacre – 1979

HALILU, Adamu (b. 1936, Garkida, Nigeria)
After a spell with the Film Unit in Northern Nigeria, Halilu received his training at the Overseas Film and Television Centre and the Shell Film Unit in London. On his return to Nigeria he made numerous documentaries: *It Pays to Care* (1955), *Hausa Village* (1958), *Northern Horizon* (1959), *Durbar Day* (1960), *Giant in the Sun* (1960), *Eye Care* (1962), *Rinderpest* (1963), *Welcome Change* (1965), *Tourist Delight* (1967), *Back to the Land* (1967), *Pride of the Nation* (1974), *Black Heritage* (1977), *Child Bride* (1977). The leading Hausa-language film-maker, Halilu has made a number of features which have received very little distribution:

Shehu Umar (1977)
Kanta of Kebbi (1978)
Moment of Truth (1981)

HONDO, Med (b. 1936, Mauritania)
Hondo has lived since 1958 in France, where he worked in theatre before turning to the cinema. All his features have been made in exile.

Soleil O – 1970
The Black-Wogs Your Neighbours/Les bicots-nègres vos voisins – 1974
We Have the Whole of Death for Sleeping/Nous avons toute la mort pour dormir – 1977
West Indies – 1979
Sarraounia – 1986

KABORE, Gaston (b. 1951, Bobo-Dioulasso, Burkina Faso)
Kabore studied history and film-making in Paris. President of FEPACI (Fédération panafricaine des cinéastes). After a number of short films – *I'm Coming Back From Bokin/Je reviens de Bokin* (1977), *Store and Preserve Grain/Stockez et conservez le grain* (1978), *A Look at the Sixth FESPACO/Regard sur le VIᵉ FESPACO* (1979) and *The Use of New Energies in Rural Areas/Utilisation des énergies nouvelles en milieu rural* (1980) – he made an international reputation with his first two features:

God's Gift/Wend Kuuni – 1982
Zan Boko – 1988

KAMWA, Daniel (Cameroon)
An actor and stage director, Kamwa came to cinema with a short film, *Boubou cravate* (1973), adapted from a story by Francis Bebey. Though his two French-language features were among the most commercially successful of African films, he has since made only short films and commercials.

Rickshaw/Pousse-pousse – 1975
Our Daughter/Notre fille – 1980

KHAN, Mohamed (b. 1942, Cairo, Egypt)
Khan studied film in London where he published a short book in English on Egyptian cinema. Since then he has been as notable for the quality of his output as for its quantity, and is arguably the leading figure of the New Egyptian Realists. 1980s features:

Vengeance/Al-thar – 1980
Bird on the Road/Tair 'alal-tariq – 1981
Dinner Date/Maw'ad 'alal-'asha – 1981
Half a Million/Nasf arnab – 1982
The Streetplayer/Al-harrif – 1983
Missing Person/Kharaj wa lam ya'ud – 1984
Omar's Journey/Mishwar 'Omar – 1985
Youssef and Zeinab/Youssef wa Zeinab – 1986
Return of a Citizen/'Awda muwatin – 1986
Wife of an Important Man/Zauja rajul muhimm – 1987
Dreams of Hind and Camelia/Ahlam Hind wa Camelia – 1988
Supermarket – 1990

KHEMIR, Nacer (b. 1948, Tunis, Tunisia)
Sculptor, writer and performing storyteller, Khemir is concerned to inject Arab cinema with its forgotten cultural heritage.

The Drifters/ Al-haimoun – 1984
The Lost Ring of the Dove/Tawq al-hamama al-mafqud – 1990

KHLEIFI, Michel (b. 1950, Nazareth, Palestine)
After studying cinema at Belgium's INSAS, Khleifi did a full-length documentary on Palestinian women. His first fictional feature, shot in the occupied territories and produced through Franco-Belgian support, has by some been called unduly Orientalist.

Fertile Memories/ Al-dhikrayat al-khasibah – 1981
Wedding in Galilee/'Urs al-jalyl – 1987
Song of the Stones/Nashid al-hijara – 1988

LAHHAM, Doreid (Syria)
Improbable as it may seem, Lahham came to cinema via a career teaching physics. He subsequently worked as an actor in theatre, television and film. Actor or director, his genius lies in comedy.

Borders/ Al-hudud – 1984
The Report/ Al-taqrir – 1986
The Attachment/ Al-mahabba – 1990

LAHLOU, Nabyl (b. 1945, El Jedida, Morocco)
Having studied theatre in Paris, Lahlou shuttles back and forth between stage and screen, as both actor and director in his own, fairly outrageous satires.

The Governor General/ Al-hakim al-'am – 1980
Brahim Yach – 1984
The Soul's Braying/Nahiq al-ruh – 1984

LAKHDAR-HAMINA, Mohamed (b. 1934, M'sila, Algeria)
Though Lakhdar-Hamina's most recent work is said to be Euro-oriented, and though when head of Algeria's national film organization he was said to be extravaganza-bound, he is none the less one of the pioneers of Algerian cinema, and one of its most competent directors.

Wind of the Aures/Rih al-Awras – 1966
Hassan Terro – 1968
December/Décembre – 1972
Chronicle of the Years of Ashes/Waqai' sinin al-jamr – 1975
Sandstorm/Vent de sable – 1982
The Last Image/La dernière image – 1986

LLEDO, Jean Pierre (b. 1947, Tlemcen, Algeria)
A graduate of VGIK, Moscow's cinema school, Lledo wrote some interesting articles in Algeria's now defunct *The Two Screens (Les deux ecrans/Al-shashatan)*, and followed this up with a whacky but controversial film on cinema in Algeria.

Empire of Dreams/Mamlakat al-ahlam – 1982
Lights/Adwa – 1990

al-MAANOUNI, Ahmed (b. 1944, Casablanca, Morocco)
After studies at Belgium's cinema school, INSAS, al-Maanouni has made his main impact through his imaginative handling of documentary material.

Oh the Days, Oh the Days/Al-ayyam, al-ayyam – 1978
Trances/Ahwal – 1980

MALASS, Mohamed (b. 1948, Kuneitra, Syria)
A graduate of the Moscow Film Institute and widely admired for his first feature film, Malass, like others, fills the gaps with shorts, one of which, the 1980 work on Palestinians, *The Dream/Al-manam*, illustrates his skill in framing and pacing.

Dreams of the City/Ahlam al-madina – 1984
Advertising for a City/I'lanat 'an madina – 1990

MARZUQ, Sa'id (b. 1940, Cairo, Egypt)
After several years away in television, Marzuq has re-emerged in Egypt's cinema of the 1980s with a couple of films particularly notable for their formal innovation.

My Wife and the Dog/Zaujati wal-kalb – 1970
Fear/Al-khauf – 1972
I Want a Solution/Uridu hallan – 1974
The Guilty/Al-mudhnibun – 1975
Save What We Can/Inqadh ma yumkin inqadhuhu – 1985
Days of Terror/Ayyam al-ru'b – 1988
The Rapists/Al-mughtasibun – 1989

al-MIHI, Raafat (b. 1940, Cairo, Egypt)
A graduate in English literature, al-Mihi first made his name as a scriptwriter. As a director he veers from unconventionally moving family drama to eccentric and biting comedy.

Unsleeping Eyes/'Uyun la tanam – 1980
The Lawyer/Al-avocato – 1984
A Last Love Story/Lil-hubb qissa akhira – 1986
The Gentlemen/Al-sadat al-rijal – 1987
Hurley Burley/Samak, laban, tamar hindi – 1988
Ladies and Young Ladies/Sayyidati, annisati – 1990 (French title: *Desmoiselles?*)

MOHAMED, 'Ussama (b. 1948, Syria)
A graduate of the Moscow Film Insitute, Mohamed's first feature film fulfilled the promise of his previous short films.

Stars of the Day/Nujum al-nahar – 1988

al-NAGGAR, Mohamed (Egypt)
A 1978 graduate of the Egyptian Higher Cinema Institute, al-Naggar already sees his first film used there as an example of visual inscriptions.

The Time of Hatem Zahran/Zaman Hatem Zahran – 1987

NEW TUNISIAN THEATRE COLLECTIVE
Both the films made by the collective have been transpositions of stage works, co-directed by two men with theatre backgrounds, Fadhel JAIBI (b. 1948, Tunis, Tunisia) and Fadhel JAZIRI (b. 1948, Tunis, Tunisia). The second of these films is reputed to herald a new Arab film language.

The Wedding/Al-'urs – 1978
Arab/'Arab – 1988

OGUNDE, Chief Hubert (b. 1916, Ososa, Nigeria)
One of the pioneer figures in the Yoruba touring folk theatre, Ogunde began his theatrical career (comprising over fifty stage works) in 1944 with a religious opera. He moved on to political and folkloric themes. He moved from music theatre to spoken plays at the beginning of the 1950s, and satirical comedies of contemporary life form a major part of his later theatrical output. His first contact with the cinema came when Ola Balogun filmed a version of his play *Aiye* (1980). Features:

Jaiyesimi – 1981 (co-director Freddie Goode)
Aropin N'Tenia – 1982 (co-director Freddie Goode)

OUEDRAOGO, Idrissa (b. 1954, Banfora, Burkina Faso)
Ouedraogo studied film-making at INAFEC (Institut africain d'études

cinématographiques) in Ouagadougou and at the IDHEC in Paris. He made a number of shorts: *Poko* (1981), *The Bowls* (1983), *The Funeral of Larle* (1983), *Ouagadougou, Ouaga Two Wheels* (1984), *Issa the Weaver* (1985), before turning successfully to features:

The Choice/Yam daabo – 1987
Yaaba – 1989
Tilali – 1990

RACHEDI, Ahmed (b. 1938, Tebessa, Algeria)
In on the very beginnings of Algerian cinema via the film units of the Resistance, Rachedi later directed the national cinema organization for a while. He has made perhaps his best films in the 1980s.

Dawn of the Damned/Fajr al-mu'adhdhibin – 1965
Opium and the Stick/Al-afyun wal-'asa – 1969
Ali in Wonderland/Ali fi bilad al-sarab – 1980
The Mill of M. Fabre/Tahunat al-sayyid Fabre – 1982

al-RAWI, Abdel Hadi (b. 1938, Rawah, Iraq)
Having studied cinema in the Soviet Union, al-Rawi returned to Iraq in 1968 to concentrate on documentaries. He moved into feature films in the 1980s.

Love in Bahgdad/Al-hubb fi Baghdad – 1986

REGGAB, Mohamed (b. 1942, Morocco)
A graduate of the Moscow film school, Reggab first worked in Morocco on a collectively made film with, among others, Derkaoui, then on his own in Morocco for a particularly anguished portrait of marginality.

The Cinders of the Yard/Les cendres du clos – 1979 (with Derkaoui)
The Barber of the Poor Quarter/Hallaq darb al-fuqara – 1982

SALEH, Tewfik (b. 1926, Alexandria, Egypt)
Saleh is a graduate in English literature and ranks with Abou Seif and Chahine in his generation. Despite his low output and the exigencies of foreign production, some of his films are outstanding for their handling of visual technique and for their taut rhythm.

Alley of Fools/Darb al-mahabil – 1955
Struggle of the Heroes/Sira' al-abtal – 1961
The Rebels/Al-mutamarridun – 1966
The Journal of a Country Prosecutor/Yawmiyyat naib fil-aryaf – 1968

Al-Sayyid al-Bolti/Zuqaq al-sayyid al-Bolti – 1969
The Dupes/Al-makhdu'un – 1972
The Long Days/Al-ayyam al-tawila – 1981

SAMB-MAKHARAM, Ababacar (b. 1934, Dakar, Senegal; d. 1987)
Trained at OCORA (Office de coopération radiophonique) in Paris and
at the Centro sperimentale in Rome, he founded a Paris-based theatre
company, Les Griots, before making his first short, *And the Snow Was
No Longer There/Et la neige n'etait plus* (1964). His two features focus on
questions of African culture:

Kodou (1971)
Jom (1981)

SEDDIKI, Tayyeb (b. 1937, Essaouira, Morocco)
Already well-known in France and Morocco for his theatrical
innovations, Seddiki surprised the audiences of his first film by his
adroit manipulation of cinematic techniques.

Zift – 1984

SEFRAOUI, Najib (b. 1948, Fez, Morocco)
After studying film, art and archaeology in Paris, Sefraoui came into
feature film making via political essays and documentary work.

Chams – 1985

SEMBENE, Ousmane (b. 1923, Ziguinchor, Senegal)
Sembene received little formal education, dropping out of school at 14.
He fought in the French army during World War Two; subsequently he
worked as a docker in Marseilles and became a union activist. In 1956 he
published his first novel, and his career as a French-language writer has
continued into the 1980s alongside his work as a film-maker: *Le Docker
noir* (1956), *O pays, mon beau peuple* (1957), *Les Bouts de bois de dieu*
(1960) – in English as *God's Bits of Wood* (1962) – *Voltaique* (1962) – in
English as *Tribal Scars and Other Stories* (1963) – *L'Harmattan* (1964),
Vehi ciosane, ou Blanche genèse, suivi du mandat (1965) – in English as
The Money Order, with White Genesis (1972) – *Xala* (1974) – in English as
Xala (1976) – *Le dernier de l'empire* (1981) – in English as *The Last of the
Empire* (1983) – *Niwam, suivi de Taaw* (1987). Sembene was almost 40
when he received a scholarship enabling him to study film-making for a
year at the Gorki Studio in Moscow under Mark Donskoi and Sergei
Guerassimov. On his return to Senegal he made a number of short films

– *Borom Sarret* (1963), *Niaye* (1964), *Black Girl/La noire de . . .* (1966), *Taw* (1970) – and features which put him in the forefront of African film-making. For ten years he has sought funding for an epic study of Samori Toure's struggle against the French invaders. Feature films:

The Money-Order/Mandabi – 1968
Emitai – 1971
Xala – 1974
Ceddo – 1977
Camp Thiaroye/Camp de Thiaroye – 1988 (co-director Thierno Faty Sow)

SMIHI, Moumen (b. 1945, Tangiers, Morocco)
A student of the Paris film school IDHEC, Smihi has moved from his 1975 stark portrayal of solitude to films more centred on history, performance and dream.

El Chergui – 1975
Forty-four, or Bedtime Stories/Quarante-quatre, ou les récits de la nuit – 1982
Caftan of Love/Quftan al-hubb – 1988

SROUR, Heini (Beirut, Lebanon)
Not only one of the Arab world's few women directors, Srour is also one of its most intrepid, having taken on almost the whole real or imagined experience of Levantine women in her first feature film.

Leila and the Wolves/Layla wal-dhiab – 1984

al-TAYYEB, Atef (b. 1947, Cairo, Egypt)
Al-Tayyeb graduated from Cairo's Higher Cinema Institute in 1970 and though his large output since then is not always up to his capacities, his film *The Bus Driver* is one of the most stunning of the New Egyptian Realist films. Several of his others are both venturesome and popular.

Murderous Jealousy/Al-ghirat al-qatila – 1982
The Bus Driver/Sawwaq al-autobis – 1983
The Clink/Al-takhshiba – 1984
The Piper/Al-zammar – 1985
On File for Morals/Malaff fil-adaab – 1986
The Innocent/Al-bari – 1986
Love above the Pyramid/Al-hubb fawq al-haram – 1986
The Basement/Al-badrun – 1987
Sons and Killers/Abna wa qatala – 1988

The World on the Wing of a Dove/Al-dunya 'ala janah yamama – 1988
The Firing Squad/Katibat al-i'dam – 1989
Heart of the Night/Qalb al-layl – 1989
The Escape/Al-hurub – 1990

TCHISSOUKOU, Jean-Paul (b. 1942, Pointe-Noire, Congo; d. 1987)
After receiving his film training at OCORA and INA in Paris,
Tchissoukou made two short films – *Illusions* (1971) and *The Child and
the Family/L'enfant et la famille* (1977) – and two well-received features
before his early death:

The Chapel/La chapelle – 1979
The Wrestlers/M'Pongo – 1982

TRAORE, Mahama Johnson (b. 1942, Dakar, Senegal)
Traore studied film-making at the CICF in Paris. After his debut with
the medium-length *Dianka-bi* (1969), he made a further medium-length
fictional film, *Reou-Takh* (1972), and five features in the early 1970s:

The Innocents' Hell/L'enfer des innocents – 1970
Diegue-bi – 1970
Lambaye – 1972
Garga M'Bosse – 1974
N'Diangane – 1975

TSAKI, Brahim (b. 1946, Sidi Bel Abbes, Algeria)
A student of Belgium's film school INSAS, Tsaki has directed two films
which, though about children and though almost mute, have far-
reaching impact and implications.

Children of the Wind/Abna al-rih – 1981
Story of an Encounter/Hikaya liqa – 1983

VIEYRA, Paulin Soumanou (b. 1925, Porto Novo, Benin; d. 1987)
Vieyra studied at IDHEC in Paris and later acquired his doctorate at the
Université de Paris X. Co-director of the first short to be made by black
African film-makers, *Africa on the Seine/Afrique sur Seine* (1955).
Vieyra was the leading historian of African cinema, and published
numerous articles and four books: *Le cinéma et l'Afrique* (1969),
Ousmane Sembène, cinéaste (1972), *Le cinéma africain des origines à 1973*
(1975) and *Le cinéma au Sénégal* (1983). Resident in Senegal, he made
some twenty documentary films between *Mol* (begun 1957; completed
1966) and his final films, *Birago Diop, Storyteller/Birago Diop, conteur*

(1982) and *Iba N'Diaye, Painter/Iba N'Diaye, peintre* (1983). His sole feature film was:

Under House Arrest/En résidence surveillée – 1981

YASHFIN, Ahmed (Morocco)
After studying cinema in Los Angeles, Yashfin returned to Morocco to make this film about a particularly Moroccan dilemma.

The Nightmare/Al-kabus – 1984

al-YASSIRI, Faisal (b. 1923, Iraq)
Trained as a television director in Vienna, al-Yassiri also worked for television in East Berlin before returning to Iraq to make feature films for the Iraqi state organization.

The Head/Al-ras – 1976
The River/Al-nahr – 1977
The Sniper/Al-qannas – 1981
The Princess and the River/Al-amira wal-nahr – 1982
Babylon my Beloved/Babel habibiti – 1988

ZEMMOURI, Mahmoud (b. 1946, Boufarik, Algeria)
A student of the Paris film school IDHEC, Zemmouri has made his films mostly in France in a brash, racy style that appeals especially to young second-generation Algerian immigrants.

Take 1,000 Quid and Shove Off/Prends dix mille balles et casses-toi – 1981
The Mad Years of the Twist/Les folles années du twist – 1983
From Hollywood to Temerraset/De Hollywood à Temerraset – 1990

ZIKRA, Samir (b. 1948, Latakia, Syria)
A graduate of the Moscow Film Institute, Zikra's acute films are part of a projected trilogy on facets of contemporary Syrian life.

The Half Metre Incident/Hadith al-nasf metr – 1983
Events of the Coming Year/Waqai' al-'am al-muqbil – 1986

Notes

1. Cinema Under Colonialism

1. Thoraval, 1975, p. 7.
2. Megherbi, 1982, p. 15.
3. Khleifi, 1970, p. 29.
4. Berrah *et al.*, 1981, p. 206.
5. Vieyra, 1983, p. 18.
6. Opubor and Nwuneli, 1979, p. 2.
7. Otten, 1984, p. 17.
8. al-Haraty, 1988, p. 2.
9. *Arab Cinema and Culture*, 1965, vol. 3, p. 54.
10. al-Mafraji, 1978, n.p.
11. Opubor and Nwuneli, 1979, p. 2.
12. Thoraval, 1975, p. 7.
13. al-Haraty, 1988, pp. 3–4.
14. Megherbi, p. 264.
15. Thompson, 1985, pp. 146–7.
16. Guback and Varis, 1982, p. 30.
17. Roitfeld, 1980, pp. 71–8.
18. Ochs, 1986, p. 112.
19. Bakr *et al.*, 1985, p. 17.
20. Ochs, 1986, p. 68.
21. Ochs, 1986, p. 77.
22. Ochs, 1986, p. 85.
23. Ochs, 1986, p. 57.
24. Ochs, 1986, p. 86.
25. Ochs, 1986, p. 68.
26. Chelbi, 1985, p. 164.
27. Chelbi, 1985, p. 165.
28. Soyinka, 1983, p. 41.
29. Soyinka, 1983, p. 108.
30. Graham, 1988, p. 17.
31. Bakr *et al.*, 1985, pp. 14–15.
32. Anderson, 1983, p. 123.
33. Fanon, 1980, p. 61.
34. Chelbi, 1985, pp. 160–1.
35. Soyinka, 1983, p. 107.
36. Soyinka, 1983, p. 108.

37. Soyinka, 1983, p. 109.
38. Soyinka, 1983, p. 109.
39. See Roberts, 1987, pp. 189–227.
40. Convents, 1986, p. 59.
41. Gould, 1986, p. 191.
42. Gould, 1980, p. 216.
43. Bernal, 1987, p. 2.
44. Said, 1985, p. 1.
45. Said, 1985, p. 3.
46. Said, 1985, p. 6.
47. Said, 1985, p. 25.
48. Graham, 1988, pp. 16–17.
49. Ranger, 1983, p. 248.
50. Ranger, 1983, p. 247.
51. Ranger, 1983, pp. 249–50.
52. Ranger, 1983, p. 250.
53. Ranger, 1983, p. 262.
54. Boughedir, 1982, p. 100 (amended translation).
55. Richards, 1973, p. 4.
56. Boulanger, 1975, p. 17.
57. Boulanger, 1975, p. 5.
58. Nicholls, 1988.
59. Megherbi, 1982, pp. 62–3.
60. Megherbi, 1982, p. 13.
61. Boughedir, 1982, p. 102.
62. Willemen, 1978, p. 32.
63. Hennebelle and Ruelle (eds.), 1978, p. 115.
64. Notcutt and Latham, 1937, p. 21.
65. Notcutt and Latham, 1937, p. 247.
66. Curran and Porter, 1983, p. 246.
67. Sellers, 1958, p. 42.
68. Notcutt and Latham, 1937, p. 11.
69. Notcutt and Latham, 1937, p. 183.
70. Notcutt and Latham, 1937, pp. 183–4.
71. Smyth, 1988, p. 287.
72. Smyth, 1988, p. 287.
73. Sellers, 1958, p. 293.
74. Gover, 1958, pp. 54–8.
75. Fenuku, 1983, p. 49.
76. Smyth, 1983, pp. 131–47.
77. Opubor and Nwuneli, 1979, pp. 2–3.
78. Megherbi, 1982, p. 42.
79. Megherbi, 1982, p. 50.
80. Megherbi, 1982, p. 55–6.
81. Diawara, 1984, p. 29.
82. Scohy, 1958, p. 76.
83. Van den Heuvel, 1958, p. 85.
84. Diawara, 1984, p. 36.
85. Mansfield, 1978, p. 220.
86. Clawson, 1981, p. 91.

87. Barber, 1987, p. 9.
88. Barber, 1987, p. 13.
89. Jan Mohamed, 1983, p. 4.
90. Memmi, 1974, p. 87.
91. Memmi, 1974, p. 105.
92. Memmi, 1974, p. 107.
93. Blair, 1976, p. 11.
94. Ngugi wa Thiong'o, 1986, p. 11.
95. Gordon, 1978, pp. 191–2.
96. Blair, 1976, p. 15.
97. Irele, 1981, p. 71.
98. Klein (ed.), 1988.
99. Killam, 1973, p. 137.
100. Gordon, 1978, p. 165.
101. Jad, 1983, p. 14.
102. Hafez, 1975, p. 100.
103. Awad, 1975, p. 183.
104. Farid, 1973, p. 38.
105. Dehni, 1966, p. 99.
106. Khoury, 1966, p. 120.
107. Long, 1979, p. 205.
108. Charkawi, 1966, p. 77.
109. Head, 1974, p. 18.
110. Thoraval, 1975, p. 14.
111. Thoraval, 1975, p. 24.
112. Farid, 1973, p. 40.
113. Thoraval, 1975, p. 108.
114. Farid, 1973, pp. 42–3.
115. Khleifi, 1970, p. 112.
116. Megherbi, 1982, p. 63.
117. Nouri, 1986, p. 58.
118. Stapleton and May, 1987, pp. 257–8.
119. Graham, 1988, p. 18.
120. Stapleton and May, 1987, pp. 260–1.
121. Stapleton and May, 1987, p. 261.
122. Stapleton and May, 1987, p. 5.
123. Barber, 1987, p. 73.
124. Stapleton and May, 1987, p. 7.
125. Iliffe, 1983, p. 37.
126. Jabre, 1966, p. 177.
127. Jabre, 1966, p. 177.

2. Cinema After Independence

1. Smith, 1983, p. 34.
2. Anderson, 1983, p. 106.
3. Anderson, 1983, p. 106.
4. Horne, 1979, p. 61.
5. Anderson, 1983, pp. 86–7.

6. Anderson, 1983, p. 49.
7. Anderson, 1983, p. 59.
8. Anderson, 1983, p. 127.
9. Anderson, 1983, p. 113.
10. Memmi, 1974, p. 111.
11. Klein, 1988, p. 11.
12. Achebe, 1975, p. 62.
13. Achebe, 1975, p. 56.
14. Barber, 1987, pp. 20–1.
15. Klein, 1988, p. 78.
16. Rosenberg, 1965, p. 21 (Rosenberg refers to the 'process of technique' in painting).
17. p'Bitek, 1973, p. 42.
18. Klein, 1988, p. 11.
19. Chinweizu, 1988, p. xvii.
20. Chinweizu, 1988, p. xviii.
21. Chinweizu, 1988, p. xx.
22. Chinweizu, 1988, p. xxvii.
23. Sembene, 1979, p. 15.
24. Stapleton and May, 1987, p. 22.
25. Graham, 1988, p. 24.
26. Graham, 1988, p. 120.
27. Stapleton and May, 1987, p. 114.
28. Stapleton and May, 1987, p. 120.
29. Stapleton and May, 1987, p. 101–2.
30. Berrah, 1987, pp. 116–20, and Ibrahim, 1987, pp. 121–30.
31. Barber, 1987, p. 25.
32. Katz and Wedell, 1978, pp. 47–8.
33. N'Gosso and Ruelle, 1983, p. 47.
34. N'Gosso and Ruelle, 1983, p. 52.
35. N'Gosso and Ruelle, 1983, p. 53.
36. Bakr et al., 1985, p. 17.
37. Bakr et al., 1985, p. 17.
38. Head, 1974, p. 359.
39. Bakr et al., 1985, p. 16.
40. Head, 1974, p. 24.
41. Katz and Wedell, 1978, p. 81.
42. Katz and Wedell, 1978, p. 212.
43. Dehni, 1987, p. 74.
44. Boughedir, 1987, pp. 24–32.
45. Cheriaa, 1979.
46. Head, 1974, p. 18.
47. Mansfield, 1978, p. 322.
48. Farid, 1973, p. 47.
49. Malkmus, 1988, p. 33.
50. Boughedir, 1987, p. 29.
51. Boughedir, 1987a, p. 71.
52. Ibrahim, 1987, p. 80.
53. Malkmus, 1988, p. 33.
54. al-Ariss, 1987, pp. 49–58.

55. Bachy, 1982; Bachy, 1986.
56. Ricard, 1983, pp. 160–7.
57. Barber, 1987, p. 31.
58. Smihi, 1987, p. 101.
59. Smihi, 1987, p. 104.
60. Smihi, 1987, p. 105.

3. The Epic

1. Toumi, 1977, p. 171.
2. Jolles, 1972, p. 35.
3. Megherbi, 1985, p. 117.
4. Ma'ruf, 1989, p. 43.
5. Toumi, 1977, p. 159.
6. Toumi, 1977, p. 169.
7. Toumi, 1977, p. 158.
8. Semsek, 1987, p. 280.
9. Megherbi, 1985, p. 161.
10. Nasri, 1988, p. 10.
11. Amr, 1987, p. 131.
12. Jolles, 1972, p. 53.
13. al-Kilani, 1989, p. 41.
14. Not to be confused with the Egyptian film of the same name, directed in 1983 by Ashraf Fahmy.
15. Frye, 1973, p. 208.
16. Frye, 1973, p. 209.
17. Deleuze, 1983, p. 202.
18. Frye, 1973, p. 58.
19. See Sperl, 1977, pp. 20–35.

4. The Comic

1. See Thoraval, 1975, pp. 27–8, 45, 52–3; and Cluny, 1978, pp. 87–8.
2. See Anon., 1988a, pp. 39–42.
3. This is an unfortunate title, but it is the official one; a better translation would be *Thick as Thieves*.
4. Cavell, 1985, p. 281.
5. Hamuda, 1988, p. 39.
6. Hamuda, 1988, p. 39.
7. Frye, 1973, p. 43.
8. Propp, 1968, pp. 82–3.
9. Deeb, 1979, differentiates between substitution and metaphor in terms of the Arab tradition.
10. See Noeldeke, 1961, p. 53.
11. Ferreri, 1989, p. 56.
12. Khayati, 1988, p. 39.

5. The Dramatic

1. Ramzi, 1987, p. 28.
2. Laroui, 1982, p. 189.
3. Garcia, 1986, p. 50.
4. Kilito, 1985, p. 62.
5. Deleuze, 1985, p. 160.
6. Robbe-Grillet, 1982, p. 58.
7. Kilito, 1985, p. 61.
8. Some titles are: *Mulberries and Cudgels/Al-tut wal-nabut* (Niazi Mustapha, 1985), *Hunger/Al-ju'* (Ali Badrakhan, 1986), *The Market/Al-suq* (Nasir Husayn, 1987).
9. Ibn Khaldun, 1967, pp. 136–42.
10. Farid, 1987, pp. 54 and 56.
11. Farid, 1984, pp. 55–6.
12. Thoraval, 1975, p. 26.

6. Scene

1. al-Mazzaoui, 1964, p. 134.
2. Bensmaïa, 1982, p. 28.
3. B., 1982, p. 25.
4. See Boughedir, 1981, pp. 207–12.
5. Farid, 1981, p. 64.
6. Thoraval, 1975, p. 69.
7. Mohamed Ali, 1988, p. 42.
8. Boukella, 1987, p. 153.
9. Alea, 1987, pp. 58–9.
10. Alea, 1987, pp. 58–9.
11. Metz, 1978, p. 145.
12. This is an argument I consider essentialist and reductive. For the strange bedfellows it creates, see Gabriel, 1985, al-Mazzaoui, 1964, Diawara, 1987, and (for a provocative synthesis and critique) Willemen, 1987.
13. al-Dasuqi, 1988, p. 30.
14. Jost, 1983, p. 195.
15. Khayati, 1973, p. 50.
16. al-Dasuqi, 1988, p. 29.
17. Salah, 1988, p. 15.
18. Berrah, 1981, p. 44.
19. I say 'apparently' because unfortunately I have not yet seen the film, but the point seemed interesting enough to cite. I rely on various personal sources.
20. Deleuze, 1985, p. 226.
21. See Nasri, 1988a, p. 11.
22. Lagny, 1984, p. 84.
23. Tomachevski, 1965, p. 287.

7. Sound

1. Braudy, 1985, p. 414.
2. Thoraval, 1975, p. 13.
3. Khayati, 1986, p. 41.
4. See Ezzedine, 1966, pp. 48–53.
5. Amr, 1987, p. 127.
6. Bounfour, 1977, p. 423.
7. Jakobson, 1963, p. 89.
8. Fano, 1981, p. 110.
9. Bakhtine, 1978, p. 380.
10. Mulvey, 1986, p. 199.
11. Djebar, 1981, p. 108.
12. Cited in Abdel Hamid, 1988, p. 57.
13. Malkmus, 1987, n.p.
14. Music by Ziad Rahbani, son of Feiruz.
15. Berque, 1964, p. 189.
16. Berque, 1964, p. 190.
17. al-Said and Ayse Parman, 1976, pp. 136–40.
18. Welch, 1979, p. 24.
19. Gardenal, 1988, p. 21.
20. Kilito, 1985, p. 19.
21. Kilito, 1983, p. 28.
22. Bakhtine, 1978, p. 380.

8. Sign

1. See Charkawi, 1966, pp. 26–32.
2. Anon., 1988, p. 10.
3. Khayati, 1986, p. 40.
4. Anon., 1989, p. 40.
5. Deleuze, 1985, p. 289.
6. Barthes, 1979, p. 156.
7. Maherzi, 1980, p. 244.
8. Bounfour, 1977, p. 422.
9. Hall, 1989, p. 80.
10. See Sperl, 1977, pp. 20–35.
11. Khatibi, 1977, p. 20.
12. Khatibi, 1977, p. 20.
13. Cluny, 1978, p. 350.
14. Cluny, 1978, p. 347.
15. Laroui, 1982, p. 177.
16. Statie, 1966, p. 16.
17. Sahin, 1988, p. 29.
18. Daniel, 1984, p. 13.
19. Hamori, 1975, p. 89.
20. Hamori, 1975, p. 81.
21. Hatmal, 1988, p. 37.
22. Interview with the author, 1985, Paris.

23. Hatmal, 1988, p. 39.
24. Hatmal, 1988, p. 39.
25. Hatmal, 1988, p. 39.
26. Kilito, 1979, p. 165.
27. Elsaesser, 1986, p. 540.
28. Elsaesser, 1986, p. 546.
29. Elsaesser, 1986, p. 540.
30. Braudy, 1985, p. 413.
31. Sellin, 1988, p. 171.
32. Vernet, 1989, p. 153.

9. Voice

1. Sembene, 1982, p. 78.
2. Lawson, 1982.
3. Prédal, 1982, pp. 62–76.
4. Serceau, D., 1985, p. 88.
5. Nee Owoo, 1989, pp. 84–5.
6. Vieyra, 1983, p. 63.
7. This and all subsequent quotations from film commentaries and dialogue
    are taken directly from the films.
8. Serceau, D., 1985, p. 34.
9. Prédal, 1985, p. 39.
10. Landy, 1982, and Spass, 1982.
11. Serceau, M., 1985, p. 35.
12. Sembene, 1972, pp. 5–6.
13. Sembene, 1972, p. 6.
14. Gregor, 1978, p. 37.
15. Hennebelle, 1979, p. 85.
16. Martin, 1979, p. 18.
17. Martin, 1979, p. 18.
18. Finnegan, 1976, p. 383.
19. Hennebelle and Ruelle, 1978, pp. 108–10.
20. Hennebelle and Ruelle, 1978, pp. 102–4.
21. Diawara, 1987a, pp. 38–9.
22. Pfaff, 1984, pp. 29–42.
23. Finnegan, 1976, p. 2.
24. Finnegan, 1976, p. 5.
25. Julien, 1983, p. 150.
26. Julien, 1983, p. 150.
27. Propp, 1968.
28. Diawara, 1987a, p. 40.

10. Space

1. Gardies, 1989, p. 171.
2. Hennebelle and Ruelle, 1978, p. 108.

3. Scheinfeigel. 1985a. p. 33.
4. Gardies. 1989. p. 22.
5. François. 1982. pp. 22–38.
6. Gardies. 1989. pp. 22–3.
7. Bordwell *et al.*. 1985. pp. 70–84.
8. Pfaff. 1984. pp. 129–30.
9. Robbe-Grillet. 1965. p. 151.
10. Copans. 1985. pp. 57–9.
11. Pfaff. 1984. p. 166. confirms this (independently made) observation.
12. Leahy. 1988a. p. 10.
13. Mpoyi-Buata. 1981. p. 162.
14. Nee Owoo. 1989. p. 85.

11. Story

1. Serceau. D.. 1975a. p. 43.
2. Cham. 1984. p. 84.
3. Hennebelle and Ruelle. 1978. p. 117.
4. Taylor. 1966. p. 184.
5. My analysis of Hollywood story structure owes much to the seminars by Robert McKee organized by the International Forum in London in 1989.
6. Cheriaa. 1985. p. 110. For an opposing view. see Gardies and Haffner. 1987. p. 174.
7. Cham. 1984. p. 84.
8. Leahy. 1988. p. 8.
9. Cheriaa. 1985. p. 109.
10. McArthur. 1972. pp. 26–8.
11. For an opposing view. see Pfaff. 1984. p. 177.

Bibliography

Abdel Hamid, Bandar (1988) interview with Samir Zikra, *Cinema Life* (Damascus), 33–4, summer (in Arabic).

Achebe, Chinua (1975) *Morning Yet on Creation Day*. London, Heinemann.

'African Dossier: Hondo, Gerima, Sembene' (1978), *Framework* (London), 7–8, spring.

Ajami, Fouad (1981) *The Arab Predicament*. Cambridge, Cambridge University Press.

Alea, Tomas Gutierrez (1987) 'Memories of underdevelopment: the viewer's dialectic III', *Jump Cut* (Berkeley), 32.

Ali, Muhsin Jassim (1983) 'The socio-aesthetics of contemporary Arabic fiction: an introduction', *Journal of Arabic Literature*, XIV.

Allouache, Merzak (1987) *Omar Gatlato* (script). Algiers, Cinémathèque algérienne, Editions LAPHOMIC.

Amr, Ibrahim (1987) 'Consommation et décalages culturels en Egypte', in Stauth and Zubaida (eds.) (1987).

Anderson, Benedict (1983) *Imagined Communities*. London, Verso.

Anon. (1988) 'Ahmed Badir is remaking *Quai no 5* in a satirical form', *Alwan* (Beirut), 1–7 October (in Arabic).

Anon. (1988a) 'The comic film in Egypt', *Alwan* (Beirut), 474–5, July (in Arabic).

Anon. (1989) 'First directing experiment', *Video 2000* (Beirut), April (in Arabic).

Arab Cinema and Culture: round table conferences (1965). 3 vols. Beirut, Arab Film and Television Centre.

al-Ariss, Ibrahim (1978) *The Image and the Reality (Al-sura wal-waqi')*. Beirut, Arab Organization for Studies and Publication (in Arabic).

al-Ariss, Ibrahim (1979) *A Voyage Through Arab Cinema (Rihla fil sinema al-'arabiyya)*. Beirut, Dar al-Farabi (in Arabic).

al-Ariss, Ibrahim (1987) 'Du côté du nouveau cinéma égyptien: les enfants de Salah Abou Seif, de la rue et de coca cola', in Berrah *et al.* (eds.) (1981).

Armes, Roy (1985) 'Black African cinema in the eighties', *Screen* (London), 26: 3–4.

Armes, Roy (1987) *Third World Film Making and the West*. Berkeley, University of California Press.

Awad, Louis (1975) 'Problems of the Egyptian theatre', in Ostle (ed.) (1975).

al-'Awdat, Husayn (n.d.) *Cinema and the Palestine Question (Al-sinema wal-qadiyat al-falastiniyya)*. Damascus, Al-Ahali (in Arabic).

Awed, Ibrahim M., Hussein M. Adam and Lionel Ngakane (eds.) (1983) *First*

Mogadishu Pan-African Film Symposium. Mogadishu, Mogpafis Management Committee.

Aziza, Mohamed (1970) *Regards sur le théâtre arabe contemporain.* Tunis, Maison tunisienne de l'édition.

B., Abdou (1982) 'Le dernier tabou', *Les Deux Ecrans* (Algiers), 44, April.

Bachy, Victor (1978) *Le Cinéma de Tunisie.* Tunis, Société tunisienne de diffusion.

Bachy, Victor (1981) 'La distribution cinématographique en Afrique noire', *Filméchange*, 15, summer.

Bachy, Victor (1982) *Le Cinéma au Mali.* Brussels, OCIC.

Bachy, Victor (1982a) *Le Cinéma en Côte d'Ivoire.* Brussels, OCIC.

Bachy, Victor (1982b) *La Haute Volta et le cinéma.* Brussels, OCIC.

Bachy, Victor (1986) *Le Cinéma au Gabon.* Brussels, OCIC.

Bachy, Victor (1987) *To have a History of African Cinema.* Brussels, OCIC. Also published in French and Spanish.

Bakhtine, Mikhail (1978) *Esthetique et théorie du roman.* Paris, Gallimard.

Bakr, Yahya Abu, Saad Labib and Hamdy Kandil (1985) *Development of Communication in the Arab States: needs and priorities.* Paris, UNESCO.

Balogun, Françoise (1984) *Le Cinéma au Nigéria.* Brussels and Paris, OCIC and L'Harmattan.

Banned films (1981), *Index on Censorship* (London), 10:4, (special issue).

Barber, Karin (1987) 'Popular arts in Africa', *African Studies Review* (London), 30:3, September.

Barthes, Roland (1979) *Sur Racine.* Paris, Editions du Seuil (Collection Points).

Bensmaïa, Reda (1982) 'Primat de la narration', *Les Deux Ecrans* (Algiers), 46, June.

Bernal, Martin (1987) *Black Athena.* London, Free Association Books.

Berque, Jacques (1964) 'Le problème de la langue', in *Cinéma et culture arabes* (1964), vol. 1.

Berrah, Mouny (1981) 'Lumières captives' (interview with Yusuf Sahraoui), *Les Deux Ecrans* (Algiers), 45, May.

Berrah, Mouny (1987) 'Les falbalas du mélo égyptien' in Berrah *et al.* (eds.) (1987).

Berrah, Mouny, Victor Bachy, Mohand Ben Salama and Hamdy Kandil (eds.) (1981) *Cinémas du Maghreb.* Paris, *CinémAction*, 14, and Papyrus Editions.

Berrah, Mouny, Jacques Lévy and Claude-Michel Cluny (eds.) (1987) *Les Cinémas arabes.* Paris, *CinémAction* 43, Editions du Cerf and Institut du Monde Arabe.

Binet, Jacques, Ferid Boughedir and Victor Bachy (eds.) (1983) *Cinémas noirs d'Afrique.* Paris, *CinémAction*, 44, and L'Harmattan.

Blair, Dorothy (1976) *African Literature in French.* Cambridge, Cambridge University Press.

Bordwell, David, Janet Staiger and Kristen Thompson (1985) *The Classical Hollywood Cinema.* London, Routledge and Kegan Paul.

Bosséno, Christian (1978) 'Le cinéma en Algérie', *La Revue du Cinéma–Image et son* (Paris), 327.

Bosséno, Christian (1983) 'Le cinéma tunisien', *La Revue du Cinéma* (Paris), 382.

Bosséno, Christian (ed.) (1985) *Youssef Chahine l'Alexandrin.* Paris, *CinémAction*, 33 and Editions du Cerf.

Boughedir, Ferid (1976) 'Cinéma africain et décolonisation'. Unpublished thesis (*doctorat de 3ᵉ cycle*), University of Paris III.

Boughedir, Ferid (1981) 'Les quatre voies du cinéma marocain', in Berrah *et al.* (eds.) (1981).

Boughedir, Ferid (1982) 'Report and prospects', in Fulchignoni (ed.) (1982).

Boughedir, Ferid (1984) 'Le cinéma en Afrique et dans le monde', *Jeune Afrique plus* (Paris), 6, April.

Boughedir, Ferid (1986) 'Economie et thématique des cinémas africains 1960–1985'. Unpublished thesis (*doctorat d'état*), University of Paris VII.

Boughedir, Ferid (1987) *Le Cinéma africain de A à Z*. Brussels, OCIC.

Boughedir, Ferid (1987a) 'Panorama des cinémas maghrébins', in Berrah *et al.* (eds.) (1987).

Boujedra, Rachid (1971) *Naissance du cinéma tunisien*. Paris, François Maspéro.

Boukella, Djamel (1987) 'En finir dans les films avec le "tout politique"', in Berrah *et al.* (eds.) (1987).

Boulanger, Pierre (1975) *Le cinéma colonial*. Paris, Seghers.

Bounfour, Abdellah (1977) 'La raison orpheline', in Sartre (ed.) (1977).

Braudy, Leo (1985) 'Genre: the conventions of connection', in Mast and Cohen (eds.) (1985).

Brossard, Jean-Pierre (1981) *L'Algérie vue par son cinéma*. Locarno, International Film Festival.

Calder, Angus, Christopher Fife, Toby Garfitt and Mario Relich (1983) *African Fiction and Film: three short case studies*. Milton Keynes, Open University Press.

Cavell, Stanley (1985) 'Types: cycles as genres', in Mast and Cohen (eds.) (1985).

CESCA (ed.) (1985) *Camera nigra*. Brussels and Paris, OCIC and L'Harmattan.

Chahine, Yusuf (1985) *Alexandrie pourquoi?* (script), *L'Avant-scène du cinéma* (Paris), 241, June.

Cham, Mbye Baboucar (1982) 'Film production in West Africa', *Présence africaine* (Paris), 124.

Cham, Mbye Baboucar (1984) 'Art and ideology in the work of Sembene Ousmane and Haile Gerima', *Présence africaine* (Paris) 129.

Charkawi, Galal (1966) 'Representing the Prophet of Islam on the screen', in Sadoul (ed.) (1966).

Charkawi, Galal (1966a) 'History of the UAR cinema, 1896–1962', in Sadoul (ed.) (1966).

Charkawi, Galal (1970) *An Essay in the History of Arab Cinema (Risala fi tarikh al-sinema al-'arabiyya)*. Cairo, Egyptian Printing and Publishing Company (in Arabic).

Château, Dominique, André Gardies and François Jost (eds.) (1981) *Cinémas de la modernité*. Paris, Klincksiek.

Chelbi, Mustapha (1985) *Musique et société en Tunisie*. Tunis, Editions Salammbô.

Cheriaa, Tahar (1979) *Ecrans d'abondance . . . ou cinémas de libération en Afrique?*. Tunis, Société tunisienne de diffusion.

Cheriaa, Tahar (1985) 'Le groupe et le héros' in CESCA (ed.) (1985).

Chinweizu (ed.) (1988) *Voices from Twentieth Century Africa*. London, Faber and Faber.

Cinéma arabe – cinéma dans le tiers monde – cinéma militant (1976). *Dérives* (Quebec), 3–4 (special issue).

'Cinéma d'Afrique noire' (1984) *Vivant univers* (Namur), 352, July/August.

Cinéma et culture arabes (1964), 3 vols. Beirut, Arab Film and Television Centre. Also published in English (1965).

Cinéma et l'Afrique au sud du Sahara: rapport général du groupe ciné-photo, section du Congo-Belge et du Ruanda-Urundi, Le (1958). Brussels, Exposition universelle et internationale.

Cinémas des pays arabes (1977), 3 vols. Algiers, Cinémathèque algérienne and Cinémathèque française (photocopy).

Clawson, Patrick (1981) 'The development of capitalism in Egypt', *Khamsin* (London), 9.

Cluny, Claude-Michel, and Salah Dehni (1975) 'L'expérience du cinéma en Syrie', *Cinéma 75* (Paris), 197, April.

Cluny, Claude-Michel (1977) 'Actualité du cinéma arabe', *Cinéma 77* (Paris), 178-9.

Cluny, Claude-Michel (1978) *Dictionnaire des nouveaux cinémas arabes.* Paris, Sindbad.

Convents, Guido (1986) *Préhistoire du cinéma en Afrique 1897-1918: à la recherche des images oubliées.* Brussels, OCIC.

Copans, Jean (1985) 'Entre l'histoire et les mythes', in D. Serceau (ed.) (1985).

Curran, James and Vincent Porter (eds.) (1983) *British Cinema History.* London, Weidenfeld and Nicolson.

Dadci, Younes (1970) *Dialogues Algérie-cinéma.* Paris, Editions Dadci.

Daniel, Charles (1984) 'Musique et narrativité', *Hors cadre* (Paris), 2.

al-Dasuqi, Mohamed (1988) 'The simple man in the street dominates the screen', *Video Arab* (Beirut), July (in Arabic).

Deeb, Abu (1979) *Al Jurjani's Theory of Poetic Imagery.* Warminster, Aris and Phillips.

Dehni, Salah (1966) 'History of Syrian cinema, 1918-1962', in Sadoul (ed.) (1966).

Dehni, Salah (1987) 'Quand cinéma et télévision se regardent en chiens de faïence: le cas syrien', in Berrah *et al.* (eds.) (1987).

Deleuze, Gilles (1983) *L'Image-mouvement.* Paris, Editions de minuit.

Deleuze, Gilles (1985) *L'Image-temps.* Paris, Editions de minuit.

Dhote, Alain, (ed.) (1989) *Cinéma et psychanalyse.* Paris, *CinémAction*, 50, and Corlet.

Diawara, Manthia (1984) 'African Cinema: the background and economic context of production'. Unpublished thesis, Indiana University.

Diawara, Manthia (1986) 'African Cinema: FESPACO, an evaluation', *Third World Affairs 1986* (London).

Diawara, Manthia (1987) 'Sub-Saharan African film production: technological determinism', *Jump Cut* (Berkeley), 32.

Diawara, Manthia (1987a) 'Oral literature and African film: narratology in *Wend Kuuni*', *Présence Africaine* (Paris), 142, second quarter.

Diawara, Manthia (1989) 'African cinema today', *Framework* (London), 37.

Djebar, Assia (1981) 'J'ai recherché un langage musical', in Berrah *et al.* (1981).

Downing, John D. H., (ed.) (1987) *Film and Politics in the Third World.* New York, Praeger.

'Écrans colonisés' (dossier) (1982), *FilmAction* (Paris), 2, February-March.

Elsaesser, Thomas (1986) 'Primary identification and the historical subject', in Rosen (ed.) (1986).

Ezzedine, Salah (1966) 'The role of music in Arab films', in Sadoul (ed.) (1966).

Fano, Michel (1981) 'Le son et le sens', in Château *et al.* (eds.) (1981).

Fanon, Frantz (1967) *The Wretched of the Earth.* Harmondsworth, Penguin.

Fanon, Frantz (1980) *A Dying Colonialism.* London, Readers and Writers Publishing Cooperative.

Farid, Samir (1973) 'Les six générations du cinéma égyptien', *Ecran* (Paris), 15, May.

Farid, Samir (1979) *Arab Cinema Guide.* Cairo, Arab Cinema Guide.

Farid, Samir (1981) *On Arab Cinema.* Beirut, Dar al-Tali'a (in Arabic).

Farid, Samir (1984) 'The image of women in Arab cinema', *Cinema Life* (Damascus), 11, spring (in Arabic).

Farid, Samir (1987) 'Neo-realism is born in Egypt', *Cinema Life* (Damascus), 31–32 (in Arabic).

Fenuku, R. O. (1983) 'Country report on Ghana' in Awed *et al.* (eds.) (1983).

Ferreri, Michel (1989) 'Au-delà du plaisir du film: spectateur-enfant' in Dhote (ed.) (1989).

Festival panafricain du cinéma de Ouagadougou: FESPACO 1983 (1987). Paris, Editions présence africaine.

Finnegan, Ruth (1976) *Oral Literature in Africa.* Nairobi, Oxford University Press.

Fisher, Lucy (1980–1) '*Xala*: a study in black humour', *Millennium Film Journal,* 7–9, winter–fall.

Fisher, William (1989) 'Ouagadougou', *Sight and Sound* (London), 58: 3, summer.

François, Pierre (1982) 'Class struggles in Mali', *Review of African Political Economy* (Sheffield), 24, December.

Frye, Northrop (1973) *Anatomy of Criticism.* Princeton, Princeton University Press.

Fulchignoni, Enrico, (ed.) (1982) *Cinema and Society.* Paris, ITFC and UNESCO.

Gabriel, Teshome (1982) *Third Cinema in the Third World: the aesthetics of liberation.* Ann Arbor, UMI Research Press.

Gabriel, Teshome (1982a) '*Xala*: a cinema of wax and gold', *Jump Cut* (Berkeley), 27, July.

Gabriel, Teshome (1985) 'Towards a critical theory of Third World films', *Third World Affairs 1985* (London).

Ganda, Oumarou (1981) *Cabascabo* (script), *L'Avant-scène du cinéma* (Paris), 265, April.

Garcia, Roger (1986) 'The melodramatic point of view', *Papers of the Hong Kong Film Festival 1986.*

Gardenal, Philippe (1988) 'Le caractère arabe pris au pied de la lettre', *Libération* (Paris), 25 May.

Gardies, André (1987) 'L'espace dans la narration filmique: l'exemple du cinéma d'Afrique noire francophone'. Unpublished thesis (*doctorat d'état*), University of Paris VIII.

Gardies, André (1989) *Cinéma d'Afrique noire francophone.* Paris, L'Harmattan.

Gardies, André, and Pierre Haffner (1987) *Regards sur le cinéma négro-africain.* Brussels, OCIC.

Georgakas, Dan, and Lenny Rubenstein (eds.) (1984) *Art Politics Cinema: the Cineaste interviews.* Chicago, Lakeview Press.

Gordon, David G. (1978) *The French Language and National Identity.* The

Hague, Mouton.

Gould, Stephen Jay (1980) *Ever Since Darwin*. Harmondsworth, Penguin.

Gould, Stephen Jay (1986) *The Flamingo's Smile*. Harmondsworth, Penguin.

Goux-Pelletan, Jean-Pierre (1971) 'Petite planète du cinéma: Liban', *Cinéma 71* (Paris), 161, December.

Gover, Victor (1958) 'A brief review of the services provided by the Overseas Film and Television Centre for film units working in Africa', in *Le Cinéma et l'Afrique au sud du Sahara* (1958).

Graham, Ronnie (1988) *Stern's Guide to Contemporary African Music*. London, Zwan Publications and Off the Record Press.

Gregor, Ulrich (1978) interview with Ousmane Sembene, *Framework* (London), 7–8, spring.

Guback, Thomas, and Tapio Varis (1982) *Transnational Communication and Cultural Industries*. Paris, UNESCO.

Hafez, Sabry (1975) 'Innovation in the Egyptian short story', in Ostle (ed.) (1975).

Haffner, Pierre (1978) *Essai sur les fondements du cinéma africain*. Paris, Nouvelles editions africaines.

Haffner, Pierre (1986) 'Le cinéma et l'imaginaire en Afrique noire'. Unpublished thesis (*doctorat d'état*), University of Paris X.

Haffner, Pierre (ed.) (1989) *Kino in Schwarzafrika*, Munich, CICIM.

Hall, Stuart (1989) 'Cultural identity and cinematic representation', *Framework* (London), 36.

Hamori, Andras (1975) *On the Art of Mediaeval Arabic Literature*. Princeton, Princeton University Press.

Hamuda, Huda (1988) interview with Saleem al-Basri, *al-Ufuq* (Nicosia), 21 July (in Arabic).

al-Haraty, Salem Ahmad (1988) 'Study on the history of cinema in the Libyan Popular Socialist Arab Jamahiriya'. Unpublished thesis, London International Film School.

Hatmal, Jamil (1988) 'Imagination is a lifeboat' (interview with Nacer Khemir), *Cinema Life* (Damascus), 33–4, summer (in Arabic).

Haustrate, Gaston, Claude-Michel Cluny, Françoise Chevalier and Mireille Amiel (1976) 'Le cinéma algérien', *Cinéma 76* (Paris), 207, March.

Hawal, Qasim (n.d.) *Palestinian Cinema (Al-sinema al-falastiniyya)*. Beirut, Dar al-Hadaf, Dar al-'Awda (in Arabic).

Head, Sydney W., (ed.) (1974) *Broadcasting in Africa*. Philadelphia, Temple University Press.

Hennebelle, Guy, (ed.) (1972) Les Cinémas africains en 1972. Paris, *L'Afrique littéraire et artistique* (Paris), 20, and Société Africaine d'Edition.

Hennebelle, Guy, (ed.) (1975) 'Le cinéma syrien', *L'Afrique littéraire et artistique* (Paris), 36.

Hennebelle, Guy (1975a) *Quinze ans de cinéma mondial*. Paris, Editions du Cerf.

Hennebelle, Guy (1976) 'Arab cinema', *Merip Reports* (Washington), 52, November.

Hennebelle, Guy, (ed.) (1979) *Cinémas de l'émigration*. Paris, *CinémAction* 8, summer.

Hennebelle, Guy, and Janine Euvard (eds.) (1978) *Israël–Palestine: que peut le cinéma?*. Paris, *L'Afrique littéraire et artistique*, 47, and Société africaine d'édition.

Hennebelle, Guy, and Khemais Khayati (eds.) (1977) *La Palestine et le cinéma*. Paris, E 100.

Hennebelle, Guy, and Catherine Ruelle (eds.) (1978) *Cinéastes d'Afrique noire*. Paris, *CinémAction*, 3, and *L'Afrique littéraire et artistique*, 49.

Hobsbawm, Eric, and Terence Ranger (eds.) (1983) *The Invention of Tradition*. Cambridge, Cambridge University Press.

Horne, Alistair (1979) *A Savage War of Peace: Algeria 1954–1962*. Harmondsworth, Penguin.

Hourani, Cecil (ed.) (1982) *The Arab Cultural Scene*. London, Namara Press.

Ibn Khaldun (1967) *The Muqaddimah* (trans. Franz Rosenthal). London, Routledge and Kegan Paul.

Ibrahim, Abbas Fadhil (1987) 'Trois mélos égyptiens observés à la loupe', in Berrah *et al.* (eds.) (1987).

Ibrahim, Abbas Fadhil (1987a) 'Le cinéma irakien: un accouchement de quarante ans', in Berrah *et al.* (eds.) (1987).

Iliffe, John (1983) *The Emergence of African Capitalism*. London, Macmillan.

Irele, Abiola (1981) *The African Experience in Literature and Ideology*. London, Heinemann.

Al-'Isa, Rima, and Hassan Abou Ghanima (1983) *From the Other Side of Cinema Culture (Min al-janib al-akhir lil-thaqafat al-sinemaiyya)*. Amman, Arab Organization for Studies and Publication (in Arabic).

Jabre, Farid (1966) 'The industry in Lebanon, 1958–65', in Sadoul (ed.) (1966).

Jad, Ali B. (1983) *Form and Technique in the Egyptian Novel, 1912–1971*. London, Ithaca Press.

Jakobson, Roman (1963) *Essais de linguistique générale*. Paris, Editions de minuit.

Jan Mohamed, Abdul R. (1983) *Manichean Aesthetics: the politics of literature in colonial Africa*. Amherst, University of Massachusetts Press.

Jargy, Simon (1971) *La Musique arabe*. Paris, PUF.

Jegede, Dele (1987) 'Popular culture and popular music: the Nigerian experience', *Présence Africaine* (Paris), 144: 4.

Jolles, André (1972) *Formes simples*. Paris, Editions du seuil.

Jost, François (1983) 'Narration(s): en deçà et au-delà', *Communications* (Paris), 38.

Julien, Eileen (1983) 'Of traditional tales and short stories in African literature', *Présence africaine* (Paris), 125: 1.

Kamphausen, M. (1972) 'Cinema in Africa: a survey', *Cineaste* (New York), 5:3.

Katz, Elihu and George Wedell (1978) *Broadcasting in the Third World: promise and performance*. London, Macmillan.

Khan, M. (1969) *An Introduction to the Egyptian Cinema*. London, Informatics.

Khatibi, Abdelkebir (1977) 'Le Maghreb comme horizon de pensée', in Sartre (ed.) (1977).

Khayati, Khemais (1973) interview with Salah Abou Seif, *Cinéma 73* (Paris), 182.

Khayati, Khemais (1986) interview with Niazi Mustapha, *al-Yaum al-Sabi'* (Paris), 25 August (in Arabic).

Khayati, Khemais (1988) interview with Rifat al-Mihi, *al-Yaum al-Sabi'* (Paris), 12 September (in Arabic).

Khleifi, Michel (1988) *Noce en Galilée* (script), *L'Avant-scène du cinéma* (Paris), 372, June.

Khleifi, Omar (1970) *L'Histoire du cinéma en Tunisie*. Tunis, Société tunisienne de diffusion.
Khoury, Lucienne (1966) 'History of the Lebanese cinema', in Sadoul (ed.) (1966).
al-Kilani, Khair (1989) 'Opinion', *Alwan* (Beirut), July (in Arabic).
Kilito, Abdelfattah (1979) 'Sur le métalangage métaphorique des poéticiens arabes', *Poétique* (Paris), 38, April.
Kilito, Abdelfattah (1983) *Les Séances*. Paris, Sindbad.
Kilito, Abdelfattah (1985) *L'Auteur et ses doubles*. Paris, Seuil.
Killam, G. D. (1973) *African Writers on African Writing*. London, Heinemann.
Klein, Leonard S., (ed.) (1988) *African Literatures in the Twentieth Century: a guide*. Harpenden, Oldcastle Books.
al-Ktozai, Mohamed A. (1984) *The Development of Early Arabic Drama, 1847–1900*. London, Longman.
Lagny, Michèle (1984) 'Les français en focalization interne', *Iris* (Limoges), 2:2.
Landy, Marsha (1982) 'Politics and style in *Black Girl*'. *Jump Cut* (Berkeley), 27, July.
Laroui, Abdallah (1982) *L'Idéologie arabe contemporaine*. Paris, Maspéro.
Lawson, William (1982) *The Western Scar: the theme of the been-to in West African fiction*. Athens, Ohio University Press.
Leahy, James (1987) 'Tributaries of the Seine', *Monthly Film Bulletin* (London), vol. 54, No. 639, April.
Leahy, James (1988) '*Sarraounia*', *Monthly Film Bulletin* (London), vol. 55, No. 648, January.
Leahy, James (1988a) interview with Med Hondo, *Monthly Film Bulletin* (London), vol. 55, No. 648, January.
Long, Richard (1979) *Tafiq al Hakim: playwright of Egypt*. London, Ithaca Press.
Maarek, Philippe J., (ed.) (1983) *Afrique noire: quel cinéma?*. Paris, Association du ciné-club de l'Université Paris X.
al-Mafraji, Ahmed Fayadh (1978) *The Cinema in Iraq*. Baghdad, Ministry of Culture and Information.
Maherzi, Lotfi (1980) *Le Cinéma algérien*. Algiers, SNED.
Malkmus, Lizbeth (1985) 'A desk between two borders', *Framework* (London), 29.
Malkmus, Lizbeth (1986) 'Arab cinema: avoiding the ghetto', *Third World Affairs 1986* (London).
Malkmus, Lizbeth (1987) unpublished interview with Samir Zikra.
Malkmus, Lizbeth (1988) 'The "new" Egyptian cinema: adapting genre conventions to a changing society', *Cineaste* (New York), XVI: 3.
Mansfield, Peter (1978) *The Arabs*. Harmondsworth, Penguin.
Martin, Angela (1979) 'Four West African film-makers', *Framework* (London), 11, autumn.
Martin, Angela (1982) *African Films: the context of production*. London, British Film Institute.
Martin, Angela (1984) *Africa on Africa*. London, Channel 4.
Martin, Angela (1988) *Arab Cinema*. London, Channel 4.
Ma'ruf, Mahmud (1989) interview with Ali Badrakhan, *al-Ufuq* (Nicosia), 19 January (in Arabic).
Mast, Gerald and Marshall Cohen (1985) *Film Theory and Criticism*. New York,

Oxford University Press.
al-Mazzaoui, Farid (1964) 'Viabilité d'un cinéma né chétif face à une télévision géante', in *Cinéma et culture arabes*, Vol. 1.
McArthur, Colin (1972) *Underworld USA*. London, Secker and Warburg.
Megherbi, Abdelghani (1982) *Les Algériens au miroir du cinéma colonial*. Algiers, Editions SNED.
Megherbi, Abdelghani (1985) *Le Miroir apprivoisé*. Algiers, ENAL.
Megherbi, Abdelghani (1985a) *Le Miroir aux alouettes: lumière sur les ombres hollywoodiennes en Algérie et dans le monde*. Algiers and Brussels, ENAL, OPU, GAM.
Memmi, Albert (1974) *The Colonizer and the Colonized*. London, Souvenir Press.
Metz, Christian (1978) *Essais sur la signification au cinéma*. Paris, Klincksieck.
Mohamed Ali, Mahdi (1988) 'About the New Realism', *Cinema Life* (Damascus), 33–4 (in Arabic).
Mpoyi-Buata, Th. (1981) '*Ceddo* de Sembène Ousmane et *West Indies* de Med Hondo', *Présence africaine* (Paris), 119: 3.
al-Mufraji, Ahmed Fiyad (1981) *Sources for the Study of Cinema Activity in Iraq 1968–1979 (Masadir dirasat al-nashat al-sinema fil-'Iraq)*. Beirut, Arab Organization for Studies and Publication (in Arabic).
al-Mufraji, Ahmed Fiyad (1981a) *Cinema Artists in Iraq (Fananu al-sinema fil-'Iraq)*. Beirut, Arab Organization for Studies and Publication (in Arabic).
Mulvey, Laura (1986) 'Visual pleasure and narrative cinema', in Rosen (ed.) (1986).
Nagakane, Lionel and Keith Shiri (1991), *Africa on Film*, London, BBC.
Nasri, Samir (1988) interview with Farid Chauqi, *al-Nahar* (Beirut), 30 April (in Arabic).
Nasri, Samir (1988a) interview with Sa'id Marzuq, *al-Nahar* (Beirut), 21 March (in Arabic).
Nee Owoo, Kwate (1989) interview with Ousmane Sembene, *Framework* (London), 36.
Ngansop, Guy Jérémie (1987) *Le cinéma camerounais en crise*. Paris, L'Harmattan.
N'Gosso, Gaston Samé and Catherine Ruelle (1983) *Cinéma et télévision en Afrique: de la dépendance a l'interdépendance*. Paris, UNESCO.
Ngugi wa Thiong'o (1986) *Decolonising the Mind*. London, James Curry.
Nicholls, Harcourt (1988) 'Black British Actors and the Film Industry, 1935–1960'. Unpublished thesis, Middlesex Polytechnic.
Noeldeke, Th. (1961) *Delectus Veterum Carminum Arabicorum*. Wiesbaden, Harroassowitz.
Notcutt, L. A. and G. C. Latham (1937) *The African and the Cinema*. London, Edinburgh House Press.
Nouri, Shakir (1986) *A la recherche du cinéma irakien, 1945–1985*. Paris, L'Harmattan.
Obiechina, Emmanuel (1975) *Culture, Tradition and Society in the West African Novel*. Cambridge, Cambridge University Press.
Ochs, Martin (1986) *The African Press*. Cairo, American University in Cairo Press.
Opubor, Alfred E. and Onuora E. Nwuneli (1979) *The Development and Growth of the Film Industry in Nigeria*. Lagos, Third Press International.

Ostle, R. C., (ed.) (1975) *Studies in Modern Arabic Literature*. Warminster, Aris and Phillips.

Ostor, Akos (1984–5) 'Cinema and society in India and Senegal: the films of Satyajit Ray and Ousmane Sembene', *Cinewave* (Calcutta), 7.

'Other Cinemas, Other Criticisms' (1985) *Screen* (London), 26: 3–4 (special issue).

Otten, Rik (1984) *Le Cinéma au Zaire, au Rwanda et au Burundi*. Brussels and Paris, OCIC and L'Harmattan.

p'Bitek, Okot (1973) *Africa's Cultural Revolution*. Nairobi, Macmillan.

Pfaff, Françoise (1984) *The Cinema of Ousmane Sembene: a pioneer of African film*. Westport, Greenwood Press.

Pfaff, Françoise (1988) *Twenty-five Black African Filmmakers*. Westport, Praeger/Greenwood Press.

Pines, Jim, and Paul Willemen (eds.) (1989) *Questions of Third Cinema*. London, British Film Institute.

Pommier, Pierre (1974) *Cinéma et développement en Afrique noire francophone*. Paris, Pedone.

Prédal, René (1982) *Jean Rouch, un griot gaulois*. Paris, CinémAction, 17, and L'Harmattan.

Prédal, René (1985) '*La noire de . . .* : premier long métrage africain', in D. Serceau, (ed.) (1985).

Propp, Vladimir (1968) *The Morphology of the Folktale*. Bloomington, Indiana University Press.

Rachety, Gehan, and Khalil Sabat (n.d.) *Importation of Films for Cinema and Television in Egypt*. Paris, UNESCO.

Racism, Colonialism and Cinema (1983) *Screen* (London), 24: 2 (special issue).

Ramzi, Kamal (1987) 'The Cairo International Film Festival 1986', *Cinema Life* (Damascus), 31–2 (in Arabic).

Ranger, Terence (1983) 'The invention of tradition in Africa', in Hobsbawm and Ranger (eds.) (1983).

Ricard, Alain (1983) 'Du théâtre au cinéma yoruba: le cas nigérian', in Binet *et al.* (eds.) (1983).

Ricard, Alain (1986) *L'Invention du théâtre: le théâtre et les comédiens en Afrique noire*. Lausanne, L'Age d'Homme.

Richards, Jeffrey (1973) *Visions and Yesterday*. London, Routledge and Kegan Paul.

Rida, Mohammed (n.d.) *The Book of Cinema (Kitab al-sinema)*. Beirut, al-Khulud (in Arabic).

Robbe-Grillet, Alain (1985) *Snapshots and Towards a New Novel*. London, Calder and Boyars.

Robbe-Grillet, Alain (1982) *Oeuvres cinématographiques*. Paris, Ministère des Relations Extérieurs (édition vidéographique).

Roberts, Andrew (1987) 'Africa on film to 1940', *History in Africa*, 14.

Roitfeld, Pierre (1980) *Afrique noire francophone*. Paris, Unifrance.

Rosen, Philip, (ed.) (1986) *Narrative, Apparatus, Cinema*. New York, Columbia University Press.

Rosenberg, Harold (1965) *The Anxious Object*. London, Thames and Hudson.

Rugh, William A. (1979) *The Arab Press*. London, Croom Helm.

Sadoul, Georges, (ed.) (1966) *The Cinema in the Arab Countries*. Beirut, Arab Film and Television Centre.

Sahin, Saifi (1988) interview with Rifat al-Mihi, *Alwan* (Beirut), 17–23 September (in Arabic).

Said, Edward W. (1985) *Orientalism*. Harmondsworth, Penguin.

al-Said, Isaam, and Ayse Parman (1976) *Geometric Concepts in Islamic Art*. Guildford, Scorpion and WIFT.

Salah, Ahmed (1988) 'Dreams of servant girls and dreams of Egyptian cinema', *Video 2000* (Beirut), fall (in Arabic).

Salmane, Hala, Simon Hartog and David Wilson (eds.) (1976) *Algerian Cinema*. London, British Film Institute.

Sartre, Jean-Paul, (ed.) (1977) *Du Maghreb, Les Temps Modernes* (special issue), October.

Scheinfeigel, Maxime (1985) '*Borom Sarret*, la fiction documentaire', in D. Serceau (ed.) (1985).

Schmidt, Nancy (1988) *Sub-Saharan African Films and Filmmakers: an annotated bibliography*. London, Hans Zell.

Scohy, André (1958) 'L'action du gouvernement général du Congo-Belge dans l'éducation des masses par le cinéma', in *Le Cinéma et l'Afrique*.

Sellers, William (1958) 'The Production and Use of Films for Public Informational and Educational Purposes in the British African Territories', in *Le Cinéma et l'Afrique au sud du Sahara* (1958).

Sellin, Eric (1988) 'Obsession with the white page in Maghrebian fiction', *International Journal of Middle East Studies* (Cambridge), 20: 2.

Semaine du cinéma arabe du 14 au 21 décembre 1987, La (1987). Paris, Institut du Monde Arabe.

Sembene, Ousmane (1972) *The Money Order*, with *White Genesis*. London, Heinemann.

Sembene, Ousmane (1979) 'Observations', in *Symposium on Cinema*.

Sembene, Ousmane (1979a) *Borom Sarret* (script), *L'Avant-scène du cinéma* (Paris), 229, June.

Sembene, Ousmane (1982) 'Tu nous regardes comme des insectes', in Prédal (ed.) (1982).

'Séminaire sur le rôle du cinéaste dans l'éveil d'une conscience de civilisation noire – Ouagadougou 8–13 avril 1974' (1974), *Présence africaine*, Third World Foundation for Social & Economic Studies, London, 90.

Semsek, Hans Günther (1987) 'Popular culture versus mass culture', in Stauth and Zubaida (eds.) (1987).

Serceau, Daniel, (ed.) (1985a) *Sembène Ousmane*. Paris: CinémAction, 34.

Serceau, Daniel (1985a) '*Emitai*: l'échec d'une transposition dramatique', in D. Serceau, (ed.) (1985).

Serceau, Michel (1985) '*Niaye*: l'Afrique sans masque', in D. Serceau, (ed.) (1985).

'Situation du cinéma du tiers-monde' (1975), *Cinéma 75* (Paris), 195, January.

Smihi, Moumen (1987) 'Si l'image arabe venait à disparaître . . .', in Berrah *et al.* (eds.) (1987).

Smith, Anthony D. (1983) *State and Nation in the Third World*. Brighton, Wheatsheaf Books.

Smyth, Rosaleen (1983) 'The Central African Film Unit's images of empire, 1948–1963', *Historical Journal of Film, Radio and Television* (Abingdon), 3: 2.

Smyth, Rosaleen (1983a) 'Movies and mandarins: the official film and British colonial Africa', in Curran and Porter (eds.) (1983).

Smyth, Rosaleen (1988) 'The British Colonial Film Unit and sub-Saharan Africa, 1939–1945', *Historical Journal of Film, Radio and Television* (Abingdon), 8: 3.

Soyinka, Wole (1983) *Aké*. London, Arrow.

Spass, Lieve (1982) 'Female domestic labour in *Black Girl*', *Jump Cut* (Berkeley), 27, July.

Sperl, Stefan (1977) 'Islamic kingship and Arabic panegyric poetry in the early ninth century', *Journal of Arabic Literature* (Leiden), VIII.

Stapleton, Chris and Chris May (1987) *African All-stars: The Pop Music of a Continent*. London, Quartet.

Statie, Salah (1966) 'Islam and the image', in Sadoul (ed.) (1966).

Statistics on Film and Cinema: 1955–1977 (1981). Paris, UNESCO.

Stauth, Georg, and Sami Zubaida (eds.) (1987) *Mass Culture, Popular Culture and Social Life in the Middle East*. Frankfurt, Campus Verlag.

Steven, Peter, (ed.) (1985) *Jump Cut: Hollywood, politics, and counter cinema*. Toronto, Between the Lines.

Symposium on Cinema in Developing Countries (1979). New Delhi, Ministry of Information and Broadcasting.

Tamzali, Wassyla (1979) *En attendant Omar Gatlato*. Algiers, Editions EnAP.

Taylor, Clyde (1985) 'Decolonizing world cinema', *Third World Affairs 1985* (London).

Taylor, John Russell (1966), interview with Harold Pinter, *Sight and Sound* (London), 35: 4, autumn.

al-Tayyar, Rida (1981) *The City in Iraqi Cinema (al-madina fil-sinema al-'iraqiyya)*. Beirut, Arab Organization for Studies and Publication (in Arabic).

'Third World Film' (1982), *Jump Cut* (Berkeley), 27, July.

Thompson, Kristin (1985) *Exporting Entertainment*. London, British Film Institute.

Thoraval, Yves (1975) *Regards sur le cinéma égyptien*. Beirut, Dar el-Mashreq.

Todorov, Tzvetan, (ed.) (1965) *Théorie de la littérature*. Paris, Seuil.

Tomachevski, B. (1965) 'Thématique', in Todorov (ed.) (1965).

Tomaselli, Keyan (1989) *The Cinema of Apartheid*. London, Routledge.

Toumi, Mohsen (1977) 'De l'état', in Sartre (ed.) (1977).

Tradition orale et nouveaux médias (Fespaco') (1989). Brussels, OCIC.

Turvey, Gerry (1985) '*Xala* and the curse of neocolonialism', *Screen* (London), 26: 3–4.

Ukadike, Nwachukwu Frank (1989) 'Black African Cinema'. Unpublished thesis, New York University.

Van den Heuvel, Alexandre (1958) 'Convient-il de faire du 'film pour Africains'?', in *Le Cinéma et l'Afrique au sud du Sahara* (1958).

Van Wert, William F. (1979) 'Ideology in the Third World: a study of Sembene Ousmane and Glauber Rocha', *Quarterly Review of Film Studies* (New York), 4: 2.

Vernet, Marc (1989) 'Autour du suspens, réflexions sur le fétichisme', in Dhote (ed.) (1989).

'Vers un "cinema novo" égyptien' (1973) *Ecran* (Paris), 73, May.

Vieyra, Paulin Soumanou (1969) *Le Cinéma et l'Afrique*. Paris, Présence africaine.

Vieyra, Paulin Soumanou (1972) *Ousmane Sembène cinéaste*. Paris, Présence africaine.

Vieyra, Paulin Soumanou (1975) *Le Cinéma africain des origines à 1973*. Paris, Présence africaine.

Vieyra, Paulin Soumanou (1983) *Le Cinéma au Sénégal*. Brussels and Paris, OCIC and L'Harmattan.

Weaver, Harold (1982) 'The politics of African cinema', in Yearwood (ed.) (1982).

Welch, Anthony (1979) *Calligraphy in the Arts of the Muslim World*. Austin, University of Texas Press.

Willemen, Paul (1978) interview with Haile Gerima, *Framework* (London), 7–8, Spring.

Willemen, Paul (1987) 'The third cinema question', *Framework* (London), 34.

World Communications (1964) (1975). Paris, UNESCO.

Yearwood, Gladstone, (ed.) (1982) *Black Cinema Aesthetics*. Athens, Ohio University Center for Afro-American Studies.

Index

Zed Books Ltd

is a publisher whose international and Third World lists span:

- **Women's Studies**
- **Development**
- **Environment**
- **Current Affairs**
- **International Relations**
- **Children's Studies**
- **Labour Studies**
- **Cultural Studies**
- **Human Rights**
- **Indigenous Peoples**
- **Health**

We also specialize in Area Studies where we have extensive lists in African Studies, Asian Studies, Caribbean and Latin American Studies, Middle East Studies, and Pacific Studies.

For further information about books available from Zed Books, please write to: Catalogue Enquiries, Zed Books Ltd, 57 Caledonian Road, London N1 9BU. Our books are available from distributors in many countries (for full details, see our catalogues), including:

In the USA
Humanities Press International, Inc., 165 First Avenue, Atlantic Highlands, New Jersey 07716.
Tel: (201) 872 1441;
Fax: (201) 872 0717.

In Canada
DEC, 229 College Street, Toronto, Ontario M5T 1R4.
Tel: (416) 971 7051.

In Australia
Wild and Woolley Ltd, 16 Darghan Street, Glebe, NSW 2037.

In India
Bibliomania, C-236 Defence Colony, New Delhi 110 024.

In Southern Africa
David Philip Publisher (Pty) Ltd, PO Box 408, Claremont 7735, South Africa.